Islamic Finance

Islamic Finance

Principles and Practice

Hans Visser

Professor Emeritus of Money and Banking and International Economics, Faculty of Economics and Business Management, VU University, Amsterdam, the Netherlands

Edward Elgar

Cheltenham, UK • Northampton, MA, USA

Published by
Edward Elgar Publishing Limited
The Lypiatts
15 Lansdown Road
Cheltenham
Glos GL50 2JA
UK

Edward Elgar Publishing, Inc.
William Pratt House
9 Dewey Court
Northampton
Massachusetts 01060
USA

A catalogue record for this book
is available from the British Library

Library of Congress Control Number: 2009922751

ISBN 978 1 84542 525 8

Printed and bound by MPG Books Group, UK

Contents

Abbreviations

AAOIFI:	Accounting and Auditing Organization for Islamic Financial Institutions
BCCI:	Bank of Credit and Commerce International
BMA:	Bahrain Monetary Authority
CBI:	Central Bank of Iran
CMC:	Central Bank *Musharaka* Certificates (Sudan)
DJI:	Dow Jones Islamic Market Index
DJS:	Down Jones Sustainability World Index
DJW:	Dow Jones World Index
EURIBOR:	Euro Interbank Offered Rate
FSA:	Financial Services Authority (UK)
GII:	Government Investment Issues (Malaysia)
IAS:	International Accounting Standards
IDB:	Islamic Development Bank
IFSB:	Islamic Financial Services Board
IIFM:	International Islamic Financial Market
IIRA:	Islamic International Rating Agency
LIBOR:	London Interbank Offered Rate
NPP:	National Participation Paper (Iran)
PLS:	Proft-and-Loss Sharing
REIT:	Real Estate Investment Trust
SMEs:	Small- and Medium-Sized Enterprises
SPV:	Special Purpose Vehicle
UAE:	United Arab Emirates

Acknowledgements

I am indebted to a number of people who at various stages offered advice, gave useful information, drew my attention to relevant literature or brought me into contact with practitioners of Islamic finance. I wish to thank in particular Ms Rachida Talal, Mr Robert Kranenborg, Professor Harald Motzki, Ms Marjorie Sinke, Dr Jan Slomp, Professor Meine Pieter van Dijk, Mr Arjan Gelderblom and Dr Hari Sunarto.

Introduction

This book is about Islamic finance. It builds on an earlier booklet (Visser 2004) and explores the products and practices of Islamic finance against the background of its ideology, including the tensions that may arise between the ideology and the practices. Islamic finance is an especially interesting phenomenon because it presents itself as an alternative to conventional finance not only in Muslim countries but in the rest of the world as well, at times broadening its appeal to non-Muslims. In the aftermath of the first oil crisis of 1973–74, which put large amounts of money into the hands of Middle Eastern investors, the first full-fledged Islamic bank, Dubai Islamic Bank, was founded in 1975. A good 30 years later we have hundreds of Islamic financial institutions and specialized Islamic subsidiaries, in more than 75 countries. Exact figures are hard to get. Estimates of total assets worldwide in mid-2006 ranged from \$205 billion to \$750 billion and observers quote annual growth figures of some 15 per cent (Tett 2006).[1] *The Banker*'s listing of the 'Top 500 Islamic Financial Institutions (TIFI)' showed a growth rate of 29.7 per cent of sharia-compliant assets over 2006, reaching a total of \$500 billion, with strong indications of serious underreporting (Timewell and Divanna 2007). Impressive as these figures may look at first sight, they should be seen in proportion to the rest of the financial industry. The biggest banks in the world each individually have a larger size than all Islamic financial institutions together. Total assets of UBS of Switzerland alone amounted to \$1533 billion in 2005, Citigroup came to \$1484 billion and Mizuho Financial Group of Japan \$1296 billion (Raphaeli 2006). Citigroup's assets as per 31 March 2008 reached \$2.2 trillion (National Information Center 2008), which means a growth rate of a similar order of magnitude as the 15 per cent often quoted for the Islamic finance industry, though admittedly far below the 2006 figure from *The Banker*.

It is well known that Islamic finance is based upon the prohibition of interest, but that is not the only reason for rejecting part of the conventional range of financial instruments, there are also others. There is a fair dose of 'thou shalt not' in all this, but Islamic economics, of which Islamic finance is the most developed branch, or perhaps the only reasonably developed branch, is made up of more than injunctions to refrain from a number of activities or to steer clear of certain financial instruments.

It also includes a couple of positive recommendations, or even religious commandments.

One would be mistaken to assume that it is always unambiguously clear what is admissible and what is forbidden for a devout Muslim. First of all, it is a moot point to what extent the texts and traditions from the early centuries of Islam, which provide the foundation of Islamic finance, apply to the modern world. Muslims are deeply divided over this question, but even those who want to fully hold on to the traditions have to grapple with the fact that the world has changed since the seventh century and that the old texts and traditions have to be reinterpreted before they can be applied to situations and financial instruments unknown at the time.

In countries with a Muslim majority the legal system may be based on Islamic precepts that have an impact on the way the economy functions. Areas that come to mind are inheritance law, land ownership and sharecropping, and restrictions imposed on women. What sets Islamic finance apart is that it can, at least in part, also function within non-Islamic legal systems.

The Medieval Christian Church wrestled with similar problems about what to accept and what to reject as present-day Muslims. Discussions in the Medieval Church went on and on, even if there was a final authority, the Church Councils that assembled irregularly (the dogma of papal infallibility only dates from the First Vatican Council of 1870). If Medieval Church Council resolutions did not provide final answers to economic questions, it is hardly surprising that there is no end of discussion among Muslims about what is admissible and what is forbidden, from a religious point of view. After all, the Sunni community, to which between 85 and 90 per cent of Muslims belong, knows no church-like hierarchy and, like Protestantism, no final authority. With Shiism it is different. Shiites distinguish themselves by holding that the religious and political leader of the Muslim community, the *imam*, is divinely appointed and can only be a direct descendant of the Prophet Muhammad, starting with his cousin and son-in-law Ali (Shia means Party, that is, Party of Ali). He was also the fourth Caliph, or successor of Muhammad as ruler of the Islamic world, for the Sunnites. The most numerous Shiite group, the Twelvers, or Ithna Asharis, holds that the last imam, the twelfth one, went into occultation. The Sevener sect maintains it was the seventh imam, the last one in their line of imams. In the fullness of time, many Shiites believe, the last imam will return as the Mahdi (Guided One), who will bring justice to the world for a number of years before the coming of the Day of Judgement, even if the Quran is silent on the Mahdi. The imam is as infallible as post-1870 popes of the Roman Catholic Church when proclaiming dogmas *ex cathedra*, and during the time of the last imam's occultation other religious leaders borrow at least some of his authority (Douwes 2004; Slomp 2005, pp. 114–17). Unlike Sunni Islam, Shia Islam does have clerical hierarchies, in the case of the Twelvers headed by *ayatollahs* (ayatollah is an honorific title for an outstanding legal scholar). These ayatollahs in their turn may accept guidance by *grand ayatollahs*, of which there may be one, as in Iraq, or more than one, as in Iran. In the latter case, Shiites decide for themselves which ayatollah to follow as their source of authority. Shiites differ on whether the religious leaders should keep some distance from politics during the time of occultation (de Bruijn 2008).

Although many Muslims do not subscribe to the need for an Islamic financial system, whereas its advocates disagree on a number of points, a distinctly Islamic system has come into existence. This system cannot be understood without some knowledge of Islamic thought on ethics and law. This is, therefore, dealt with first. The structure of the book is as follows. Chapter 1 traces the motives for setting up a separate Islamic financial system; Chapter 2 describes the legal reasoning behind Islamic precepts and its religious foundations; Chapter 3 analyses what Islamic finance is all about, put against the backdrop of an Islamic economy; Chapter 4 gives an overview of Islamic financial instruments; Chapter 5 discusses the peculiarities of Islamic banking; Chapter 6 does the same for Islamic investment, insurance and other special activities; Chapter 7 goes into the problems confronting the central bank and the Treasury if they decide to follow Islamic principles and Chapter 8 finally tries to find an answer to the question of what can be seen as the successes and failures of Islamic finance, both from the point of view of conventional economics and in the eyes of some prominent Muslim scholars. Appendices contain relevant texts from the Quran and the Bible and a list of web addresses. The reader will become acquainted with quite a number of latinized Arab words. In the latinization of these words, diacritical marks have been left out.

NOTE

1. The difference between the low estimate and the high one can at least partly be explained by the inclusion or exclusion of some categories. The General Council of Islamic Financial Institutions in Bahrain estimated in 2006 that on-balance sheet assets of Islamic financial institutions amounted to nearly $300 billion. If we add some $200 billion for Iran, which is not a member of this Council, and a similar figure for the Islamic activities of Western banks, we arrive at the higher estimate. These are no more than guestimates, however (see Gassner 2007a). KPMG gives an estimate of over $300 billion bank assets plus $400 billion in the form of investments (KPMG 2006, p. 2). It is not made clear what exactly is subsumed under the latter heading.

1. Why Islamic finance?

1.1 INTRODUCTION

This chapter is about the motives for Muslims to advocate the use of financial instruments that obey specific Islamic requirements. The movement for an Islamic economy, and an Islamic financial system in particular, is rooted in the experience of Muslims in what they, or at least some of them, felt in the past was an unfriendly non-Muslim environment. A new impetus was given with the rise in oil wealth in a number of Muslim countries after the 1973–74 oil crisis and the success of Malaysia as a fast grower, both of which may have contributed to a formerly unknown level of self-confidence that made it possible for Muslim governments and firms to develop new financial instruments in close cooperation with Western firms, without the feelings of resentment that underlay the first attempts to Islamize the economy. The history of the movement for Islamic finance, and Islamic economics in general, is sketched and the chapter ends with highlighting the diversity of views among Muslims on this matter.

1.2 THE ORIGINS: MAULANA MAUDUDI

Islamic finance is a way to put Islamic principles about the economy into practice. Attempts to develop a specific Islamic type of economy, based upon the precepts of the holy book of Muslims, the *Quran*, and on Islamic religious law, the *sharia*, can be seen as a manifestation of the wish harboured by Muslims to retain, or regain, their own identity vis-à-vis the capitalist West and, until the fall of communism, the socialist East. There is a deep-rooted idea among large parts of the Muslim intelligentsia, in particular in the Middle East, that the forces of the globalizing world, in their view characterized by materialism and sex, are incompatible with the values cherished by Muslims (Najjar 2005). Thus, Islamic economics can also be seen as an attempt to prevent Muslims from assimilating in this globalizing world dominated by Western culture (Kuran 1996, 2006, ch. 4).

The idea of Islamic economics was introduced around the time of the Partition of India by a number of people, first of all maulana or mawlana Sayyid Abu'l-A'la Maududi (1903–79).[1] Maududi (also spelled Mawdudi or Maudoodi) had already delivered an address on the subject in 1941 (Maududi 1941). An economy based on Islamic principles was also advocated by Anwar Iqbal Qureshi in 1946 (Qureshi 1991), who was influenced by Maududi, Naiem Siddiqhi in 1948 and Sheikh Mahmud Ahmad in 1952 (see Gafoor 1996, p. 37; Mahmud Ahmad 1999). It should not come as a surprise that pre-Partition India and later Pakistan provided a fertile environment for developing ideas on an Islamic economy, as Pakistan was founded expressly to be a homeland for Muslims. Maududi is the main figure behind the movement to organize society along orthodox, fundamentalist lines (Slomp 2003, p. 239). Sayyid Qutb (1906–66), a prominent leader of Egypt's Muslim Brotherhood, and Muhammad Baqir al-Sadr (1931–80) from Iraq were also in the forefront of the development of Islamic economics.

One important motivation for developing specific Islamic views on the economy was the conviction that Islam was seen as backward by the dominant European civilization, which had little time for the tenets of Islam in the economic sphere. From the nineteenth century on, Islam was not taken seriously and was regarded as rather benighted and incompatible with modern scientific views, people such as Maududi, Qutb and al-Sadr felt; and not without some justification (see the Introductions by Syed Sulaiman Nadvi and Manazir Ahsan Gilani to Qureshi 1991; Kuran 2006, pp. 86–7). Maududi, as editor of a journal he founded in 1932, wrote about its objective:

> The plan of action I had in mind was that I should first break the hold which Western culture and ideas had come to acquire over the Muslim intelligentsia, and to instill in them the fact that Islam has a code of life of its own, its own culture, its own political and economic systems and a philosophy and an educational system which are all superior to anything that Western civilization could offer. I wanted to rid them of the wrong notion that they needed to borrow from others in the matter of culture and civilization. (Quoted from Slomp 2003, p. 240)

They said farewell to the defensive attitude and went on the offensive, in their discussion on economics in particular impugning existing interest theories and justifications of interest (extensively in Qureshi 1991, ch. I). Mahmud Ahmad even states that intellectual bankruptcy is the hallmark of every theory of interest (Mahmud Ahmad 1999, p. 30).

Communism could not find favour with Maududi, as, in his words, Islam does not approve of any political or economic organization that seeks to submerge the individual in the society, and stultify the flowering of his personality (Maududi 1999, p. 5). Nationalization of all means of production would lead to social regimentation, read: dictatorship (Maududi 1999, pp. 5, 27). Fascism and national-socialism are as bad as communism in this respect (Maududi 1999, pp. 28–9, this is still from his 1941 address). On the other hand, Islam, according to Maududi, also abhors laissez faire, because that would open the way for individuals to pursuit their own ends at the cost of society as a whole. Capitalism is associated, in his view, with the French revolution, which propagated individual liberty, liberalism, capitalism and the system of secular democracy (Maududi 1999, p. 107). For French revolution we may probably read Enlightenment.

Maududi was the most outspoken advocate of an Islamic economy. He was born in 1903 in Aurangabad, in the Muslim state of Hyderabad in the Deccan. His family belonged to the upper crust of Indian Muslims and claimed to descend from the relatives of the Prophet. His father was strongly under the influence of a movement that, in reaction to the European values that had come to India with the British, strove to purify Islam from syncretistic practices and revive the strength of the Muslim community. Maududi himself, as editor-in-chief of a variety of Muslim journals, was opposed to Muhammad Ali Jinnah's All-India Muslim League and its ideal to found an independent Muslim state, because Islam pretends to express universal values and should not be used as an ideological foundation for a nation state. Rather, he would bolster the Islamic community in order to prepare for life in an independent India dominated by Hindus often hostile to the Muslim minority (Kuran 2006, pp. 83–4). Some people suspect a personal antipathy vis-à-vis Jinnah (Mazari 1998). Nonetheless, after the Partition he moved to Lahore and propagated the view that the moral and ethical principles of Islam can only be put into practice if the state imposes them.

Maududi founded a political party, the *Jamaat-e-Islami* (Islamic Society or Party) in 1941. This party, which is still active in Pakistan, is based on the idea that all present-day problems can be solved with the help of the Quran and the *sunna* (from *sunnat al-nabi* or practices of the Prophet, see Chapter 2), as delivered in the *ahadith*, or traditions. Maududi distinguished himself by combining a strictly literal interpretation of the Quran with modern political terminology in order to show the relevance of the Quran and the sunna for twentieth-century society. Maududi's ideal society was the supposedly pure one under the Prophet and his four successors before the Umayyad dynasty took over, Abu Bakr, Umar, Uthman and the Prophet's cousin and son-in-law Ali, collectively known as the rightly-guided caliphs. Remember that the first three are not acknowledged by Shiites, as they were no relatives of Muhammad.

It was all fine and well to have a Muslim state, or a state for Muslims, but that was still far removed from an Islamic state. What Maududi was after was a fundamentalist theocracy, which he dubbed a 'theo-democracy', a form of government that should not only be forced upon Pakistan or the Muslim world, but on the whole human race. The Muslim population should freely choose a leader, but with the choice restricted to people, or rather males, with an impeccable sunna-respecting track record. He only differed from traditionalist *ulama*, or religious scholars, in that he still left a small place for the modernization of Islamic law, as traditional Islamic law does not have the answer to each and every problem confronting present-day Muslims. His views did not go down too well with the modernists in the Pakistani government and the army, nor were these enamoured of the well-organized Jamaat-e-Islami machinery that spread his message. Maududi was several times imprisoned and in 1953 he was even sentenced to death by a court martial, but under public pressure the sentence was commuted to two years imprisonment. He died in 1979 in New York, where he had gone for heart surgery. In the same year his follower Kurshid Ahmad became a cabinet minister (1979–80) under President Muhammad Zia ul-Haq (1977–88), who declared Pakistan an Islamic state and began to enforce sharia law (see on Maududi Adams 1966; Aziz Ahmad 1967; Otto 2001; Slomp 2003).

Maududi held strong views on the way society should be run. He advocated strict gender separation and was strongly in favour of the death sentence for apostates, even if prominent Muslim scholars argue that in the early times of Islam the death sentence was only issued for soldiers that converted to Judaism or Christianity, in order to evade military service (Slomp 2002). He was very strict as regards expenditure on leisure and even culture. Muslims, in his eyes, should not only stay away from such things as wine and gambling, but also from 'music and dances and other means of self-indulgence' and are furthermore forbidden to wear silken dresses, to use golden ornaments and jewels (except in the case of women, parentheses Maududi's), or to decorate their house with pictures and jewels (Maududi 1999, p. 31). This rejection of culture sounds not too different from the views of some of the more puritan currents within Protestantism, and, like there, cannot be seen as representative of the views of the whole community of believers.

1.3. DIGRESSION: THE ISLAMIZATION OF THE FINANCIAL SYSTEM IN PAKISTAN; A CHEQUERED HISTORY

The ideas about what an Islamic economy should look like took some time to develop. For the founding fathers in British India and later Pakistan it was a process of trial and error; they did not start out with a detailed blueprint. Also harsh realities impeded a fast adoption of the principles of Islamic economics. Anwar Iqbal Qureshi notes that he, as Economic Advisor to the Government of Pakistan after Partition, actively tried to introduce interest-free banking, but did not pull it off because of practical difficulties (Qureshi 1991, p. 199). An important step in the process was that President Muhammad Zia ul-Haq, who had seized power in 1977, in February 1979 decided that interest-based transactions were to be phased out. Banks were ordered to offer interest-free alternatives to conventional savings accounts and to completely switch to interest-free banking within five years. Zia started in the same year by making three financial institutions interest free. Even if some specialized credit institutions were quick to shift to interest-free financial products, in the commercial banking field the process proved time-consuming and the government itself did not refrain from fixed-interest borrowing activities. In the mid-1980s the Islamization of the financial sector ran out of steam, but the Sharia Bench of Pakistan's Supreme Court became active with a verdict given in December 1991 under which a number of laws based on *riba* or interest were declared unlawful. The governments that followed upon Zia's death in an air accident that nobody believes was an accident, did all they could to stymie the efforts of the Court and its supporters.[2] The struggle has been dragging on since. The Sharia Bench had ordered the government to eliminate interest from the economy by 30 July 2002. An appeal by Pakistani banks for the court to review its earlier decision was backed by the government, which claimed that the initial ruling was flawed and that modern banking did not conflict with Islamic principles. The government also argued that interest-free banking would create financial anarchy in the country. The Supreme Court on 24 June 2002, a few weeks before its earlier deadline, duly reviewed the earlier judgement and remanded the case back to the Federal Sharia Court for a fresh decision (Supreme Court of Pakistan 2003, pp. 35–8).[3] So banking is to a great deal interest-free, but interest-based transactions are still possible.

1.4 ISLAM AGAINST THE REST OF THE WORLD?

Maulana Maududi can be credited with launching the idea of an Islamic economy. In his approach, it is associated with an ideology where the state sees to it that Islamic rules are strictly observed. This idea of an Islamic economy not only proved attractive to Pakistanis, but also to non-Pakistanis in search of an Islamic answer or alternative to capitalism and communism. It was embraced by the Muslim Brotherhood in Egypt, which, like Maududi, advocated Islamic forms of finance as part and parcel of a rather aggressive drive to Islamize society at large. Members of the Muslim Brotherhood also played a prominent role in the establishment in 1977 of the first Islamic bank in Sudan, Faisal Islamic Bank (rival groups set up their own Islamic banks, see Coutsoukis 2004). Indeed, *political Islam*, the ideology that seeks the establishment of an Islamic state based on the sharia, is commonly seen as having been born with the establishment of the Muslim Brotherhood in 1928. In the eyes of the leader of one of its more radical wings, Sayyid Qutb, who was executed by the Nasser regime in 1966, people have to choose between 'God's absolute rule' and 'total pagan ignorance' (*jahiliyyah*). People who are deemed not to follow 'God's absolute rule' have to be struck by *takfir*, that is, they are declared unbelievers, *kuffar*. Muslims that turn unbelievers are guilty of apostasy and deserve the death penalty. Sunnites are not allowed to rise against a Muslim ruler, but declaring him an unbeliever frees the way for insurgents. Through takfir, attempts on the life of Muslim rulers that stand in the way of the establishment of a fully Islamized society can be justified (Best et al. 2004). The Muslim Brotherhood and similar movements attacked, after their countries had gained independence, the ruling classes in their own societies, who they felt were guilty of social injustice and oppression. A return to what they preached to be the true Islamic way of life was seen as necessary to end these evils (Hoebink 2008). As a reaction, some argue, the ruling classes embraced the cause of Islamic finance in order to legitimize their rule and evade takfir (Barenberg 2004–05). Timur Kuran (2006, pp. xii, 73), for instance, suggests that in countries where the propagandists of political Islam or Islamists do not eschew violence, such as Pakistan, politicians and intellectuals have supported efforts to introduce Islamic economic institutions, including Islamic banks, not out of conviction, but for fear of being branded insufficiently Islamic. In countries such as Egypt and Turkey, where critics have been assassinated, intellectuals hesitate to speak out openly against the economic ideas of Islamists.

Advocates of a distinct Islamic way of life and Islamic institutions come in all shapes and sizes. Apparently, there is more than one way to read the holy scriptures. After the sources of Islamic law have been discussed in Chapter 2, we shall bring in a bit of nuance by presenting Tariq Ramadan's classification of Muslims according to their way of reading and interpreting the sources.

Against the voices advocating an Islamic economic system totally different from and even isolated from the non-Muslim rest of the world, we have people such as the leading Muslim economist Mohammad Nejatullah Siddiqi, who takes his brethren (and sisters, but they are less vociferous) to task for what he sees as a 'hostile-West syndrome' that puts all the

Muslim countries' woes down to the pernicious influence of the West (Siddiqi 1994). He deems it futile to try and develop an Islamic economic system that is totally different from the West. To him, Islamic finance and Islamic economics are more a question of ethics and morality. He sees these as a step forward in the development of more equitable economic and financial arrangements which the whole world needs and in which Muslim individuals and countries should participate (Siddiqi 2002).

This shows that embracing Islamic finance can follow without any antagonism to non-Muslims. Many Muslims who take their religion seriously are eager to obey what they see as the precepts of the Quran and the sunna as much as possible, even if they are not inclined to impose their views on those who do not share their convictions or to shut themselves off from the non-Muslim world. The ideas on Islamic economics may have been developed as a reaction to colonialism and capitalist and communist economic systems and it may be true that Islamization of the financial sector in Iran was an instrument in the hands of the revolutionaries who had overthrown the Shah, but it still seems the case that these ideas can be adopted without necessarily accepting at the same time the political ideas of Maududi or Sayyid Qutb. No anti-Western feelings need be involved, as Siddiqi argued. Muslims have no compunction making use of the services of Islamic windows of American and European banks in predominantly Muslim countries. Western banks such as HSBC, Citigroup and Deutsche Bank have been in the forefront of developing Islamic financial instruments. Moreover, the International Monetary Fund has built up cordial relationships with the Islamic financial world and the Institute of Islamic Banking and Insurance, set up in London in 1991, calls it a good omen that major international financial organizations are involved in Islamic finance and that there is an active interaction between those organizations and Islamic bodies. Others find that it is only to be applauded if non-Muslim institutions accept sharia conditions and offer sharia-compliant products (Yaqubi 2000). They may be inclined to see this as a step forward on the way to a fully Islamized economy, however.

It seems that Islamic finance may fulfil different roles in different circumstances. In countries where it is the only form of finance allowed, it is clearly part of an Islamization drive that leaves little choice to their inhabitants. If, however, Islamic finance is offered alongside conventional finance, the range of products offered to the public is widened. Greater choice is in principle a good thing, provided there are no forces working behind the scenes to completely replace conventional finance in the end by Islamic finance. As so often in the Muslim world, opinions differ widely. One observer, the Turkish columnist Uğur Mumca, saw Islamic banking as part of, in the words of Timur Kuran (2006, p. 55) 'a sinister ploy to advance Islamism, isolate Muslims from global civilization, and force Muslim nations into a despotic political union established on medieval principles'. Mr Mumca was murdered in 1993, and there are strong indications that this was on orders from Iran. The results apparently can be disastrous if the most extreme views clash, but generally the world of Islamic finance itself gives the impression that the interest in earning money in a sharia-compliant way is more prevalent than any hatred of critics. Still, some theorists of an Islamic economy may have more fundamentalist and antagonistic convictions than the practitioners.

In the case of Islamic finance offered in Western countries one may take the positive view that it is to be applauded if Muslim inhabitants have a choice and feel themselves taken seriously. From the viewpoint of Western financial institutions it is probably best to see the market for Islamic financial products as a potentially interesting niche. But there is more to it than that. Islamic finance is not only touted as the answer to Muslims who feel uncomfortable with conventional finance for religious reasons, but also as beneficial for others. It is claimed that Islamic finance is ethically superior and one observer states that 'Islamic Banking and Finance marketing strategies may be undergoing a subtle shift, toward the "ethical" and "socially responsible" labels and away from the "faithbased" and "Islamic" labels' (Maurer 2003, p. 198). Though the September 11 attacks in 2001 may have played a role in this strategy and the phenomenon is first of all an American one, it is a potentially attractive one for Islamic financial institutions, in particular Islamic funds, in other countries as well, as it might broaden the potential market.

1.5 CONCLUSIONS

It should be realized that, as just described, the Muslim world itself is divided on the desirability of Islamic economics. Islam harbours as divergent views as Christianity. Many Muslims do not agree that the Quran and the sunna forbid the financial instruments rejected by Islamic finance. One Pakistani writer, Izzud-Din Pal, sees the whole drive to introduce Islamic finance and an Islamic economy as a plot by traditionalist religious scholars, the ulama, and their political supporters, first of all president general Muhammad Zia-ul Haq, to revive the institutional framework of the Middle Ages (Pal 1999, p. 143). He deplores the fact that there is little place for 'Islamic modernism which embraces those Muslims who believe that the Qur'anic verses should be examined in the context of the social framework in which they were revealed and their message reconstructed in the light of modern times' (Pal 1999, p. ix). He does not hesitate to label the brand of Islam which dominates the mainstream literature in Pakistan, that is, the literature inspired by the ideas of Maududi and Qureshi, as pharisaic (Pal 1999, p. xx). But if not all Muslims feel attracted to Islamic financial products, some non-Muslims may do. The most well-known characteristic of Islamic finance is the prohibition of interest and if Malaysia's former Prime Minister, Dr Mahathir Mohamad, claims that Islamic finance puts an end to the slavery of debt and makes for a fair distribution of risk between lenders and borrowers, that may ring a bell with those in the West who are sympathetic to the diatribes against interest from such people as the poet Ezra Pound in his Cantos 45 and 51 (Pound 1968, see Brooke-Rose 1971 on his economic views). Also they might feel that Islamic investment funds answer their needs for ethical ways of investing their money. Indeed Western banks such as Switzerland's UBS target both Muslim and non-Muslim investors with their Islamic investment products (Iley and Megalli 2002).

There is thus a wide variety of views concerning the desirability of Islamic forms of finance. Some of these views may be incompatible with each other, but a pluralistic society should at least be able to accommodate Islamic forms of finance, whatever the ideas of the theorists.

NOTES

1. 'Maulana' or 'mawlana' is a title used for a scholar of Persian and Arabic in countries such as India and Pakistan.
2. See Maududi's disciple Khurshid Ahmad (1997) for an account from the point of view of Maulana Maududi's Jamaat-e-Islami party.
3. See Mehmood (2002) on the history of the attempts to Islamize Pakistan's economy.

2. Sources of Islamic law

2.1 INTRODUCTION

A Muslim's life ideally is ruled by Islamic religious law, the sharia. Literally, the word 'sharia' can be translated as 'the path that leads to the spring' (Ramadan 2004, p. 31). Figuratively, it means 'a clear path to be followed and observed'. Islamic religious law springs from various sources. These are discussed in this chapter, along with the different ways in which the law is interpreted. Separate attention is paid to the question of how Muslims living among a non-Muslim majority should observe the sharia.

2.2 PRIMARY AND SECONDARY SOURCES

There are various sources of Islamic legal knowledge. The first one of course is the Quran itself, which, Muslims believe, was revealed to the Prophet Muhammad, also called the Messenger of God (Rasulullah), by the angel Jibril (Gabriel). The second one is the sunna, that is, the deeds, utterances and tacit approvals of the Prophet, as related in the ahadith or traditions (the singular *hadith* is also used for tradition in general), handed down through a dependable chain of transmitters.[1] Sometimes, the term sunna is used in a wider sense, including the deeds of Muhammad's Companions and successors.[2] Note that this is not a critical study of the origins of Islamic law. We try to understand the Muslim view of Islamic law. Eminent Islam scholars such as Joseph Schacht (1902–69), following Ignaz Goldziher (1850–1921), argued that the sunna is in reality the practice of the Umayyad rulers of Damascus, only supported by ahadith of dubious authenticity (see Schacht 1949, 1975, p. 4). More recent scholarship, however, tends to concentrate on the authenticity of individual ahadith, rejecting wholesale branding of the ahadith as forgeries (Motzki 2008; Sentürk 2007). All this, however, lies outside the purview of this book.

The Quran and the sunna are the primary sources. They are thought to contain God's infallible and immutable will, or sharia in a narrow sense. Of course present-day Muslims, living some 15 centuries after the time of Muhammad, see themselves confronted with problems on which the

Quran and the sunna are silent. The Hadith dwells at great length on such subjects as 'the sale of gold necklace studded with pearls' (Muslim, book 10, chapter 38) and 'the selling of the camel and stipulation of riding on it' (Muslim, book 10, chapter 42), but contains precious little on, say, corporate government, public utilities or intellectual property, let alone complex financial products. Furthermore, the Quran and the sunna leave room for different interpretations. Muslims therefore often have to resort to secondary sources of law. Sharia in a wide sense includes all Islamic legislation. In so far as this is based on secondary sources, it is not necessarily valid for all times and all places.

In the authoritative classification developed in the early ninth century by al-Shafii (the founder of the Shafii school of law, see below), there are two secondary sources of law: *ijma*, or consensus, and *qiyas*, or analogy. Together with the primary sources they are the four principal *usul al-fiqh* or roots of law in Sunni Islam (Table 2.1).

- *Ijma*, consensus. The underlying idea of ijma as a source of law is that truth is safe with the community of believers (Cragg 1964, p. 145). Support is provided by a hadith according to which Muhammad said that 'my community will never agree on an error' (Esposito 2003, p. 134). Thus, after Allah and the Prophet, the Muslim community or *umma* can also be a source of law (Cragg 1964, p. 16). The trouble is that there is no consensus about what consensus consists of. Some, following al-Shafii, define consensus as agreement among the entire community of believers whereas others restrict ijma to agreement among the scholars. Some political modernisers in the Muslim world give a liberal twist to consensus and see it as a foundation for democracy, with parliament as the body that produces ijma.[3]

Table 2.1 Sources of Islamic law

Primary sources	Quran
	sunna, Hadith
Secondary sources	ijma (consensus)
	qiyas (analogy)
	ijtihad (individual interpretation)
	ray (expert private interpretation)
Some principles	istihsan (juristic preference)
	istislah (public interest)
	urf (custom)
	darura (necessity)

- *Qiyas* or analogy is the second important secondary source, or the fourth 'root', of Islamic law. The idea is that, if a ruling is required on a situation not covered in the Quran or the sunna, a comparison can be made with situations which the Quran or the sunna did provide for. If, for instance, the Quran prohibits the use of wine, the use of other toxicants, with similar deleterious effects, can be assumed to fall under the prohibition as well (Cragg 1964, p. 145).

The classification is not logically watertight, in the sense that it covers all sources of law without overlap. Ijma, for instance, may use qiyas, and other sources of law are also accepted by many Muslims. It is not surprising, therefore, that al-Shafii's classification has not been universally followed. Many scholars, down from al-Ghazali (Abu Hamid al-Ghazali, 1058–1111), see ijtihad as the third secondary source of Islamic law.

- *Ijtihad* is the independent reasoning by a qualified jurist leading to new legal rules. Such a jurist may, or rather should, use qiyas (El-Gamal 2006, p. 17).

There is no unanimity on the question of whether there is still a place for ijtihad in the modern world. Some Muslim scholars opine that the 'door of ijtihad' or 'gate of ijtihad' was closed early in the tenth century, as at about that time scholars of the law schools felt that all important questions had been settled (Schacht 1982, p. 70). Others say it took place in the thirteenth century (El-Gamal 2006, p. 24). A modern case of (collective) ijtihad, according to Yaqubi (2000), are the accounting standards developed by the Accounting and Auditing Organization for Islamic Financial Institutions (AAOIFI) (see Section 5.4.4). In Sudan ijtihad was reintroduced in 1983 by the military dictator Jafar al-Numayri when he established Islamic law as the law of the state (Esposito 2003, p. 301). In cases not foreseen in statute law, the Sudanese civil court may apply the sharia as it interprets it and if necessary exercise ijtihad (Layish 2004, p. 99). It is in the character of ijtihad laws that they can be changed if circumstances change, which allows many economic laws to be adapted to new circumstances (see, for example, Maududi 1999, p. 295).

A special case of ijtihad in early Islam was ray.

- *Ray* is expert private interpretation or personal reasoning. Ray was involved in the instructions that the Prophet and the early Caliphs gave to the people responsible for the administration of justice in conquered territories and in their *ex post* sanctioning of it (Gardet 1967, pp. 79–81; *A Field Guide*). It did not use qiyas, as there were not yet rules or examples that could be used as an analogy. According to Schacht, by the ninth century ray was no longer acceptable (Schacht 1982, p. 70).

Instead of following al-Shafii's classification, it would perhaps be more logical to group ijma and ijtihad together, as these concepts bear on the people who are qualified to make binding rules, whereas qiyas refers to a method that can be applied in ijma and ijtihad. Indeed, some regard ijtihad as the main secondary source, encompassing ijma (Ramadan 2004, pp. 44–5).

If qiyas is not sufficient to find an answer, jurists may also base their rulings on considerations of istihsan, istislah, urf and darura.

- *Istihsan* means 'juristic preference' and points to exceptions that a jurist can make to strict or literal legal interpretations (Esposito 2003, p. 152; Schacht 1982, pp. 37, 299). Istihsan can be applied when qiyas, or any other method, does not provide a definite answer, or when a ruling based on qiyas would put unreasonable burdens on the believers. Istihsan is concerned with equity.[4]
- *Istislah* literally means 'seeking the good' (Ramadan 2004, p. 38), or taking the public interest, *maslaha,* into account.[5] Jurists have differed over the scope of istislah or maslaha as a source of law. Some see no place for it, others want to consider it as legal only to the extent that it can be seen as part of another source of law, such as qiyas, but still others accept istislah or maslaha as an independent source of law, even in cases where it cannot be based on quotations from the Quran or the sunna. The principle of istislah can be invoked, for instance, in decisions about blood transfusions and organ transplants, where there are no historical precedents and qiyas therefore cannot show the way (Esposito 2003, p. 152).
- *Urf* is custom. It can be an argument behind istihsan and istislah. Custom can also function as a supplementary source of law in contract law. It will determine the rights and duties of contracting parties in cases where no conditions have been stipulated (Libson 1997, pp. 153–4).
- *Darura* or necessity. The principle of necessity says that a law need not be followed in cases where it would be unreasonable to demand strict obedience to the laws and rules. This is simply the old adage that necessity knows no law. It can be seen as a kind of source of law, even if it is a principle that is not used to formulate laws, but only to determine when laws should not apply. A ruling under the heading of darura may be based on custom (Libson 1997, p. 138). In the Quran itself a case of darura can be found in Chapter, or Sura, 2:185, where it is said about travellers and the ill, who are not able to observe the rules of fasting: '(. . .) whoever is ill or upon a journey shall fast a similar number of days later on. Allah intends your wellbeing and

> does not want to put you to hardship.' To those for whom fasting is under any circumstances difficult, such as the old and infirm, Quran 2:184 offers a choice: 'For those who can not endure it [for medical reasons], there is a ransom: the feeding of one poor person for each missed day.' The message is that Islam does not demand the impossible from the believers.

The sharia distinguishes between things and actions that are strictly forbidden, or *haram*, and those that are permitted, or *halal*. But decisions on whether something is permissible or not are not simple yes or no questions. The permissible, or halal, things and actions in their turn can be subdivided into four categories:

- First, we have duties that have to be performed by all Muslims, called *fard*.
- Second, we have things that are advisable to do, *mandub*.
- Third, things about which religion is indifferent, *ja'iz*.
- Fourth, things that can better be refrained from, undesirable or *makruh*.

Duties for all Muslims, fard, include the 'five pillars of Islam':

- the profession of faith or *shahada*
- prayer or *salat*
- charity or *zakat*
- fasting or *sawm*
- pilgrimage to Mecca or *hajj*.

Additional prayers on specific occasions are mandub, air travel is ja'iz and certain kinds of fish are makruh (Fyzee 2005, p. 17).

The sharia ideally governs all actions of a Muslim, but religious law leaves some options open. It is left to the believer to make up their mind about undesirable things.

In situations where it is not clear what sharia law requires from a Muslim, individuals or a court of law can ask a legal opinion or *fatwa* (pl. *fatawa*) from a qualified Islamic fiqh scholar, a *mufti*.[6] Fiqh is the science of Islamic law, and the general term for a fiqh scholar is *faqih*, pl. *fuqaha*. Fatawa may also be promulgated by ulama or fuqaha, individually or in group deliberation, by assemblies such as the Indonesian Council of Ulama (MUI or Majelis Ulama Indonesia)[7]. In Sunni Islam a fatwa is not binding, but in Shia Islam a fatwa is binding for those who requested it (Haase 2001). A fatwa issued by a highly-respected mufti is the closest equivalent in the Muslim world to a case law precedent in the Anglo-American legal system (Masud et al. 1996, p. 4). One complication is that there are different law schools whose followers may follow different principles of jurisprudence. To these schools we now turn.

2.3 LAW SCHOOLS

Muslims differ in their views about the applicability of the various principles and secondary sources of Islamic law. There are different schools of law, *madhahib* (sing. *madhhab*), each with its own fiqh or science of law. There are four leading Sunni schools of law (before the fourteenth century there were more such schools). They may hold different views on many subjects, but these are in general mutually accepted as valid from an Islamic point of view. The four madhahib are the Hanafi, Maliki, Shafii and Hanbali Schools.

- The Hanafi school. This is the oldest one. It derives its name from Abu Hanifa, an Iranian who taught in Iraq and died in 767. It is the most flexible of the four schools, emphasizing private interpretation, ray, juristic interpretation, istihsan, and reasoning by analogy, qiyas. Ijma, consensus, is also accepted and the Hanafi school even allows a new consensus to cancel an old one (Ramadan 2004, p. 45). Hanafis furthermore grant a much larger place to custom, urf, than the other schools (Libson 1997). The Moguls in India and the Ottoman rulers were Hanafis. They can accordingly be found in Turkey, Central Asia, the Balkans, Iraq, Afghanistan, India, Pakistan and Bangladesh. Reformist movements, which try to accommodate Islam to the modern world, often are to a greater or lesser extent Hanafi (*A Field Guide*). Still, Pakistan's traditionalist Hanafi ulama believe that ijtihad and ray can no longer be allowed, as all necessary interpretations have already been made long ago (Adams 1966, p. 386; Engineer 2000).
- The Maliki school. This school was founded by Malik ibn Anas, who died in 795 in Medina. It accords qiyas a larger place than the other schools, as Malik seems to have given priority to qiyas over ahadith with a weak chain of transmitters (Al-Mukhtar Al-Salami 1999, p. 22). Nonetheless, the Malikis strongly rely on the Hadith and also on the ijma of the scholars in Medina, where Muhammad lived after he had fled Mecca. Many of the customs of Medina arguably were granted the status of hadith, which fits in with the fact that Maliki scholars from the first centuries of the Muslim era

hardly ever explicitly referred to custom (Libson 1997, pp. 133–4). But even if custom is not formally seen as a source of law, in actual practice Maliki scholars seem to refer to it quite frequently (Libson 1997, p.136). Maliki scholars may further take the principle of public welfare, istislah, into consideration, though not all accept istislah and maslaha as an independent source of law. Malikis are concentrated in Upper Egypt, Tunisia, Algeria, Morocco, Mauretania, Libya, Kuwait, Bahrain, Dubai and Abu Dhabi.

- The Shafii school. Its founder was Muhammad ibn Idris al-Shafii, an Arab who died in 819 or 820 in Egypt. He rejected the personal view of scholars (ijtihad in the form of ray), juristic interpretation (istihsan), and considerations of public welfare (istislah), but fully accepted consensus (ijma). Reasoning should be based on ijma and go along the line of analogy (qiyas). Many Shafiite ulama follow al-Shafii in his rejection of public welfare as an independent source of law, because of the danger of unrestricted subjective human opinions and also because public welfare varies over time and between places (Esposito 2003, p. 152). Apparently, in their view public welfare is too slippery a concept to provide a firm basis for rulings. Al-Shafii was the first jurist to emphasize the Hadith as an unassailable source of law but also applied a rigorous rational criticism to it, verifying every link in the chain of transmission and establishing criteria by which to judge the transmitters (Ergene n.d.).[8] Indonesia, Malaysia and the Muslim minorities in South-East Asia and the Philippines are exclusively Shafiite. Furthermore, Shafiites live in Lower Egypt, the Sudan, Ethiopia, Somalia and Yemen.
- The Hanbali school, founded by disciples of Ahmad Hanbal, who died in 855 in Baghdad. The Hanbali base themselves exclusively on the Quran and the sunna, and the only ijma that is accepted is the consensus of the Companions of the Prophet, among whom the rightly-guided Caliphs. The leading Hanbali scholar Ibn Taymiyya (1263–1328) emphasized the literal truth of the Quran and rejected independent reasoning, in line with his rejection of Aristotelian logic. Allah, after all, is not bound by human logic (Stein 2005). Ibn Taymiyya was not a typical middle-of-the-road Hanbali. His writings influenced Muhammad ibn Abd al-Wahhab (1703–92), the founder of the puritan Wahhabite sect of Saudi Arabia. Whereas the followers of the four orthodox schools accept each other as true Muslims, Wahhabites are the exception in that they regard the Hanbali School as the only legitimate one. Hanbalis live on the Saudi Arab peninsula and Qatar and the Saudi courts apply the Hanbali interpretation of the sharia (Ahmed 2005, p. 102).

Some countries follow exclusively one school, other countries have more than one school inside their borders and in Egypt all four main schools are present. To add to the confusion, whereas Syrians, Jordanians and Palestinians follow Hanafi laws, they predominantly observe Shafii rites (Gardet 1967, pp. 86–7).

Besides the four great law schools there have been others. A very strict one was the Zahiri school, whose founder Abu Sulayman Daud al-Zahiri died in 884. Laws should according to the Zahiri school be exclusively based on the literal meaning, *zahir,* of the Quran and the sunna, excluding qiyas, ray and istihsan. The only ijma that is legally valid is the consensus of the Companions of the Prophet. Zahiri represented a traditionalist reaction against the great schools of law, in particular the Hanafi and Maliki schools. It seems that, even if the school itself was extinct by the fourteenth century, Zahiri elements could quite recently still be found in the Moroccan law system (Saleh 1986, p. 156). The Zahiri view is shared by other traditionalists who want to go back directly to the Hadith.

A still existing group with a law system peculiar to its own is the Ibadi sect, which is found in Oman, on Zanzibar, in Algeria and Libya and on the Tunisian island of Jerba (Saleh 1986, p. 4; Schacht 1982, p. 66). They follow a literal interpretation of the Quran and have no place for ijma or qiyas, but accept ray (Gardet 1967, pp. 100–101; Williams 1961, p. 215).

Shiites, who are concentrated in Iraq, Iran, Afghanistan, Yemen and India, follow their own rules. The Jafari law school of the largest group in Shii Islam, the Twelvers (Ithna Asharis), accepts ijma provided its validity was recognized by Muhammad himself or an infallible Shiite imam. It also accepts ijtihad by selected scholars, predominantly living in the holy cities of Shiism such as Qum. Ray and qiyas are anathema to Ithna Ashari and some other Shiites as well (Fyzee 2005, p. 22). It may be noted that Al-Azhar University in Cairo in 1959 designated the Jafari law school as the fifth school along with the four Sunni schools (Esposito 2003, p. 154). As far as its positive content is concerned, Shii doctrines do not differ more widely from those of the Sunni law schools than these last differ among themselves, except for inheritance law (Schacht 1982, p. 16).

2.4 HOW STRICT SHOULD ONE BE IN OBSERVING THE *SHARIA*?

Liberal-minded Muslims question a literal interpretation of the Quran and the Hadith. In the sharia a distinction is made between *ibadat*, devotional matters, and *muamalat*, dealings in the political, economic and social spheres. Ibadat includes the five pillars of Islam. Islamic finance, of course, falls under muamalat, but the wider field of Islamic economics also includes zakat, one of the five pillars, and is therefore not restricted to muamalat. Liberals argue that as far as muamalat is concerned, the revelation of the sharia provides general principles and that details are to be decided upon by every generation depending on time and place, guided by maslaha, public interest. After all, Islamic law is there for the wellbeing of the believers (see Quran 2:185). One leading Islamic economist, Mohammad Nejatullah Siddiqi, contends that 'We should never lose sight of the reality that the divine part of modern Islamic finance, though crucial, is very small. The rest is man-made resulting from *Ijtihad* (efforts in understanding and applications)' (Siddiqi 2001). In one of the publications of the Minaret of Freedom Institute in Bethesda, Maryland, which is close to the very liberal pro-free-market Austrian School, it is argued that the Hadith should not be seen as a series of injunctions, but as a window on the sunna, whereas the sunna in its turn provides an illustration of how to arrive at the right way to solve problems. The sunna 'must be understood as illustrations of the application of principles rather than blindly imitated' (Imad-ad-Dean Ahmad 2004, p. 2).

The Muslim world is deeply divided over these issues. Traditionalists routinely accuse the liberals of being corrupted by detestable Western ideas. It must be noted that it is not always easy for Muslims to take up a liberal position, as activists of less liberal persuasions often are ready to see any deviation from their version of strict orthodoxy as a reason for takfir, branding someone an apostate. This is an accusation not to be taken lightly (see Section 1.4). But reducing the matter to a dichotomoy between liberals and traditionalists would be too simplistic, as the Western Muslim scholar Tariq Ramadan argues. Ramadan distinguishes six major approaches in contemporary Islam to reading the sources, without pretending to be exhaustive (Ramadan 2004, pp. 24–8).

- Scholastic traditionalism. This current is marked by strict and sometimes even exclusive reference to one school of jurisprudence. The scope for interpretation of texts is very limited and does not realistically allow development. There is no room for ijtihad and the opinions of scholars that were codified between the eighth and the eleventh centuries rule the views on applying the sharia. Examples are the followers of the Deobandi movement in the border area between Pakistan and Afghanistan, which runs thousands of religious schools, *madrassas*. Deobandi students are called Taliban. It is in favour of reimposing *hudud* law, the most strict form of Sunni law, which demands flogging, amputation and capital punishments for a number of offenses (from *hudud Allah*: boundaries established by Allah). Ramadan further mentions Indo-Pakistani groups in the

UK and the USA and Turks in Germany as scholastic traditionalists. They are concerned mostly with religious practice and isolate themselves from their non-Muslim environment.

- Salafi literalism. This current rejects any mediation of the law schools when it comes to approaching and reading the holy texts. Its followers call themselves *salafis* because they are concerned to follow the *salaf*, that is, the title given to the Companions of the Prophet and to pious Muslims of the first three generations of Islam. They take the primary sources literally. Salafis keep themselves as much as possible apart from any non-Islamic environment. In their worldview there is a sharp distinction between *dar al-Islam*, the house or territory of Islam, on the one hand, and *dar al-kufr*, the house or territory of the infidels, and *dar al-harb*, the territory of war, on the other.
- Salafi reformism. This, too, refers back to the salafs, but in contrast to salafi literalism, its approach is to adopt a reading based on the purposes and intentions of the law and jurisprudence. Salafi reformists see ijtihad as necessary. They use reason when applying the primary sources in dealing with present-day developments in society. Prominent salafi reformists were maulana Maududi and Sayyid Qutb. Salafi reformists in the Western world aim to protect the Muslim identity and religious practices, but do not isolate themselves from their non-Muslim environment.
- Political literalist salafism. This is the label given to people, often former followers of salafi reformism, who have turned into political activists or even radical revolutionaries. Ramadan cites repression in the Muslim world as the main cause. Political literalist salafists want to reinstitute the Caliphate, seen as the only true Islamic state. The Caliphate covered the period from the death of Muhammad until 1924 when Caliphs nominally ruled the Islamic world as the successors of Muhammad.[9] The Western world is uncompromisingly seen as dar al-harb. Any collaboration with it is treason and the only thing a Muslim ought to do is wage a holy war, *jihad*, against it. One group seeking the return of the Caliphate is Hizb ut-Tahrir, or Liberation Party, which is actively recruiting supporters in Western Europe, among other places.[10]
- Liberal or rationalist reformism. This is essentially born out of the influence of Western thought during the colonial period. The social and political system that resulted from the process of secularization in Europe is welcomed by liberal or rationalist reformers. They supported Atatürk's reshaping of Turkey as a secular state and in the West they are in favour of integration or even assimilation of Muslims. They set not much store by the daily practice of religion

and have no need for special Islamic dress. They do not turn to the Quran and the sunna for every detail of conducting their life.

- Sufism. Sufis are mainly oriented toward the spiritual life and mystical experience, but that does not necessarily prevent them from becoming involved with the wider community. The holy texts have, in their view, a deep meaning that requires time for meditation and understanding. Most Sufi orders, certainly in the West, provide support to their own members and keep themselves to themselves.

Apart from these currents or movements, there are all kinds of sects that see themselves as the only 'true' Muslims and are quick to brand Muslims of another ilk as unbelievers, kuffar, which effectively is a call to kill them. Perhaps there is also a sizeable group that can be placed between salafi reformism and liberal reformism. It has been noted that in Turkey the rise of Islamic capitalists helps to moderate the stance of political Islamists, at least of reformist salafist convictions. In his PhD thesis on Turkey, Jang (2005) finds support for the hypothesis that the transformation of the Islamic political party from a fundamentalist one to a moderate one is connected with the more important role played by the Islamic bourgeoisie. They want to make profits and have an interest in political stability, friendly relations with other countries and the rule of law. Such people have no interest in alienating non-Muslims or building walls around themselves. They would often prefer pragmatism over dogmatism.

Salafi reformism is the cradle of the project of an Islamic economy and Islamic finance. It grew from the attempts by maulana Maududi and his contemporaries to find an Islamic answer to the challenges of the twentieth century. It appears, however, that many Muslims with less outspoken ideas also feel attracted to Islamic finance, because it offers a way to practise Islam in the modern world and emphasize their identity without isolating themselves. This is particularly important for Muslims living among a non-Muslim majority. They are the subject of the next section. Political literalist salafists of course have other ideals. Their ideas on the economy, based on a strict dividing line between the Muslim world and the rest, will be discussed in Section 3.6.

2.5 MUSLIMS AMONG A NON-MUSLIM MAJORITY

Muslims living in countries with a non-Muslim majority are a separate group with its own problems. They are bound by laws that do not even pretend to obey the sharia and it stands to reason that the growth of the Muslim population in Europe and the USA has led to an increasing demand for legal opinions on the ways they should adapt to their new environment. What makes things complicated is that Islamic jurisprudence is not bound by precedent and that fatawa from one scholar may deviate from previous legal opinions given by other sharia scholars (Jobst 2007). Partly to solve this problem, in 1997 the Fiqh Council (Council of Islamic Law and Jurisprudence) was established in the USA and the European Council for Research and Fatwas in Europe (Ramadan 2004, p. 53). Still, unanimity is far to seek; no surprise given the enormous disparity between the various currents in Islam as depicted in Tariq Ramadan's survey.

The four orthodox Shia law schools themselves also differ on the rules to be followed by Muslims living among a non-Muslim majority. Muslims are bound to follow the sharia even in countries where they form a minority, but there are circumstances where they cannot be expected to fulfil each and every obligation from the sharia. For such cases, the fiqh scholars, the fuqaha, accept exceptions to the rules. Especially the Hanafi school allows liberal recourse to darura (necessity) in order to lighten the lives of Muslims in non-Islamic countries. Most Hanafi jurists, for instance, would not rule that Muslims must strictly observe the ban on interest in their dealings with non-Muslims in the non-Muslim world, though Hanbali, Maliki and Shafii fuqaha are less lenient (Saleh 1986, p. 31; Schacht 1982, p. 199). The Hanafi school more generally sees contracts that would not pass muster in a Muslim environment as permissible for Muslims outside dar al-Islam and allows Muslims to trade with non-Muslims following the rules in force in their countries (Jum'a 2005; Ramadan 2004, p. 96). In the same vein, the leading Iraqi Shiite Ayatollah Sistani issued fatawa allowing Muslims in countries where they form a minority to deposit funds with banks against interest and to take out mortgage loans against interest (El-Gamal 2006, p. 19).

These solutions still maintain a sharp distinction between the Islamic and non-Islamic worlds. There is a widespread tendency among Muslims, first of all political literalist salafis, to distinguish between dar al-Islam, the abode of Islam, and dar al-harb, the territory of war. In dar al-Islam Islamic law prevails, whereas dar al-harb denotes territory that does not have a treaty of non-aggression or peace with Muslims. From this it follows that there is a third category, encompassing those territories that do have a treaty with Muslim territory. This category is called *dar al-ahd*, the abode of treaty, a concept applied by a number of Islamic scholars to international organizations such as the United Nations or the Organisation of African Unity; or alternatively *dar al-sulh* (sulh means amicable settlement).

These distinctions date from the early days of Islam, when the Muslim community was heavily involved in armed conflicts. The use of this terminology today only helps to sour relationships. A much more positive attitude of Muslims in the West toward their country of residence is possible and defendable from a Muslim point of view. Tariq Ramadan (2004, pp. 63ff, 239) argues that the concepts of dar al-Islam and dar al-harb do not figure in the Quran or the sunna, apart from three ahadith of debatable authority, and do certainly not belong to the universal principles of Islam that have to be followed always and everywhere. But even if one insists on making a distinction, the non-Muslim world need not be seen as hostile, as dar al-harb: the Hanafi school denotes as dar al-Islam any country or territory where Muslims are secure and have nothing to fear by practicing their religion. Dar al-harb by contrast are those territories where Muslims are not free to practice their religion. Ramadan argues that, following the Hanafi strand of thought, one can only arrive at the conclusion that most of the Western world is dar al-Islam, much more so than the great majority of countries with a Muslim majority. This appears to tally with the views of leading Muslims such as Abdurrahman Wahid, president of Indonesia from 1999 to 2001 and earlier the leader of the Muslim mass organization Nahdlatul Ulama, with a claimed membership of 40 million, who stated that from a Muslim point of view the form of government is not very important, as long as Muslim communities are free to carry out their religious duties (Lubis 2004).

Ramadan is dead-set against applying the concept of dar al-ahd to the Western world, as it would imply that Muslims living there should always keep aloof and shun the company of others. He takes issue with the binary view of a Muslim world that is fundamentally hostile to a non-Muslim world, a view on which the concept of dar al-ahd also rests. It is a view that is no longer appropriate in today's world. If there is one view held by the ulama of the past that fits the present world, it is the Hanafi view of dar al-Islam as any territory where Muslims are free to practise their religion. Ramadan would prefer to use the concept of *dar al-dawa*, a 'place for inviting people to God', presenting what Islam is and spreading its message (Ramadan 2004, pp. 72, 239). The corollary is that Muslims is Western countries should not stand with their backs to the society in which they live, but should fully participate, at the same time observing their religious duties as much as possible. This would mean that, if they see the ban on riba as applying to the present forms of interest, they would prefer to set up Islamic banks and other financial institutions. Unlike Ramadan's political literalist salafists, they would not be in implacably hostile opposition to conventional finance, but just demand their own place in the financial landscape. For the rest, if Muslims live in the West, they have a kind of tacit or implicit agreement with their country of residence, which commits them to respect the laws of the country of which they are citizens (Ramadan 2004, pp. 94–5).

Not all problems faced by Muslims can be satisfactorily solved in this way, but it is also an accepted principle by fiqh scholars that in the real world often a choice has to be made between imperfect solutions (Ramadan 2004, p. 162). It should be noted that Ramadan, even if he enthusiastically preaches participation, is deeply opposed to the dominant economic system, which in his eyes is not only based on interest, riba, but also on speculation and is, in addition, very exploitative. It is the duty of Muslims to develop alternatives, jointly with critics of the system from other faiths, but one should not place oneself outside the system: 'if it is impossible to get involved outside the system, unless one is very wealthy, one must find liberation by stages' (Ramadan 2004, p. 198).

2.6 CONCLUSIONS

The variety of views among Muslims is probably as great as in Christianity or Jewry. There is not one common view on the authority of the various sources of Islam nor on their applicability to the modern world. This means that the ideas on Islamic finance and an Islamic economy in general to be described in the chapters that follow are not shared by all Muslims. They originate with salafi reformists, but the interesting thing is that they also seem to appeal to Muslims without a strong attachment to any particular movement or current.

NOTES

1. Muslims do not universally agree on these chains. Shiites in particular have their own ahadith, though they also accept part of the Sunni Hadith. The most authoritative collections of ahadith are those by Bukhari, or Muhammad ibn Ismail al-Bukhari (816–878, or 870 according to others) and Muslim, or Abul Husain Muslim bin al-Hajjaj al-Nisapuri (824–883, or 875 according to others).

   A wide supply of Hadith collections in Arabic with English translation is available from Islamic bookstores; see, for example, www.halalco.com. Complete Hadith collections in English translation can also be found on the Internet. Particularly comprehensive sites are those of the University of Georgia, www.uga.edu/islam/, the University of Southern California, www.usc.edu/dept/MSA, and the Library of GC University, Lahore, www.gcu.edu.pk/Library/islam.htm.
2. Muhammad's companions were people who interacted with Muhammad. Sunnis consider them the most authoritative sources of information about the views and conduct of Muhammad. They themselves are also seen as guides for the believers. Shiites hold against many of the Companions that they supported the first three Caliphs (Esposito 2003, p. 55). These are not acknowledged by Shiites, as they were not relatives of Muhammad's.
3. Sinanovic (2004) reviews the discussion on whether only scholars or all believers can participate in ijma and on whether unanimity or a majority is required. The spiritual

founder of the state of Pakistan, Muhammad Iqbal (d. 1938), saw parliament as the only suitable vehicle for ijma in the modern world (Pal 1999, p. 146).

4. See Opwis (2008) for part of the history in Islamic legal thought on the role of istihsan.
5. The word maslaha is from the same root as istislah (Ramadan 2004, p. 235).
6. Unlike judges, muftis can be women or physically handicapped people (blind or mute). There are no formal requirements for a mufti; if a scholar's judgements are seen as authoritative by a community, they can function as a mufti (see Masud et al. 1996 on the requirements for becoming a mufti). Alongside these private muftis, Islamic countries have official, state-paid muftis representing the different law schools in that country. The highest-ranking official mufti in the Ottoman empire, from the start of the fifteenth century, used to be known as *shaykh al-Islam*. A special place is taken by the fatwa committee of al-Azhar University in Cairo. Fatwas issued by this committee, made up of scholars representing the four Sunni schools of law and existing since 1935, are held in particularly high esteem (Haase 2001; Masud et al. 1996).
7. In Indonesia there are four main bodies issuing fatawa. These can be seen as the result of collective ijtihad. Muftis are unknown in Indonesia (Gillespie 2007, pp. 206–7).
8. For a more detailed account of the somewhat complicated question of the place of ijma in Shafii's thought, see Schacht (1982, pp. 58ff).
9. Strictly speaking, the Caliphate ended in 1258, when Baghdad was sacked by the Mongols. The Sultans of Turkey later assumed the title of Caliph. The father of the Turkish republic, Kamal Atatürk, abolished the Sultanate in 1922 and the Caliphate in 1924.
10. See http://en.wikipedia.org/wiki/Hizb_ut-Tahrir, www.hizb-ut-tahrir.org and www.hizb.org.uk on Hizb ut-Tahrir.

3. The Islamic economy

3.1 INTRODUCTION

Islamic jurists have by and large been silent on the financial system for centuries until interest revived after the second world war (Chapra 2007, p. 346). Then Maududi and his contemporaries stood up and sought ways to Islamize the economy. Islamic economics is about the rules that should be followed by Muslims. It is normative economics. There have also been calls to develop an Islamic theoretical system of economics, including Islamic microeconomics and Islamic macroeconomics (Chapra 2000), but these have met with little success. Masudul Alam Choudhury (2007) would have liked to see such a system to be based on a specifically Islamic epistemology, itself founded on *tawheed*, the oneness of God. His own attempts, however, go no further than the pious wish that 'In the end, by combining the totality of the *sharia* precepts with financing instruments, Islamic banks become investment-oriented financial intermediaries and agencies of sustainability of the socioeconomic order, the socio-political order and institutions of preservation of community assets and wellbeing.' This has hard to understand implications for the nature of money:

> The nature of money now turns out to be endogenous. Endogenous money is a systemic instrument that establishes complementarities between socioeconomic, financial, social and institutional possibilities towards sustaining circular causation between money, finance, spending on the good things of life and the real economy. . . . Money cannot have an exchange value of its own, which otherwise would result in a price for money as the rate of interest. Money does not have a market and hence no conceptions of demand and supply linked to such endogenous money in Islam. (Choudhury 2007, p. 34)

Apart from the fact that interest is not the price of money but the price of credit, that is, for borrowing money, it looks like Choudhury only wants to accept money as a means of exchange and a numeraire, not as an asset in its own right. This is the view generally adopted by Muslim authors. It has a distinct Aristotelian twist, as we shall see below. Whether his diffuse picture of an ideal society logically follows from a tawheed-based epistemology, or indeed from any epistemology at all, is debatable. It must be said that attempts on the Christian side to base economic analysis on a specific epistemology anchored in religion have hardly fared better. One who tried was Professor T.P. van der Kooy, who taught economics in the Law Faculty at the VU University of Amsterdam from 1950 to 1969 and sought to base economic analysis on a Calvinist philosophical system developed by others at the VU University.[1] Van der Kooy rejected the distinction between positive and normative analysis, as Choudhury does, but it led nowhere and in the end he had to admit defeat (van der Kooy 1952, 1957). A distinct religion-based epistemology of course is something quite different than an analysis of the consequences for an economy of following Islamic principles with the help of conventional micro- and macroeconomic theory (see, for instance, Choudhury 1986, 1997; Tourani Rad 1989).

Islamic economics is about the rules that should be followed by Muslims. It is normative economics and as such does not require a different epistemology. Islamic economics is first and foremost the application of ethical principles, derived from what is seen as divine law. Sharia is, after all, a system of duties. These duties rest on a few basic principles: *tawheed* and brotherhood, fair remuneration of labour and redistribution of private wealth (Choudhury 1986, ch. 1; Chapra 2000).

- *Tawheed* and brotherhood. Tawheed is the oneness of God. It has also been interpreted as the unity of God and his creation, implying 'equality' of all men (Valibeigi 1993, p. 796). Tawheed and brotherhood bear on the way people treat each other in the light of their relationship with God, in other words, on social justice. Man as God's vice-regent on earth is charged with the obligation to use His resources in a right way, a principle not unknown in Chistianity either.
- Fair remuneration of labour. The remuneration of labour should be commensurate with the character and the amount of the work done. The available resources belong to God and those who appropriate an income that is too high, given this principle, are guilty of excess.
- The right of society to redistribute private wealth. Obligatory alms giving, zakat, follows from this principle.

The first two are general principles, but zakat is a specific duty. In our discussion of the Islamic economy in this chapter we start with zakat, followed by the ban on interest or riba, including a comparison with Christian attitudes, and the bans on gambling, *maysir*, and taking unnecessary risk, *gharar*. Then the scope widens and the views of Islam, or at least prominent Muslim scholars, on the economic order are reviewed. Finally, calls for an Islamic economy to be kept apart as far as possible from the non-Islamic one are discussed.

Of course, Muslims should also refrain from consuming haram goods and services. These include alcoholic drinks, pork-related products, gambling and adult entertainment. Among the more strict believers, virtually all entertainment, including the cinema and music, is considered haram (see Maududi 1999, p. 31). No sex, drugs and rock'n'roll for them. This restriction does not require extensive explanation, but it will return in the discussion in the following chapters every now and then.

3.2 *ZAKAT*

Zakat is the third of the five pillars of Sunni Islam, as we saw in Section 2.2. The Arabic word 'zakah' or 'zakat' means 'purity' and 'cleanliness' and the idea is that one purifies one's wealth as well as one's heart by giving away a part of one's wealth to the poor (Benthall 1999, p. 29; Sadeq 2002, p. 13). Zakat comes in two forms: *zakat al-fitr* and *zakat mal. Fitr* is the breaking of the fast and zakat al-fitr is the requirement for everybody if possible to give something for the needy every year at the end of the fasting month of Ramadan. What is asked is something like 2.2 kg of the local staple food or the equivalent in money. Zakat mal is a wealth tax in the form of a levy of, in most cases, 2.5 per cent on a number of assets. It is levied from adult, sane, free Muslims on productive assets that are held for at least one lunar year, above a threshold. Zakat is generally imposed on:

- gold and silver, in any form; not on other metals
- financial assets such as cash, banknotes and stocks
- merchandise for business
- livestock
- income derived from rental business.[2]

Personal needs are not taxable. These include, among other things, clothing, household furniture, utensils, cars, diamonds, pearls and other precious or semi-precious stones. For shares held in a company, zakat is based upon the current market value. Machinery, land, fixtures and fittings, furniture, buildings and so on are exempt from zakat, as only property intended for trade is included, and one is allowed to subtract these from the value of the shares.

There is a fierce discussion on what to include in the range of assets subject to zakat. Many assets did not yet exist in the early days of Islam and it is a moot question whether they should be taxed or not. An additional complication is that even in the days of the rightly-guided Caliphs not all assets were taxed. One hard to understand case was the decision by Caliph

Umar that dates are subject to zakat, but not pomegranates (Kuran 2006, p. 116). As for newer assets, banknotes, for instance, did not exist in the time of the Prophet, and are included on the basis of qiyas, as are bank deposits. Another source of uncertainty is the fact that price ratios have changed over the centuries. In particular, silver prices have fallen relative to gold and a threshold value based on some weight of silver is now way below threshold values based on gold (Sadeq 2002, p. 29).

A literal following of the ahadith concerning zakat leads to all kinds of other inconsistencies and inequities. A not too well-off farmer, for instance, may have to pay a considerable amount of zakat, whereas much richer people who have invested their wealth in cars and other assets that did not exist in the time of the Prophet, such as old masters, pay much less. The Fiqh Academy of the Organization of the Islamic Comference has firmly come out in favour of the traditional view that only items mentioned in the Hadith can be included.[3] In a fatwa issued in its session in Jeddah in November 1985, fixed assets such as buildings, machines and equipment are excluded from zakat (Sadeq 2002, pp. 32–3). This is the line followed in Saudi Arabia, on the grounds that these fixed assets are not items of trade. More liberal currents in contrast are in favour of applying ijtihad and istihsan, that is, of reinterpreting the rules with an eye to equity. Among those liberal currents, there is lack of unanimity on whether, for instance, salaries should be brought under zakat. Nor do they agree on differentiation of zakat rates, advocated by some who would like to see higher rates for those sources of income that require less exertion of labour and a lower amount of invested capital. Some adaption to modern times was unavoidable. Saudi Arabia, for instance, has fixed the threshold value for assets in terms of gold, ignoring the threshold on silver, and zakat has been imposed on professional income (Sadeq 2002, p. 47). Even those that are against reinterpretation of the Hadith sometimes accept levying zakat on items on which the sunna is silent, in particular banknotes.

The use of zakat is strictly circumscribed. The Quran, 9:60, says:

> In fact the sadaqat [zakat] collection is for the poor, the helpless, those employed to administer the funds, those whose hearts need to be won over [to the truth], ransoming the captives, helping the destitute, in the Way of Allah and for the wayfarer. That is a duty enjoined by Allah; and Allah is All-Knowledgeable, Wise.

Still, interpretations differ widely. Jurists disagree over whether zakat should be distributed directly to needy individuals or can also be given to charities or used for welfare projects. Some are convinced that zakat must be spent on the needy in the area where it is raised, unless there is a surplus left after the needs are met or there is an emergency situation elsewhere (Ramadan 2004, pp. 89, 189). Others, following the salafi reformists Maududi and Qutb, want to include propagation of Islam, Islamic education, activities to establish an Islamic way of life by replacing anti-Islamic or secular systems, or any other struggle in righteous cause (Sadeq 2002, p. 39). Others again argue that zakat proceeds may be used for social welfare programmes and economic development projects, manpower training or education in various scientific and technical fields, on the ground that such programmes will help both the poor who directly participate in them and also others. Even using zakat proceeds for defence is seen as permissible, since an attack on a Muslim country is synonymous to an attack on Islam (ibid.). All this opens the way, of course, for financing activities that many would label as terrorist, though the worries of the US government after September 11 do not always seem to have been warranted. The anthropologist Jonathan Benthall, a specialist in this field, at least deems the leading Islamic charities from Britain, Islamic Relief Worldwide, Muslim Aid and Muslim Health, as professional, with transparant money flows (van der Aa 2007).

Zakat may not be used for payments to descendants of Muhammad, to parents, grandparents, children, grandchildren or one's husband or wife. Also excluded are institutions or organizations that do not pass zakat to the rightful recipients, but instead use zakat funds for construction, investment or salaries.

Muslim scholars disagree over whether the poor that qualify for zakat should include non-Muslims. Some state that zakat money may be paid to non-Muslims after the needs of the Muslims have been met, finding no indication in the Quran or sunna that zakat is to be used for Muslims only. Provided they do not fight against Islam and Muslims, non-Muslims qualify. Maududi, by contrast, deems non-Muslims not eligible for receiving zakat, on the basis of an hadith 'To be taken from your rich people and to be distributed to your poor people', where 'your' in his view refers to 'Muslims'. Non-Muslims should receive assistance from general welfare funds (Sadeq 2002, p. 41). These differences are reflected in the policies of charities. Islamic Relief, for instance, extends zakat funds to non-Muslims in Africa, Muslim Aid only supports Muslims (Benthall 1999, p. 31).

The fiqh schools differ on the sums to be given to the poor. According to the Hanafi school, they should be given an amount that brings them up to the minimum taxable income; the Maliki school and most Hanbalis demand an amount sufficient to cover their needs for a year and the Shafii school requires an amount sufficient for the whole of their life. All this does not mean that the poor should be on perpetual welfare, they should rather get an opportunity to rise from their misery and take control of their own lives; they should become self-sufficient. Some Islamic scholars therefore have advised to provide the poor not only with food and shelter, but also to enable them to buy tools, animals and goods for trade (Ramadan 2004, pp. 192–3).

In most Muslim countries zakat giving is voluntary, but in some countries, including Pakistan (since 1979), Sudan (since 1983), Saudi Arabia, Yemen and Malaysia, it is an obligatory tax. In Pakistan and Saudi Arabia not only individuals but companies are subject to zakat levies (Sadeq 2002, p. 43; Kuran 2006, p. 21). In Indonesia a law enacted in 1999 charged the government with regulating zakat, so that it is no longer a private affair of individual Muslims (Lubis 2004, p. 102). In countries such as Morocco and Oman zakat contributions are completely left to the individual's conscience and Jordan is somewhere in between. There is a zakat directorate under the Ministry of Religious Affairs, but local zakat committees are also allowed to raise and distribute charitable funds (Benthall 1999, p. 29). In Kuwait and Bangladesh the state administers zakat funds, but contributions are voluntary.

State zakat collectors cannot always be trusted to channel the best part of their funds to the poor. Evidence from zakat offices at the level of individual states in Malaysia (Malaysia is a federation) from the 1970s and the 1980s shows that no more than between 11 and 15 per cent went to the poor, with a much larger share set aside for the zakat collectors – in the state of Negeri Sembilan during 1978–82 52 per cent – and to religious education. For Sudan, administrative costs to the tune of 18 per cent have been reported. Whereas zakat in Malyasia and Sudan may be disbursed to all the categories mentioned in the Quran, Pakistan and Saudi Arabia are reported to disburse mainly to the poor and the destitute (Sadeq 2002, pp. 17, 51–2; Kuran 2006, p. 25).

Quite a lot of self-congratulatory noises are made about the institution of zakat, but available evidence suggests that it is neither a fair nor a very helpful tax. It is not fair, because the rich, at least in Pakistan, Saudi Arabia and Malaysia, don't pay much, partly because of evasion and partly because assets such as housing are not taxed. In Malaysia relatively poor rice growers pay disproportionately. It is not very helpful, because the sums brought together are not impressive. In Pakistan zakat tax brought in no more than 0.35 per cent of GDP in 1987–88 and in Saudi Arabia it was even less, 0.04 per cent in the 1970s (Kuran 2006, pp. 21–2). Still, rather overblown claims are being made, to the effect that zakat has other beneficial effects besides alleviating poverty. Qureshi (1991, p. 185) argues that zakat increases what Keynes in Chapter 17 of *The General Theory of Employment, Interest and Money* called the carrying cost of money and thus makes it less attractive to hold deposits (carrying costs are the pecuniary costs, as distinct from the opportunity costs, involved in holding an asset) (Keynes 1936 [1961], p. 225). This should stimulate wealth holders to invest their money and try and get some return rather than increase their idle balances, thus preventing economic stagnation. It is an echo of Silvio Gesell's idea that people should be made to pay for maintaining the value of their money, in his blueprint by buying stamps to be affixed on banknotes (Gesell 1931). The argument is not convincing. As in the case of inflation, which also acts as a tax on money holdings, people will switch to foreign currency or invest in real estate, without contributing to sustained higher growth. Moreover, with the amounts involved one can hardly expect zakat to have a measurable impact on aggregate spending and unemployment. Furthermore, a lack of spending need not always be a pressing problem. These arguments can also be advanced against the idea that zakat implies a redistribution of goods that should lead to a higher demand for labour-intensive consumption goods (Sadeq 2002, p. 22). Zakat can only play a minor role in addressing poverty. For financing today's social spending levies from a much wider tax base at much higher rates are required than zakat can ever hope to attain.

3.3 *RIBA*

3.3.1 The Prohibition of *Riba*

If there is one distinguishing characteristic of the Islamic economy, it is the prohibition of riba. This is nothing new. The ban on riba was already observed in the medieval Muslim world (Udovitch 1979) and famous scholars such as al-Ghazali took the ban on riba for granted (Ghazanfar and Islahi 1990). The literal meaning of riba is 'increase' or 'addition' or 'surplus'. In the sharia, riba stands for an addition to the principal and, by implication, for a payment for the use of money which has been fixed beforehand. It is a form of excess, of unjustified appropriation of income, and it therefore is at variance with the principle of tawheed and brotherhood and with Islamic ideas about income distribution (Choudhury 1986, p. 11).

The prohibition of riba is based on a number of verses from the Quran, in particular *Sura* 2:275, 276 and 278, *Sura* 3:130, *Sura* 30:39 and *Sura* 4:161 (see Appendix A). The last two may not include an outright ban on riba, they only state that riba earnings are not blessed by God, respectively, that riba was forbidden for the Jews, but the other verses do. It is not quite clear what the Quran exactly means by the term riba, and people have to rely on the sunna to find an answer. The first Caliph, Umar, is reported to have complained that 'The last [of Quran] that was revealed was the verse on *riba* [2:275–278]; and, behold, the Apostle of God passed away before having explained its meaning to us' (Meherally 2007).

For those who see the ban on riba as the cornerstone of Islamic economics, all forms of interest are forbidden and no discussion is possible on this fundamental tenet (for example, Uzair 1978, p. 4). It may be noted that a Western Muslim such as Tariq Ramadan, who is an outspoken proponent of full participation of Western Muslims in their various national societies, is adamant in defending the ban on riba (Ramadan 2004, ch. 8). The relevance of the ban on riba for the present-day world is, however, a moot point. One form of riba concerned a pre-Islamic Arabic custom which prevailed in transactions of gold and silver. If a debt was not paid on maturity (after one year), the principal was doubled (Qureshi 1991, p. 54). Quran 3:130, which talks about 'doubling', probably refers to this custom. The ban on riba was aimed, in the view of some commentators, to prevent the debtor being enslaved (Kuran 1995, pp. 156–7; Fazlur Rahman,[4] cited in Haque 1995, p. 35). That would make the ban on riba irrelevant for present-day banking and finance, as it would only bear on *riba al-jahiliyya*, the riba practised by the Arabs in the pre-Muslim 'time of ignorance'. Riba and interest in these views are different things. Various Muslim scholars, including the great reformer Muhammad Rashid Rida (1865–1935), have accordingly concluded that riba manifested itself in Muhammad's time in very specific forms and that a ban cannot simply be carried over to all forms of interest found today. According to Imad-ad-Dean Ahmad of the Minaret of Freedom Institute of Bethesda, Maryland, riba stands for any unjustified increase, and in the Quran specifically concerns consumption loans to people experiencing financial distress (Imad-ad-Dean Ahmad 1996). Others, however, contend that the Quranic injunction refers to business loans, needed for financing long-distance trade (Chapra 2006). Much depends on the way one reads the Quran and the Hadith. If one only looks at the literal statements, one may be inclined to reject interest totally; people who look at the rationale for an injunction may argue that a ban on riba is justified when charging interest brings injustice and not when it does not. They may, for instance, consider riba on consumer loans as haram and riba for productive purposes as halal. Those who see the ban restricted to riba al-jahiliyya either conclude that compound interest or that excessively high interest, usury in the connotation it has in common parlance, is forbidden (Talal 2007).

Especially in Egypt, conventional forms of interest have been defended. Already in the mid-1980s Egypt's highest-ranking judge, Said al-Ashmawy, ruled that the interest charged and paid by commercial banks is quite something else than riba. This was after sharia boards of Islamic banks had come under suspicion of fraud and corruption (Botje 1987). Islamic banks and other financial institutions have such a sharia board or committee made up of religious scholars in order to convince their clientele of the Islamic character of their products (see Section 5.4.5 on sharia boards). Al-Ashmawy's argument that riba is not well-defined, as the Prophet had died before he had been able to give a final explanation of the Quran verses on riba and furthermore the four orthodox schools of law disagree on the subject, seems to have been unable to make many converts (see Botje 1988). Still, Egyptian religious and secular authorities have been loth to condemn interest outright. Some religious leaders have argued that interest as paid by conventional banks to their depositors can be seen as a share in the profits made by productive investments and, by that token, are fundamentally different from the riba that is forbidden by the sharia (El-Gamal 2001a, p. 2). One former Egyptian cabinet minister, Dr 'Abd-Al-Mun'im Al-Nimr, saw the ban on riba as a means of protecting debtors, which, in his view, is irrelevant in the case of bank accounts, the bank being the debtor. Egyptian muftis have accordingly issued fatwas authorizing interest-yielding bank deposits (El-Gamal 2000, p. 29). The political situation in Egypt may have played a role, or perhaps the scandals in which dubious firms masquerading as Islamic financial institutions were involved. After a number of pyramid funds had gone bust, one of the leading religious leaders, the mufti of Cairo, issued a fatwa ruling that interest payments provide security to small investors and, therefore, are halal, or permitted according to the sharia (Drummond 2000). Quite an uproar was caused by a fatwa issued on 2 December 2002, by the rector of Al-Azhar University, Muhammad Sayid Tantawi, permitting prespecified fixed-rate bank deposits, in response to a query by the Chairman of the Board of Directors of Arab Banking Corporation and after discussion in the Islamic Research Institute of Al-Azhar.[5] The fatwa sees banks as agents for permissible investment and regards interest paid on bank deposits as profit distributions that are pre-specified by mutual consent (El-Gamal 2003a notes that the fatwa applies not to all bank deposits, but only to investment accounts, see Chapter 4). The leading Muslim organizations in Indonesia have been lukewarm towards banning interest as well.[6] In 1938 the Nahdlatul Ulama stated in its national congress that bank interest benefits the customers and society at large and is therefore halal (Lubis 2004, p. 103). The other Indonesian Muslim mass movement, Muhammadiyah, was less sure and tended to accept interest-based banking on the ground of darura (necessity), given the lack of sharia-based financial institutions, but in 1993 it had come round to condemning all forms of interest and advocating the founding of Islamic financial institutions (Lubis 2004, p. 104).

Those who see the ban on riba as relevant for the modern world generally distinguish two broad categories, *riba al-nasia* and *riba al-fadl*.

- *Riba al-nasia*, or riba by way of deferment, is produced by delaying completion of an exchange of countervalues and includes interest in the conventional sense of a predetermined payment for a loan, which may be a loan of money or a loan of goods.
- *Riba al-fadl*, or riba by way of excess, refers to an excess or increase paid in a direct exchange of commodities. It looks at first sight a bit like the idea of 'unequal exchange', seen by Marxists as characteristic of capitalist society (see Emmanuel 1969). The resemblance, of course, is no more than superficial, as Muslims do not subscribe to the labour theory of value which underlies Marxist analysis. Nonetheless, the strongly anti-capitalist Muslim author Haque (1995) is quite close to it. In his eyes, 'unequal exchange' or riba al-fadl is characteristic of capitalist societies.

Many Muslim scholars see riba al-jahiliyya as a form of riba al-nasia, but some consider it a separate category. *Riba al-jahiliyya* is related to transactions in which no increase was stipulated at the time of advancing a loan; however, if the debtor could not pay the principal amount at the time of maturity, the creditor used to offer him two options: either to pay the principal or to increase the amount in exchange for an additional term allowed by the creditor. Those who deem riba al-jahiliyya a separate category see it as the riba condemned in the Quran, whereas the other two forms were dealt with in the sunna. If riba al-jahiliyya is included in riba al-nasia, one of course cannot but conclude that the injunctions in the Quran against riba concern the latter category.

Obviously, then, riba in general is more than the mere phenomenon of a predetermined payment of a sum of money for a loan. The concept of riba covers not only money loans, but also the exchange of goods. It refers to a surplus gain, whether in the form of money or in kind.

From the description given here it is not immediately clear where the dividing line between halal, or permitted, and haram, or forbidden, transactions runs. This, indeed, is a matter for continuing dispute and the various law schools hold different views on the subject.[7] Take the ban on riba al-fadl. This is based on ahadith such as the following:

> Ubida b. al-Simit (Allah be pleased with him) reported Allah's Messenger (may peace be upon him) as saying: Gold is to be paid for by gold, silver by silver, wheat by wheat, barley by barley, dates by dates, and salt by salt, like for like and equal for equal, payment being made hand to hand. If these classes differ,

> then sell as you wish if payment is made hand to hand. (Muslim, book 10, number 3853)

This is interpreted as a ban on exchanging, say, two low-quality dates for one high-quality date, even if it is permitted to sell the low-quality dates for money and use the receipts for buying a high-quality date, according to the Hadith:

> Narrated Abu Said Al-Khudri and Abu Huraira: Allah's Apostle appointed somebody as a governor of Khaibar. That governor brought to him an excellent kind of dates (from Khaibar). The Prophet asked, 'Are all the dates of Khaibar like this?' He replied, 'By Allah, no, O Allah's Apostle! But we barter one Sa of this (type of dates) for two Sas of dates of ours and two Sas of it for three of ours.' Allah's Apostle said, 'Do not do so (as that is a kind of usury) but sell the mixed dates (of inferior quality) for money, and then buy good dates with that money'. (Bukhari, vol. 3, book 34, no. 405; see also Muslim, book 10, number 3875)

It is not quite clear what the rationale for the ban on riba al-fadl is. Possibly, it was meant to protect people against sharp traders (Talal 2007). Whatever the case, the question that immediately arises is: must the list be seen as an exhaustive account or not? Hanafis, with their liberal application of qiyas (analogy), generalize the ban to all goods that are measurable by weight or volume. Zahiris, by contrast, reject all forms of qiyas and restrict the ban on riba al-fadl to the six commodities mentioned in the Hadith. The curious thing is that, as a result of their dogmatic rigour, they end up with a more liberal view on riba al-fadl than less strict schools of law.

Only the slightest form of qiyas has to be applied in order to extend the ban on riba al-fadl to the exchange of money against claims on money. This would imply that money and claims on money can only be traded if those claims are traded at par, effectively banning conventional interest again. It may be different if the claims on money are backed by real goods, because the claims on money can in that case be interpreted as claims on goods.

It may be noted that riba al-fadl does not seem to make a transaction null and void. It is argued by some Muslim jurists that the implementation of the prohibition of riba al-fadl is the responsibility of individual Muslims (Usmani 2000, para. 107). In general, the verdict on a contract tainted by riba often seems to be defective, and if sharia courts find that riba was involved in a contract, the transgressor has to donate the amount involved to the poor. This also applies to riba al-nasia.

One interesting question concerning loans is whether if a predetermined interest payment is not allowed, that also precludes giving and receiving an inflation compensation. Generally, Muslim scholars think it does.

Indexation has found little favour with them, on the grounds that rules of riba or any other divine rule cannot be relaxed for man-made problems like inflation. What is needed is an effective check on inflation through rational macroeconomic policies and not an acceptance of inflation (Obaidullah 2005, p. 28). Others, however, see a place for inflation compensation. A.L.M. Abdul Gafoor (1996, ch. 2, 2000), for instance, regards inflation compensation as a separate component of the cost of borrowing, quite distinct from interest. In his view, the interest charged by conventional banks can be split up in six components, namely services costs, overhead cost, a risk premium, profit, inflation compensation and interest proper. Only the last category, which banks pass on to depositors, is subject to the ban on riba. Islamic banks would, in Mr Gafoor's view, perfectly well obey the sharia if they charged their clients a fee which covered the first five categories and left interest out. Depositors would not receive interest, but the value of their balances would be guaranteed, the real value, that is, they would receive an inflation compensation.

Mr Gafoor's ideas appear to be largely ignored in the world of Islamic finance. Still, one authoritative Islamic organization, the Islamic Fiqh Academy of the Organization of the Islamic Conference, has moved just a few steps in his direction. It draws a distinction between foreseen and unforeseen inflation. A loan contains a gift element, because the provider of the loan could have invested the money in other, more profitable, ways. After all, according to Maududi (1999, p. 167), the profound objective of the ban on riba was to replace the stinginess and selfishness of the capitalist mentality with generosity and a cooperative spirit. If there is foreseen inflation, the gift element simply is larger and it does not give the loan provider the right to demand compensation. If, however, inflation is unforeseen, the loan provider may lose more in real terms than was his intention. The Academy advises to resort to arbitration in such cases. If that should be impossible, losses above the, admittedly arbitrary, limit of 33 per cent should be compensated (El Gamal 2000, pp. 32–3).

A question on a more theoretical plane is whether the Islamic rejection of interest on loans precludes a recognition of a time value of money. Many Muslim scholars, following Maududi (1999, pp. 175–7), amongst others, are convinced that the whole concept of a time value of money or time preference is devoid of sense. There is no unanimity on the subject though. El-Gamal (2002, pp. 3–4) argues that not all forms of interest fall in the category of forbidden riba and that not all riba is interest. Riba and interest are not the same thing. In Chapter 4 we shall discuss mark-up and leasing contracts that involve an increase in the purchase price, and El-Gamal regards such an increase as a fully justified compensation to the trader or the financier for the opportunity cost of providing credit (cf. the Scholastic idea of *lucrum cessans* in Section 3.3.3 below). Whether we denote this compensation as interest or not is immaterial. The point is that, as we have already seen in *Sura* 2:275, trade is permitted but riba is not. El-Gamal (2000, p. 12) shows that the traditional jurists of the various schools of law saw sales in which the price is increased in case of deferment as permitted, whereas an increase in the amount of debt was seen as riba, and thus as not permitted. Credit sales can therefore be used as a form of finance, but interest-bearing loans not. Why this is so, only God knows (El-Gamal 2000, p. 13). The notion of a time value of money is thus fully accepted, according to El-Gamal. So, even if in many cases the fees or mark-ups that sellers and financiers demand look suspiciously close to conventional interest, there is one requirement that most Islamic scholars emphasize can never be disregarded, and that is that all financial transactions should be asset-backed, unless done at par. Whether the conditions of a financial transaction smack of interest is in the last analysis less important than this coupling of a financial transaction to a real transaction.

Part of the condemnation of riba can be found in the Hadith. If the authority of the Quran is unassailable, the authority of a hadith is dependent on a reliable chain of transmitters. Fazlur Rahman saw contradictions between the different ahadith condemning riba, which led him to the conclusion that they are unlikely to be authentic (Pal 1999, p. 53). This strengthened his conviction that the ban on riba refers exclusively to riba al-jahiliyya, as described in the Quran, with its exorbitant increase in the capital sum when the term of payment of a debt is extended. This did his name no good among the more conservative ulama in Pakistan.

3.3.2 Secular Arguments for the Prohibition of *Riba*

The injunctions against riba in the Quran and the sunna were given without a justification. Muslims simply have to follow the commands of God, whether they understand the rationale of those demands or not. Nevertheless, Muslim scholars have tried to give a secular justification for the ban, showing why it should be beneficial for mankind. Some argue that money in itself is not a factor of production and that a loan of money which does not go hand in hand with at least some entrepreneurial risk taking should not bring a reward. Money, or capital, can only be seen as a factor of production when combined with entrepreneurship (for example, Uzair 1978, pp. 14–21; Maududi 1999, p. 170). We shall return to this argument in Section 3.3.3.

Some justifications look a bit far-fetched. Choudhury (1986, p. 11) follows a Kalecki-like reasoning, arguing that capitalists reinvest their income. Capital accumulation makes the rate of profit fall, but interest rates will increase and in order to maintain profits, the capitalist will lower wages or dismiss workers. Riba thus leads to exploitation and unemployment. This reasoning smacks of Marxist business cycle analysis and is far from compelling. For one thing, it is not made clear why the interest rate should increase when the rate of profit falls.

A common justification of the ban on riba is that interest means a transfer of wealth from the poor to the rich, turns people away from productive enterprise or makes people selfish and stone-hearted (Siddiqi, quoted by Kuran 2006, p. 8). One would be hard put to detect such effects in, say, widows and orphans living from the interest on government bonds. Some Muslim scholars, among whom Mahmoud A. El-Gamal, consequently make short shrift of the alleged danger of exploitation (El-Gamal 2001a). After all, that would imply that the US government is exploited by investors in treasury bills or that banks are exploited by holders of savings accounts. This does not mean that he wants to throw the ban on riba overboard. He rather looks for another rationale. His approach marries microeconomic theory to the ideas of the Maliki scholar Ibn Rushd, or Averroes (1126–98), who, in this case, leaned to Hanafi views, which means that he generalized the ban on riba al-fadl. The ban on riba al-fadl sees to it that partners in a transaction collect information about the market valuation of goods. This prevents trade taking place at non-equilibrium prices, which would happen under imperfect information, and leads to Pareto-optimality. Goods in this situation are exchanged against each other at a ratio that equals both the ratio of the marginal utilities and the ratio of market prices. If the outcome is an unacceptable distribution of income, that should be taken care of by *ex post* reallocations of wealth, in particular by zakat. With riba al-fadl there is an informational argument that can be used to justify its banning. With riba al-nasia there is an additional argument, namely that the dimension of time adds another source of inefficiency in the form of dynamic inconsistency. A ban on riba al-nasia provides a precommitment mechanism in financial contracts that effectively deals with this dynamic inconsistency. El-Gamal argues that people do not always make rational choices. There are, in particular, anomalies in the discounting of expected future costs and benefits. El-Gamal attacks the problem with the help of a three-period model in which investments yield a profit in the third period. Investments are partly financed by loans. Now economic agents will be tempted to take one-period loans rather than two-period loans, as short-term loans carry lower interest rates. The danger is that economic agents deviate in period two from the plans they made in period one, presumably jeopardizing the financing of the project in the process. If finance is provided in the form of a participation instead of a loan, agents are not free to, say, suddenly increase consumption in period two over and above what was planned in period one, at least not without the agreement of the partners. This should, in El-Gamal's eyes, go a long way to prevent dynamic inconsistency and, with it, loss of efficiency. Financial instruments based on participation provide a form of precommitment and therefore are not only preferable over interest-paying loans but also over halal forms of loans.

The argument looks a bit far-fetched, even if it is presented in the language of modern economics. It should make clear, though, to what lengths Muslim economists working in the Western world and fully acquainted with modern economic theory go to link economic analysis with the precepts of the Quran and the sunna.

3.3.3 Digression: Parallels in Medieval Christianity

The condemnation of interest has not been confined to Islam. Based on passages from the Bible, the Christian Church at various times took a strong stand against demanding and paying interest. The term used for interest was *usura*, which is a technical term that includes 'normal' interest and what is commonly seen as exorbitant rates of interest, or usury, but also excessive profits (van Straaten 2002, p. 9). In the Old Testament, or Tenach, it was forbidden to demand interest on loans, but not entirely, as interest could be charged on loans to foreigners, and the ban sometimes was restricted to loans to the poor (Exodus 22:24; Leviticus 25:35–36; Deuteronomy 23:20–21, see Appendix C). Money was not borrowed for productive purposes, but out of dire necessity, and the ban on interest was most probably intended to prevent people profiting from a deplorable situation of the poor (van Straaten 2002, p. 13). In the New Testament the negative attitude is less absolute. In the parable of the talents (Matthew 25:14–30; Luke 19:11–27), paying interest is apparently not frowned upon, and though other passages are perhaps less positive, they do not seem to contain an outright condemnation (see Luke 6:27–38).

Whereas Leviticus 25:36 and Deuteronomy 23:20 forbid demanding interest from one's countrymen, older translations have 'brothers' instead of countrymen, and Christians were inclined to set great store by the universal brotherhood of man. This led to a wholesale rejection of interest by the Church. One of the first to speak out against interest was the holy Clemens of Alexandria (†220). The Council of Nicea (325) forbade interest payments among the clergy. The First Council of Carthago (345) disapproved of interest payments by laymen, even if it did not go so far as to forbid them. The Second Lateran Council (1139) excommunicated 'usurers' and the Third Lateran Council (1179) denied them Christian burial. Pope Eugene III in 1148 condemned mortgage loans as indirect usury. The Fourth Lateran Council (1215) berated Christians who did business with Jewish usurers and the Second Council of Lyon (1274) added foreign usurers. The Council of Vienne (1311–12) extended the threat of excommunication to authorities who permitted usury or protected usurers. Those who let a house to usurers could be excommunicated as well. It furthermore declared all secular legislation in favour of usury null and void. The last encyclical against usury, promulgated by Pope Benedict XIV, dates from 1745.[8] The French bishops issued a decree on 12 October 1789, during the Revolution, repealing the ban on interest but it took until 1838 before the Vatican followed suit, in a pastoral letter to confessors (see on the attitude of the Church Beutels 1990; Gelpi and Julien-Labruyère 2000; Le Goff 1979; O'Brien 2001; van Straaten 2002; Wood 2002).

Medieval Scholastics, like present-day Muslims, marshalled not only theological but also secular arguments to the defence of a ban on interest, or rather usury. St Thomas Aquinas (1225–74) argued that interest is a price paid for the use of money while money, seen from the point of view of the individual agent, is consumed, used up, when it is used, in the same way as goods such as wine. Money cannot be used without decreasing the existing stock, unlike durables such as houses, land or horses. To demand interest for the use of money means that a payment is demanded for something that in the case of money does not exist, namely a use distinct from consumption (Aquinas 1965, Question LXXVIII). This would be an injustice, because it would amount to asking for double payment: first for the use and then for the return of the good in equal measure. This is, in the eyes of the Scholastics, fundamentally different from, say, letting a house. According to O'Brien (2001, pp. 97ff), Aquinas saw a loan contract, a *mutuum*, as a sale, because ownership passed. What matters in sales is the fixing of just prices, and in case of fungible goods, of which money is the prime example, the just price is nothing else but the return of fungibles of the same value as those lent. The amount to be returned thus is simply the amount of money borrowed.

The argument draws heavily on Aristotle, who in his *Politika* (book I, ch. 10; Aristotle 1992, pp. 85–7) argues that money has been developed first and foremost as a means of exchange and that, consequently, it should be used for making purchases and not for lending and receiving a reward for that lending. Lending money and receiving a reward for lending goes, in Aristotle's view, against nature. The Greek term for interest, *tokos*, also means offspring. But unlike nature – cattle, fields – money has no offspring, it does not produce anything, it is barren. Money does not beget money. Money is nothing more than a convention and conventions, unlike natural things, cannot produce things. His reasoning seems to have been fed by disdain for the daily activities of common people, first of all merchants; an attitude far from unique among the upper classes at the time (Engen 2004).

Another explanation, not necessarily at odds with the earlier one, is that Aristotle's main concern was maintaining a well-ordered stationary state, where people, or rather heads of households, should involve themselves only up to a modest degree in acquisitive activities and have no use for money making as an end in itself (Gordon 1993). It may all look less than compelling in our eyes, but Aristotle was intensively studied and was seen as an unassailable authority by thirteenth- to fifteenth-century theologians, including Thomas Aquinas. Thomas's teacher Albertus Magnus (c. 1200–80) was so steeped in his writings that he was nicknamed 'Aristotle's ape' (O'Brien 2001, p. 13). Aquinas fully adopted Aristotle's reasoning and saw money as sterile in itself. True, a borrower can use the money borrowed in some venture and make a profit, but such a result was seen by Aquinas and the other Scholastics as the reward for the labour applied by the borrower. The delay in the repayment of the loan could not be used as a reason for demanding interest either, because that would amount to a sale of time, and time cannot be owned.

The medieval view on interest is evident in the first part of Dante's *Divina Commedia, Hell*, which appeared around 1314. In Canto XVII Dante spots the Usurers, predominantly Florentine bankers, on the burning sand of Circle VII, Ring iii, lumped together with the Sodomites. One commentator observes that the two groups are classed together because the latter make sterile the natural instincts which result in fertility, whereas the former make fertile that which by its nature is sterile (Dante 1955, pp. 174–9). This is pure Aristotle. The pernicious effects of associating oneself with interest were somewhat later literally painted in bright colours by Quinten Metsys (1465 or 1466–1530) in his *The moneylender and his wife* (1514, Louvre, Paris, see www.louvre.fr) and in a caricatural painting of two moneylenders and their clients (Galleria Doria Pamphilj, Rome, see www.bridgemanartondemand.com). Marinus van Reymerswaele (c. 1490–1567) followed with quite a number of similar paintings. Some present-day manifestations of a negative attitude to the phenomenon of interest are JAK Banken in Sweden, a bank that provides interest-free loans but requires its clients or participants to hold funds for long periods on interest-free accounts (they in fact give up liquidity in one period for the privilege of not paying interest in another period), and action groups and NGOs such as the Dutch *Stro* social trade organization that support local initiatives for interest-free borrowing and investment (see Anielski 2003 and www.strohalm.nl). Another example was the poet Ezra Pound, already mentioned in Chapter 1, who in his Canto 45 carries on about 'usura, sin against nature'.

El-Gamal (2000, n. 3) may argue that the notion that money is sterile and does not grow by itself is part of the traditional doctrine of the Catholic Church and is alien to Islam, but it cannot be denied that the

Scholastics, including St Thomas, leaned heavily on such Islamic scholars as Al-Ghazali. Al-Ghazali, like Aristotle, argued that money is meant to express the value of goods in exchange and not for earning additional money (Hosseini 1995, p. 540). Those Islamic scholars in their turn were heavily influenced again by Aristotle (Versteegh 2008).

The ban on usury did not mean that all interest was forbidden. The Scholastics accepted various justifications for demanding and paying interest, the so-called extrinsic titles, extrinsic because they were based on circumstances outside the loan itself. These extrinsic titles were the following:

- *Lucrum cessans*, the gain foregone by lending. Acceptance of *lucrum cessans* means that the notion of opportunity cost entered the discussion (Beutels 1990, p. 320; Schumpeter 1967, pp. 103–4). *Lucrum cessans* figures for the first time in a letter from Pope Alexander III, written in 1176; it was only gradually accepted and it took until the fifteenth century before theologians accepted it universally.
- *Damnum emergens*, a loss incurred because someone else was using one's goods and the lender had to do in the meantime with inferior ones or had to borrow money himself. This title had been clearly laid down by Aquinas and had already been recognized by Albertus Magnus. Loss as a result of late repayment is also included.
- *Periculum sortis*, the danger or risk of loss, justifying a recompense for default risk. The acceptability of this title was still hotly debated in the fifteenth century.

There was furthermore a possibility to write contracts specifying a penalty for late payment, *poena conventionalis*, which met with no objections. The needs of the commercial and financial community in Europe saw to it that fictitious late payments became an accepted, though disingenuous, way of circumventing the ban on usury.

Interest paid on account of the extrinsic titles was seen as something different than usury. This interest was 'interesse', or what is between, difference. It was meant to compensate the lender for any deterioration in his condition between the moment the loan was made and the time of the repayment (O'Brien 2001, p. 100; Wood 2002, p. 181). Of course, the extrinsic titles justifying the payment of interest could hardly fail to undermine the ban on usury. The introduction of the notion of opportunity cost under the title of *lucrum cessans* can even be seen as lethal for such a ban.

Rivalry between the Order of the Dominicans, to which the leading Scholastics belonged, and the Order of the Franciscans seems to have played a role in the struggle about the ban on usury. Starting in 1462 in

Perugia, more than 200 so-called *Montes Pietatis* (mounts of compassion, or charitable pawnshops) had sprung up that lent money to the needy at 5 per cent, in order to prevent them falling into the clutches of usurers, who charged a multiple. The Franciscans urged city governments to set up such *montes pietatis* (Wood 2002, p. 203). Against Dominican opposition, the Fifth Lateran Council (1515–16) sanctioned this exception to the ban on usury (van Straaten 2002, p. 47). The Church perhaps had no choice but to agree to what had become accepted practice. It was not all-powerful. Already in 1345, the city government of Florence had decided that the church courts had no jurisdiction over its citizens. The pre-*monte pietatis* pawnbrokers did get fined at those times, but the fines were for all practical purposes licence fees (Wood 2002, p. 183).

In the fifteenth century a number of theologians, in particular from Paris and Tübingen, came to see the intentions of the lender as the proper measure of usury. If the lender did not intend to oppress the borrower, interest could not be labelled usury. The German theologian Johannes Eck (1486–1543), supported by the Fugger banking family from Augsburg, defended a 5 per cent interest rate as fully acceptable if the loan was for a bona fide business opportunity (Jones 2004). According to Eck, a fixed annual return was a guarantee for the creditor that his capital would remain intact and functioned as a kind of insurance against uncertain profit disbursements (van Straaten 2002, pp. 48–9). In fact, a fixed-rate contract could be seen as a combination of three contracts, a *contractus trinius*:

1. A partnership contract, stipulating profit sharing.
2. The sale of uncertain profit disbursements at a fixed price.
3. An insurance contract protecting the investor against any loss on the principal sum (Henning 2000).

Church law had never made any objection to any of those different contracts and, therefore, Eck reasoned, the combination should be acceptable as well. His views did not go down too well with the Church, but nevertheless deposits that paid 5 per cent soon became common in a number of German states.

The Reformation finally put an end to the ban on interest. True, Luther, who often crossed swords with Eck, was still dead set against interest, not only in the guise of usura but also as interesse, and indeed hostile to the world of banking and commerce in general (Tawney 1960, pp. 95–6; see also Luther's injunctions against usury in Kerridge 2002[9]). He grudgingly tolerated one exception, with a lot of ifs and buts: buying an annuity (Sneller 1968). His associate Melanchthon adopted a more liberal attitude and accepted the extrinsic titles (Jones 2004). The breakthrough came with

John Calvin, who argued that Deuteronomy does not ban interest per se, but only exorbitantly high interest rates, or usury in the present-day connotation. One Hebrew word for interest, *nesech*, means 'bite', and was used in the sense of 'putting the bite on the poor', but another word that also is translated as interest, *tarbit*, means 'to take legitimate increase' (Jones 2004). More importantly, Calvin argued that the injunctions of the Old Testament are not always relevant for modern societies, even the rulings of the Gospels were designed for other kinds of societies than ours. And then, of course, St Paul maintained in his Letter to the Romans, Chapter 3, that the 'New Convenant' had replaced Mosaic law, so that the Church did not have to follow Deuteronomic rules (Lewis and Algaoud 2001, pp. 204–5). Calvin also made short shrift of Aristotle's argument that money does not beget money, arguing that houses do not beget anything either, but that nobody objects when someone lets his house in return for a rent (though Aristotelians will not have been impressed, as houses are not normally used up by a tenant). Calvin, however, was careful to point out that this should not be taken as a charter to charge interest at the highest rate allowed by the law of the land. There were, in Calvin's view, all kinds of limitations to charging interest. Loans should be made available to the poor and needy without charge and the borrower must reap as much advantage as the lender (see letters by Calvin,[10] reprinted in Kerridge 2002).[11] In Calvin's Geneva the government took harsh measures against those who exceeded the interest ceiling it imposed and also, for that matter, against those that borrowed in order to purchase luxury goods (Valeri 1997). The important thing, however, is that he accepted that commerce in modern urban communities could not flourish without credit (Tawney 1960, ch. 2, section 3). A factor that most probably influenced Calvin and in general helped to weaken the aversion to interest was a shift that took place in society from consumption loans to production loans, where 'fairness' or fear of exploitation is less of an issue (Lewis and Algaoud 2001, p. 206).

Calvin's orthodox Calvinist followers were inclined to adopt his negative views on consumption loans. In the Dutch Republic, for instance, moneylenders came under fire from leading Calvinist clergy in the seventeenth century, which even led to acrimonious conflicts with the provincial governments (van Straaten 2002, pp. 64–6). Eventually, the orthodox Calvinists had to back down when the provincial governments of Gelderland and Holland in 1658 decided that church assemblies should accept that it was the secular authorities that regulated interest ceilings and that it was inappropriate for the Church to brand licensed moneylenders who charged interest rates not exceeding such ceilings as usurers. The provincial government of Utrecht followed in 1664 (van Asselt 2007, pp. 65ff). In the Roman Catholic Church resistance against the interest phenomenon lingered on until 1838, when the Vatican more or less surreptitiously said farewell to it in the pastoral letter to confessors mentioned above (Beutels 1990, p. 325). Still, given the acceptance of the extrinsic titles, even in the thirteenth century the attitude of the Church was less negative to interest than those of present-day Muslims who equate interest with riba.

3.4. *GHARAR* AND *MAYSIR*

3.4.1 The Prohibition of *Gharar* and *Maysir*

Commercial activities are permitted under Islam, but they are subject to the ban on riba. They are also subject to another restriction: the ban on gharar and maysir. *Gharar* is risk, uncertainty, and *maysir* is gambling or speculation.

The ban on gharar implies that commercial partners should know exactly the countervalue that is offered in a transaction. The word 'gharar' in the Arabic language means risk. It also has the connotation of deception and delusion. Of course, risk can never be totally avoided, certainly not by entrepreneurs, and no productive or commercial activities would be possible without a certain degree of risk and uncertainty. Only conditions of excessive risk have to be avoided (Obaidullah 2005, p. 29). The ban on gharar stands for transparency and fairness. In order to avoid gharar the parties to a contract must:

- Make sure that both the subject and prices of the sale exist, and that parties are able to deliver.
- Specify the characteristics and the amounts of the countervalues.
- Define the quantity, quality and date of future delivery, if any.

The prohibition of gharar is found in ahadith forbidding as gharar the sale of such things as 'the birds in the sky or the fish in the water', 'the catch of the diver', the 'unborn calf in its mother's womb' (El-Gamal 2001b, p. 2). These are all cases where the object of the transaction is uncertain. One may not buy tomorrow's catch of a diver, but one may hire a diver for a certain number of hours tomorrow. Also selling goods without specifying the price, such as selling at the 'going price', is haram, as is selling goods without allowing the buyer to properly examine the goods (Al-Ameen Al-Dhareer 1997). Gambling, maysir, is banned in the Quran (2:219, 5:90, 91), see Appendix B. Speculation is seen as a case of maysir.

The ban on gharar and maysir, though less well-known than the ban on riba, has consequences that are hardly less far-reaching. There are many contracts that do not stipulate the exact nature, date or value of what is received in exchange. This is especially the case with insurance and on financial markets. Hard and fast rules are difficult to discern, as it is not a priori clear when there is a case of gharar. Risk and uncertainty can hardly ever be fully excluded. If we follow Schumpeter and see the entrepreur as the creator of new combinations (‘*neue Kombinationen*’), as an innovator, risk and uncertainty, especially uncertainty in the sense of Frank H. Knight, are part and parcel of entrepreneurial activities. Gharar and maysir, therefore, do not cover each and every manifestation of risk and uncertainty, but only cases that can reasonably be avoided. But where to draw the line? Not surprisingly, interpretations of exactly under what circumstances the bans on gharar and maysir apply vary. Hanbalis, for instance, have allowed obligations from a contract to arise before the sale price is precisely known. Also, sales concluded at market prices are for the most part seen as valid even when at the time of offer and acceptance the exact market price is not known (Deutsche Bank 2007). But does the ban on gharar also mean that one may not sell agricultural products before they are harvested or picked? After all, it is not certain what the harvest will look like and the buyer is unable to examine the goods at the time of purchase. Sure enough, the different law schools have come up with diverging rulings (see for details Saleh 1986, ch. 3). But in general, futures, forwards and other derivatives are seen as gharar, as there is no certainty that the object of the sale will exist at the time the trade is to be executed (El-Gamal 2000, p. 8). We shall see, though, that some exceptions are made and that Islamic banks do not hesitate to try and stretch the limits of what is deemed acceptable by sharia boards.

There seems to be a consensus among Muslim scholars that gharar and maysir make a contract null and void. A distinction between null and void, on the one hand, and defective or voidable, on the other hand, is, however, not always made in Islamic law (Lewis and Algaoud 2001, p. 197).

3.4.2 Secular Arguments for the Prohibition of *Gharar* and *Maysir*

As with riba, commentators have tried to find a secular rationale for the ban on gharar and maysir. Muslim jurists see the ban on gharar as a means to prevent people taking advantage of naivete on the part of their counterparties, or, in the language of economics, asymmetric information (Saleh 1986, p. 49; Hassan 2002, p. 290). The weak should be protected against exploitation by the strong. There is a hadith which has Muhammad saying: ‘Do not go forward to meet the caravan [to buy from it on the way before it reaches the town]. . . . A town dweller should not sell the goods for the desert dweller’ (Bukhari, vol. 3, book 34, no. 360). In other words, the smart should be prevented from tricking people who do not yet possess full price information. Muslim jurists treat the ban on gharar as an injunction to maintain commutative justice. Like Aristotle, as interpreted by Thomas Aquinas, they tend to translate commutative justice into the idea of *iustum pretium*, the just price, seen as the competitive market price (Hassan 2002).[12] Before entering into a contract, both parties should have full knowledge of relevant facts, including the market price.

As with riba, El-Gamal tries to make sense of the ban on gharar with the help of modern economic concepts, in the process shifting the emphasis away from protection of the weak (El-Gamal 2001b). The ban on gharar can, in his view, best be approached as a prohibition of trading in risk. What falls under the ban is a question of cost–benefit analysis. Trading in risk generally is inefficient compared with other forms of risk sharing, because it does not lead to a correct pricing of risk. From this it follows that not all risks should be avoided. Three types of risk that may be implicitly traded in a contract can be distinguished:

- Ambiguity in the contract language. This may lead to uncertainty regarding the nature of the object of sale or regarding the price. An example would be: I sell you the item hidden in my sleeve, or I sell at this or that price deferred until Mr X returns from abroad, without specifying when this return might happen.
- The object of the sale may be known, but the delivery may be doubtful. This would be the case with the birds in the sky or the fish in the water mentioned in the Hadith.
- The object of the sale may itself contain risk or uncertainty, for example, the sale of an as yet unborn calf.

According to El-Gamal, the first category is not very interesting. Removing ambiguity in the contract language is the obvious solution. This would prevent costly legal disputes and would hardly have negative effects. The other two categories are more interesting, and here cost–benefit analysis gives an explanation of why some forms of gharar are permissible according to Muslim scholars. There are two prominent exceptions to the prohibition. The first are formed by *bai'salam* contracts, or sales with the price paid in advance and delivery deferred to a future date. The future existence of the object of sale, such as a harvest, is uncertain, but agriculture would suffer greatly if this form of buyer's credit were not allowed. The other case is the phenomenon of *istisna*, which is the commission to manufacture or build an object, with part of the price paid in advance. This is especially important in the building industry. Istisna is permissible, according to Islamic jurisprudence (fiqh), because of a custom that prevailed at the time of the Prophet resembling this phenomenon, following a qiyas reasoning. Istisna has also been declared halal because of the necessities of business and because of equity (Saleh 1986, p. 61). El-Gamal tries to give an economic justification for this state of affairs by showing that risk trading is in most cases negative for economic efficiency, in the sense of reducing utility. It is doubtful whether that explains the prohibition of gharar, though it may explain the exceptions.

As for the ban on maysir, there is again an idea of commutative justice that is invoked to justify it. Gambling is seen by Muslim jurists as a zero-sum game. If one party gains, it goes at the expense of the other party. It does not contribute to an increase in welfare (Tag El-Din et al. 2007).

3.5 THE ECONOMIC ORDER

A pithy description of the difference between capitalist, socialist and Islamic economies was given by Mahmud Ahmad (1999, p. 43): capitalism accepts both profit and interest, socialism rejects them both and Islam accepts the profit motive but rejects interest. It is true that the Quran is far from negative on market activities. The Quran in Chapter or *Sura* 2:275 explicitly states that commercial activities are allowed (see Appendix A). Indeed, Muhammad's first wife, Khadijah, was a trader.

Generally, Muslim scholars share Ahmad's view. They see entrepreneurship as a positive force as long as it does not degenerate into preponderantly speculative activities (Valibeigi 1993). Still, as in Christianity, views differ widely. One of the early proponents of Islamic economics, Anwar Iqbal Qureshi, was very much in favour of capitalism, but a later one, Haque, takes him to task for referring to texts from the Quran in the defending of capitalism that, in his view, have nothing to do with the subject (Haque 1995, p. 52). For Qureshi, profit is a positive phenomenon, even if it accrues to a capitalist who did not have to exert himself to earn it, as in the case of landowners earning a rent. Haque, by contrast, is very critical of capitalism and would favour a large role for the state in the economy. Profits are suspect and in his view the injunctions in the Quran against riba are meant to cover a much wider range of activities where unjustified increases or surpluses are involved than is usually thought to be the case. People such as Haque subscribe to what Valibeigi (1993, p. 796) called the 'populist' interpretation of tawheed, emphasizing the equality of all men. For them, state ownership is the primary form of ownership. Another proponent of this approach was Banisadr, the president of Iran in 1980–81. A Muslim equivalent to the Austrian School is not lacking either. The Minaret of Freedom Institute that we already met in Section

2.4 shows great admiration for the work of Murray Rothbard (1926–95), a representative of the Austrian school who even by Austrian standards went a bit over the top in his glorification of the market mechanism (see Imad-ad-Dean Ahmad n.d., 1995). Still, the most widely accepted view seems to be that private ownership is generally a good thing, but that it should not be used to exploit other people (for example, Maududi 1963). Everything belongs in the last analysis to God and man should manage his possessions as God's steward or *khalifah*. Ownership is never absolute, there are no rights without obligations, in particular the obligation of social justice.

3.6 DREAMS OF A SEPARATE MUSLIM ECONOMY

Some currents in Islam, including political literalist salafism, want to separate Muslims to a large extent from the rest of the global economy. Influential Muslim economists such as M.A. Choudhury, for instance, have spoken out in favour of a separate group of Muslim countries setting up an Islamic World Trade Organization and freeing themselves from what they call 'the yoke of Western dominance and manipulation' in international economic relations. These countries would mainly trade with each other, 'in a spirit of godliness and following the precepts of the sharia, with rules and institutions not imposed from above but developed in ongoing consultations'. This would bring 'felicitous orders of balance, growth, goodness, purpose and distributive equity', leading to 'collective self-reliant development, complementarity and growth' (Choudhury 1996, pp. 18–19). Even Western technology and science should not be imitated, as they are 'inherently socially alienating'.

Another manifestation of the drive for a separate Muslim economy can be found in the Islamic Mint, which has its seat in Malaysia.[13] The Islamic Mint officially launched the Islamic gold dinar just after the attack on the Twin Towers, namely on 7 November 2001. This dinar should, together with a silver dirham, help the Muslim world return to the days of the Caliphate. In the view of the Islamic Mint, fiduciary money is not acceptable as a currency for paying religious tax, *zakat*, or for dowries. Fiduciary money, or paper money as they call it, is a mere promise to pay, as it has no intrinsic value. Zakat and dowries require real payments, not promises to pay, in their interpretation of Islamic law as distilled from the Hadith. Furthermore, dinars and dirhams should replace paper money, in particular the US dollar, as a medium of exchange. This is because it is, again in their view, forbidden for Muslims to entrust wealth to non-Muslims, and what else is accepting US dollars, mere promises to pay, than entrusting wealth to non-Muslims? Nor are Muslims in their interpretation of sharia generally allowed to take a non-Muslim as a partner outside dar al-Islam, the territory of Islam, where Islamic law prevails, as they might cheat or use a Muslim's wealth in forbidden transactions (Islamic Mint n.d.). Within dar al-Islam these restrictions are less binding, presumably because non-Muslims can be kept under strict supervision there.[14]

In the same vein, a British-based organization, Al-Khilafah Publications, runs a website www.khilafah.com which blames capitalist economic policies for all economic ills in the Muslim world, though the siphoning off of the wealth of Muslims to Swiss bank accounts by corrupt governments plays a role as well, in their view. The solution touted is simply to restore the Caliphate.

3.7 CONCLUSIONS

Muslims who regard not only the Quran but also the sunna as a source whose injunctions and exhortations should be followed to the letter, both in matters of worship and in matters of muamalat, in social relationships, want to see the bans on gharar, maysir and riba rigorously maintained. However, it is always a question of interpretation which present-day phenomena would fall under such a ban. Interpretations differ widely, the more so as there is also the additional question of whether the relevant ahadith can really be regarded as authentic. But even if they are not that strict and feel not attracted to any form of salafism, many Muslims, including those in Western countries, feel uncomfortable with paying and receiving interest and with conventional insurance (which involves, in their view, gharar and maysir, see Section 6.2).

For the rest, a great majority of Muslim scholars are in favour of an economy with private enterprise, but as in most other religions and much of secular thought this is no licence for unrestricted profit seeking. There are currents, though, that would prefer to set up an Islamic economy largely apart from the rest of the world, where the practices of the Golden Age of the Caliphate can be reintroduced and one can live according to the Islamic ideals without any danger of getting tainted with non-Islamic stains. This dreamworld of the political literalist salafists in particular is one where non-Muslims, be they angelic or not, would fear to tread – as would many Muslims, probably. After all, golden age or not, only the first Caliph, Abu Bakr, died a natural death, the other three were assassinated. It was a time of great military successes, but also of internecine strife and discord (Waardenburg 2008).

NOTES

1. The 'Wijsbegeerte der Wetsidee', literally Philosophy of the Law-Idea but usually called Calvinist or Reformational Philosophy. It was mainly developed by Professor Herman Dooyeweerd (1915–86). Note that the VU University was staunchly Calvinist during the first 80 years or so after its founding in 1880. The 'Wijsbegeerte der Wetsidee' did not really catch on, outside a small band of enthusiasts; see van Deursen (2005).
2. www.islam.tc/alhilaal/site/zakat.html, September 2006.
3. The Islamic Fiqh Academy is an international body of Muslim jurists sponsored by the 46 nation Organization of the Islamic Conference.
4. Fazlur Rahman (1919–88) was a highly respected scholar of Islam who taught in the UK, Canada and the USA, interrupted by a short and unsuccessful stint as head of the Central Institute of Islamic Research, which was set up by the Pakistani government in order to implement Islam into daily life. Rahman was a critical thinker who, following Schacht, distrusted the reliability of ahadith, among others those on riba. He further held non-traditional views on the nature of revelation. He was branded a *kafir* or apostate by aggressive traditionalists, including Maududi, which forced him to resign from the Institute and leave the country (Pal 1999, pp. 6–7, 53).
5. The fatwa can be found in Netzer (2004), which further analyses the character of the relationship between Al-Azhar and the Egyptian government, in the light of the latter's hostility towards the Muslim Brotherhood. The fatwa is also reproduced in El-Gamal (2003a), which gives the arguments used in the discussion on the fatwa.
6. The Indonesian Ulemas Council (MUI) Edict Commission announced on 16 December 2003 that it was seriously considering to prohibit Muslims from using conventional financial institutions once sharia-compliant institutions were operating in their area (Wijaksana and Junaidi 2003). The Council's pronouncements certainly carry weight, as representatives of Indonesia's two Islamic mass organizations, Nahdlatul Ulama (NU) and Muhammadiyah, play prominent roles there, but these appeared to be less than enthusiastic. Interestingly, NU owns Nusumma Bank and Muhammadiyah manages Bank Persyarikatan, both of which are engaged in conventional banking. Muhammadiyah Chairman Ahmad Syafii Maarif called the views of the MUI a nice piece of ijtihad, but did not want to attach too much weight to it. In his view, bank interest is different from *riba* as long as there is no element of exploitation involved (Wahyuni 2003).
7. For a thorough description of the various views, see Saleh (1986).
8. English and other translations of the encyclical are easily found through a Google search.
9. M. Luther, *Grosser Sermon vom Wucher,* 1519, 1. Teil, in *Alle Bücher und Schrifften,* vol. 1, pp. 195–7, Jena 1555; M. Luther, *An die Pfarrherrn wider den Wucher zu predigen Vermanung,* 1540, 7. Teil, in *Alle Bücher und Schrifften,* vol. 7, pp. 397–9, Jena 1555–8.
10. J. Calvin, *Commentarii in Libros Mosis necum in Librum Josue,* Amsterdam, 1567; J. Calvin, *Epistolae et Responsa*, Geneva, 1575.
11. Similar ideas had earlier been developed by Heinrich Bullinger (1504–75), the successor to the Protestant reformer Zwingli in Zürich (Baker 1974).
12. Hassan (2002, p. 296) notes that the Muslims jurists were acquainted with Aristotle's ideas from his *Nichomachean Ethics* and had a similar approach, but need not consciously have followed him.
13. According to the Defamation League, officers of the Islamic Mint (who hail from England, Spain, Switzerland, Malaysia and Germany) are members of the Murabitun movement – a tiny, Western offshoot of Islam's Sufi movement, founded by a Scottish convert in the 1960s. The sect is staunchly anti-Al Qaeda and anti-Taliban and seeks to enlist Muslims worldwide in an effort to overturn world finance in favour of a 'Quranic' gold and silver system (www.adl.org/internet/e_currency.asp, 2006).
14. The idea of a gold dinar also holds attractions for people who have little inclination to separate Muslims from the rest of the world, but who, in the vein of the Austrian School, harbour a deep distrust of managed money (see Imad-ad-Dean Ahmad 1998).

4. Financial instruments

4.1 INTRODUCTION

There are a great number of financial instruments that are acceptable from a sharia point of view, others are not admissible and there is also a grey area with products that pass muster in the eyes of some but are haram in the eyes of others. As noted earlier, the pioneers of the idea of an Islamic economy had no idea how to shape such an economy; nor had the first practitioners of Islamic finance (Kahf 2004). The various financial instruments had to be developed in the practice of banking. There are by and large two sets of instruments, namely those based on profit-and-loss sharing, and the rest. Many instruments are the subject of ongoing discussions, as their legal form may be different from interest, but their economic function is not always far removed from conventional interest, or from gharar and maysir. The most widely used financial instrument, *murabaha* (see below), did not even exist in its present form when the first serious large-scale initiatives for Islamic banking were launched: the Islamic Development Bank and the Dubai Islamic Bank, both established in 1974. It was derived by Sami Hamoud, a visionary Jordanian economist,[1] from a publication by al-Shafii and only in 1976 recommended to these two banks (Kahf 2004, p. 33, n. 13).

The early writers on Islamic finance and the Islamic economy in general had to navigate in uncharted waters and came up with inchoate and sometimes incoherent proposals. On one page Qureshi plays with the idea that banks should neither pay nor charge interest and that the costs of banking should be borne by the state. Two pages further, he advocates partnerships between banks and their clients which would yield profits, apparently without any need for the state to step in (Qureshi 1991, pp. 131, 133). Mahmud Ahmad (1999, ch. 2) developed a scheme where banks provide free credit and debtors are required to furnish a counter loan, not unlike the practice of JAK Banken in Sweden (see Section 3.3.3). The counter loan would be for a smaller sum, but for a longer period, such that the total of the counter loan, measured as the amount of money times the period during which it is furnished, equalled the loan provided by the bank. Mr Qureshi's second idea won the day, but not decisively. Profit-and-loss sharing may be the ideal of Islamic finance, in practice it only plays a secondary role.

The system of Islamic finance that has emerged over the years is based on the idea that riba, gharar and maysir should be avoided. Islamic financial institutions have sprung up that provide financial instruments meeting this requirement. We shall first cover the instruments that are based on profit-and-loss sharing, and then the others. A separate section is devoted to instruments whose sharia compatibility is seen as debatable. It should be noted that Muslims need have no compunction making use of the services and products of conventional financial institutions, provided they make sure these services and products are not tainted by riba, gharar and maysir or by haram investments.

Freedom of contract is restricted in Islam. It is not enough that halal instruments and activities are avoided. Islamic contract law imposes additional restrictions. Many Muslim jurists further hold that the class of permissible contracts is restricted to those that are mentioned in the sharia, the so-called nominate contracts (El-Gamal 2006, p. 18; Sinke 2007, p. 17). This restriction hasn't proven fatal for the development of an Islamic financial sector, however, as bankers and fiqh scholars have been quite skilful in the art of dressing new financial instruments in the garb of the nominate contracts. A complete survey of these instruments is hardly possible, and would anyway soon be obsolete.[2] Nevertheless, some basic forms reappear in various guises and it is quite possible to give a reasonably comprehensive idea of current practices in the world of Islamic finance.

In this chapter we first review the financial instruments that are widely seen as halal and then in a separate section instruments that are accepted in some quarters but frowned upon by others. Another section is devoted to the requirements that Islamic contracts have to meet, which differ in several respects from conventional contracts.

4.2 HALAL INSTRUMENTS

4.2.1 Which Instruments are Considered *Halal*?

The ideal of Islamic finance is a situation where the capital provider shares the business risks of the borrowing entity, which means that it shares in its profits but also in its losses, in some cases even shouldering the losses fully. This is called profit-and-loss sharing, or PLS. The class of PLS instruments consists of two types:

- *mudaraba*, or trustee finance, also known as *qirad*, and a version developed for agriculture, *muzara*

- *musharaka*, that is, partnership financing, with its variants *musharaka mutanaqisah* or diminishing musharaka and *musaqat*, applied in orchard keeping

Alongside these PLS instruments a veritable smorgasbord of other financial instruments has sprung up. In all of them (except quard hasan in some cases), the financier receives a return in the form of a fee or a mark-up on the price of the goods that are bought with the help of the funds supplied. The underlying idea is that the Quran, 2:275, prohibits interest but applauds trade, and profit is not frowned upon. Sharia scholars generally accept these fees and mark-ups, provided the financier also bears some of the risks associated with owning the good. Not all sharia scholars find a return in the form of a mark-up acceptable, though. Still, the following instruments are generally regarded as halal:

- *murabaha*, or mark-up financing, with a variant called *musawama*
- *ijara*, leasing, with its variant *ijara wa iqtina*, which means lease to own, or lease purchase
- *bai'salam*, that is, prepaid purchase
- *quard hasan*, or beneficence loan
- *istisna*, a contract of manufacture with progressive financing
- *sukuk*, certificates or Islamic bonds
- Islamic credit cards.

These instruments will now be discussed successively.

4.2.2 *Mudaraba*

Mudaraba (stress on the second syllable) can be translated as trustee finance contract or trust financing. The Maliki and Shafii law schools also use the name *qirad*. The bank, or any other money provider, acts a *rabb al-mal* or financier, capital owner, and provides the entire capital needed for financing a project. The other party, the *mudarib* or agent, manages the venture and brings their labour and expertise in. The capital provider is similar to a sleeping partner. Parties agree beforehand on the proportion in which they share any profits. Losses are borne exclusively by the capital provider. The mudarib cannot share in any loss, because the sharia stipulates that one cannot lose what one does not contribute. Even poor management is no reason to hold the mudarib responsible, unless there is evidence of wilful or culpable negligence (Chapra 1998).

The mudaraba contract is a profit-sharing contract. Mudaraba is therefore reserved for business finance, it is not suitable for consumer finance. In farming there is a special variant of mudaraba, called *muzara*. The bank may provide funds or land, or the landowner provides land and seeds, and the harvest is divided between the farmer and the bank or the landowner. Mudaraba is used in trade finance and in investment projects with short gestation periods, but it is not very popular, apart from its use as a form of deposit taking by banks (see Section 5.2). The fact that losses are exclusively borne by the financier brings with it serious agency problems. There is little incentive for the mudarib to do his utmost to make a success of the project financed by a mudaraba contract. As we shall see in Section 5.3.3, the fact that any profits are shared between the mudarib and the financier does not help either. We shall also see that it may be difficult for the financier to find out how large profits are. Further, wilful or culpable negligence is often difficult to prove, and even if it is, the prospect of long drawn-out court cases with an uncertain outcome does little to enthuse financiers for this sort of contract. Collateral may be requested to help reduce these moral-hazard risks (more on moral hazard in Section 5.3.3). It may, for example, help to prevent the entrepreneur absconding, but this is hardly sufficient to neutralize the disadvantages.

The majority of the sharia scholars are of the opinion that the mudaraba contract is revocable, which implies that it could be cancelled by any of the two partners at any time (Sarker 1999). It may be noted that even if mudaraba is widely accepted as sharia-compliant, there are dissenters. Haque (1995, p. 51) argues that a mudaraba contract is not really about partnership, but only about profit sharing. This may have worked fine in ancient times as a method for financing long-distance trade, but in present-day economies the mudarib is wholly subject to the capitalist, and the farmer to the landowner. It has no basis in any clear text from the Quran or the Hadith and in the present time, in the words of Haque (1995, p. 162), it is only developed 'as a way to justify economic serfdom, political and social corruption, and effete morality'. This is, however, far from being the dominant view.

4.2.3 *Musharaka*

Musharaka (again, stress on the second syllable) is partnership financing. It can be seen as a kind of equity participation contract. Both profits and losses are shared according to a predetermined formula, usually in the same proportion as the partners' shares in the firm's equity capital, though profits can be shared in any equitable proportion. Losses must be shared in proportion to capital contributions. Partners may decide to share profits not only taking account of capital contributions, but also of the amounts of labour supplied. The Shafii school requires profits to be divided exclusively in proportion to capital contributions. This is because the contribution of labour, or skill and management, is difficult to measure and it is assumed that labour will be contributed equally. Profits, like losses, should also be in proportion to the risk shared. However, if two partners contribute to the capital and only one of them is actually working, then even according to the Shafii school the working partner's share in the profits should be higher than his share in the partnership's capital (Chapra 1998). There is a form of musharaka where some partners only contribute their skills and effort to the management of the business without contributing to the capital, but such partnerships are not recognized by the Maliki and Shafii schools. There are various other forms of musharaka (see Chapra 1998). In one of these, all partners have full authority to act on behalf of the others and are jointly and severally responsible for the liabilities of their partnership business, provided that such liabilities have been incurred in the ordinary course of business. In others, in particular where partners own unequal shares in the capital of the firm, their liability towards third parties is several but not joint. Like mudaraba, musharaka is exclusively meant for business finance.

Musharaka partnerships can be securitized. Musharaka certificates or notes representing ownership in the assets of the partnership can thus be traded on the secondary market, provided the assets of the partnerships are not mainly liquid assets. In that case, trade would only be sharia-compliant if the price of the certificates would reflect the nominal value of the assets, otherwise riba would be involved. Fiqh scholars seem to agree that a minimum of 50 per cent of the assets should be non-liquid (Sinke 2007, p. 32).

A special form of musharaka is *musharaka mutanaqisah* or dimishing partnership. This variant is used in home finance. Ownership of a dwelling is shared by the capital provider and the occupier. The share of the capital provider in the dwelling diminishes over time as the occupier makes regular payments to the capital provider. In orchard keeping there is another special musharaka-like contract called *musaqat*. The harvest is shared among the partners according to their respective contributions.

Unlike under a mudaraba contract, under a musharaka contract the entrepreneur, the user of the funds, also runs the risk of a financial loss. Musharaka financing is used for long-term projects, but also for projects that need flexible financing or for providing working capital. Musharaka financing requires the setting up of a joint venture that is an independent legal entity, according to some (Gafoor 1996, p. 43). The share of the capital provider may vary, but Saudi Hollandi Bank (SHB) in Saudi Arabia usually takes a 80–90 per cent share in a project. The bank can have representatives on the firm's board of directors and all parties involved have the right to participate in the management of the firm (see www.shb.com.sa).

Like mudaraba, musharaka finance runs up against agency problems. These are slightly less serious in this case, because not only profits but also losses are shared, and musharaka finance consequently is less impopular than mudaraba finance, but serious they still are, as the analysis in Section 5.3.3 will show. These difficulties are compounded by the fact that Islamic law does not allow any collateral in the case of musharaka finance, as that would undermine the idea of partnership. This ban, however, is not always strictly applied (see Section 5.3.3).

4.2.4 *Murabaha*

The most popular Islamic financial instrument is murabaha, that is, a cost-plus or mark-up contract (once again, stress is on the second syllable). The word murabaha derives from the Arabic word 'ribh', meaning profit. A murabaha contract is a trade contract, stipulating that one party buys a good for its own account and sells it to the other party at the original price plus a mark-up. The mark-up can be seen as a payment for the services provided by the intermediary, but also as a guaranteed profit margin. Payment may take place immediately, but also at a later date or in instalments. In the case of deferred payments we have in fact a combination of murabaha and a credit sale, *bai'muajjal* (Usmani n.d.). Bai'muajjal is a shortened form of *bai bithamin ajil* (Obaidullah 2005, p. 68). It has become common practice to denote a credit sale with a mark-up as murabaha, and sometimes the terms murabaha and bai'muajjal are used interchangeably.

The mark-up may openly use interest rates, such as the London Interbank Offered Rate (LIBOR), as a benchmark. The well-known sharia scholar Sheikh Muhammad Taqi Usmani explains why, with the help of an example of two brothers, A and B. A trades liquor, which is of course haram. B trades sharia-compliant soft drinks. He wants a similar return for his efforts as his brother and therefore applies the same rate of profit for his soft drinks as his brother does for the alcohol. There is no transgression on the part of B, his pricing is not haram (Deutsche Bank 2007). The use of interest rates as benchmarks for determining mark-ups, and more generally for pricing Islamic financial instruments, is widely accepted by fiqh scholars, be it with some lack of enthusiasm. Usmani states that murabaha is far from ideal from an Islamic point of view; it should only 'be used as a transitory step taken in the process of the Islamization of the economy, and its use should be restricted only to those cases where mudarabah or musharakah are not practicable' (Usmani n.d.).

Under a murabaha contract, the seller and the buyer must agree on the mark-up. The seller thus is obliged to reveal to the buyer the cost of the good to himself (*State Bank of Pakistan* 2005). It is not always possible for the seller to ascertain the cost of the goods to be sold or establish the price paid for it, and in that case a variant of murabaha applies, called *musawama*. This is identical to murabaha, except that the seller is not under the obligation to reveal his cost or purchase price, so that there is no way for buyer and seller to haggle about the size of any mark-up.

The murabaha contract is by its nature first of all a means of trade finance. It is suitable for the financing of, among other things, machinery, consumer durables, trade supplies and means of transport. Pakistan International Airlines, for instance, concluded murabaha contracts with a number of banks in 2002 to finance the purchase of airliners. There are particular risks involved when murabaha is used in longer-term transactions, as explained below.

One aspect stressed by the proponents of Islamic finance is that purely financial deals are banned, murabaha loans should always be connected with goods transactions. It has, however, proven easy to circumvent this requirement and to use murabaha as a cumbersome method to obtain a purely financial loan. The financier in this case buys commodities and sells these to its client, who resells the goods but repays the murabaha loan later. In the Gulf countries a retail banking variant, *tawarruq*, has been developed exactly for this purpose (see Section 4.3.4). The use of the murabaha contract for such pure credit transactions has been condemned in the strongest terms by the Sharia Appellate Bench of the Supreme Court of Pakistan (Usmani 2000, § 190–191). It states that a murabaha transaction by a bank may only be undertaken to finance the purchase of a good by a bank, and should only be resorted to in cases where musharaka and mudaraba are not practicable. Note that Sheikh Usmani was on the bench.

For a murabaha contract to be sharia-compliant, the financier must bear the risks associated with owning goods, in particular the risks of loss and damage (the financier may take out an insurance), but also any liability for hidden defects, until they have been delivered to the client. A murabaha contract requires the financier to sign two separate contracts, one with the supplier of the goods, who sells the goods to the financier, and one with his client, who buys the goods from the financier against deferred payment (Chapra 1998). One serious risk for the financier is that the client may have second thoughts, in which case the financier gets stuck with the goods. The client usually promises to buy the good, but fuqaha differ on whether this promise is binding for the buyer (Elhiraika 2003, p. 14; see more on this subject in Section 4.4).

It will be difficult to increase the contract period after it has been agreed, unless the financier accepts a longer repayment period without increasing the mark-up. Such an increase of the mark-up is excluded, as it would make the mark-up a function of the loan period and thus indistinguishable from interest. Rollovers are excluded. This is because the same good cannot be the subject of a new transaction (Obaidullah 2005, p. 75). As for early repayment, before the contractual time limit, this is possible, but the client has no right to a reduction of the mark-up. That may pose problems for clients that have obtained finance for a period of several years and want to sell the financed object, such as a car or a house, well before the end of the loan period. Conventional loans can be amortized without having to pay interest after amortization. Under a murabaha contract, by contrast, an amount roughly equal to the capitalized value of future interest payments under conventional loans has been added to the purchase price in the guise of the mark-up and a discount in the case of early repayment cannot be included in the contract. It would, again, make the mark-up openly time-dependent. Still, financiers are free to offer a rebate, as a gesture of kindness, but they are not allowed to promise it beforehand.

In principle, the financier may not add a penalty to the mark-up in case of late payment by the client, unless the penalty avoids riba. That means that it must be independent of time and unrelated to the capital sum of the debt. See Section 4.4 for further discussion.

4.2.5 *Ijara* and *Ijara wa iqtina*

Ijara is a contract under which the financier purchases the required item and leases it to their client. Upon expiration of the lease, the title of the item may be sold to the lessee. Parties may agree to such a sale beforehand in a separate contract. Under *ijara wa iqtina*, lease to own, or lease purchase, periodic instalments include a portion that goes toward the final purchase and transfer of ownership of the product. This can be seen as a call option premium. It gives the lessee the right to buy the good at the end of the lease period at an agreed resale price. Islamic banks and Islamic windows of conventional banks routinely offer ijara financing for periods from, say, three to seven years. This form is, again, popular for financing means of transport, including airplanes and machinery. Longer periods apply for home finance. Lease can be seen as the transfer of the usufruct of an object, to which there are no objections in the sharia. As with murabaha, penalty clauses for late payments should avoid riba (El-Gamal 2000, p. 14).

The financier may finance his own activities by issuing leasing notes. Investors buying these notes receive from the financier part of the rental payments that the financier, the lessor, in his turn receives from the lessee. The lessor may of course buy the lease object from a third party, but he may also buy the object from the lessee and lease it back, with an understanding that the lessee buys it back at the end of the lease period at an agreed price.

A necessary condition for ijara to be permissible is that the lessor remains the owner of the leased object for the whole period of the lease and bears any liabilities, such as manufacturing defects, emerging from ownership, though not any liabilities pertaining to its use. This implies that permissible ijaras are operating leases. The dividing line between operating leases and financial leases is, however, hard to draw. Ijara wa iqtina and ijara coupled with a sales contract would hardly qualify as operating leases under the definition of the International Accounting Standards (IAS) Board.[3] The fact that ijara wa iqtina and some other ijara contracts are very similar to financial leases makes some fuqaha doubt their permissibility. Long-term lease contracts shift the entire price risk to the lessee, given the fact that ijara contracts cannot be cancelled. This is particularly so with ijara wa iqtina or ijara coupled with a sales contract, if the 'residual' value of the asset, or the resale price, is fixed in advance. The quality of the asset at the end of the lease period is unknown when the lease conditions are made up, and the market-related price is also unknown. Agreeing a resale price beforehand is therefore, in the eyes of those fuqaha, a case of gharar. Even under a simple ijara contract without a sales contract, the end result for the lessee may turn out to be worse than the outright purchase of the asset through an interest-bearing loan, which is deemed unfair. Suppose the lease contract is for five years. The lessee would have to continue making lease payments even if he does not need the asset, say, after two years. In the case of a purchase of a good through an interest-bearing loan, the purchaser can sell the asset on the market and repay the loan, thus reducing his loss. This he cannot do under the terms of an ijara contract. Under an ijara wa iqtina contract there is the additional injustice that, if the lessee is unable to make lease payments, he may lose his stake in the asset even through he has paid a part of the asset price beyond the rental charge he would normally pay in an operating lease (Chapra 1998, 2007). Contracts where any purchases at the end of the lease period are only optional and the price would be market-related and not fixed in advance, would go a long way to meet the objections of the critical fiqh scholars.

4.2.6 *Bai'salam*

Bai'salam is a sales contract where the buyer pays in advance for goods. It is a purchase with deferred delivery, or buyer's credit. The goods need not already exist at the time the bai'salam contract is entered into, but they must be ascertainable, that is, they should be described exactly as to both quality and quantity, and the exact date and place of delivery must be specified in the contract. Otherwise the contract would be tainted by gharar. It remains, of course, uncertain whether the goods will be actually available. If the seller is unable to deliver, parties may agree to postpone delivery to the next crop or the seller returns the advance paid to him, without any increase (M.F. Khan 1997, p. 37). If the seller fails to deliver while able to do so, this is a breach of contract and the buyer may take the matter to court.

Bai'salam is applied to agricultural products and also to fungible manufactured goods or for providing working capital to small traders. Farmers and other small entrepreneurs would suffer disproportionally if buyer's credit were not available. Bai'salam is a bit of an exception in the Islamic financial landscape, as forward contracts are not generally acceptable. You cannot sell what you do not own and possess. Its permissibility is based on the sunna (for instance, Bukhari, vol. 3, book 35, ahadith 441–449). Bai'salam may be a forward contract, but it differs in two important aspects from the usual forwards and futures. First, under a bai'salam contract the full price of the product must be paid in advance. Second, at maturity the buyer must take delivery of the good (Al-Suwailem 2006, p. 30). Muslim scholars argue that in this way speculative activities (maysir) are prevented, but the downside is that hedging also becomes more difficult.

The ultimate buyer may act as the financier, but banks may also fulfil this role. In the latter case, the goods will be resold after the financier takes delivery. The bank may reduce its price risk if a third party, for instance a prospective customer of the farmer or trader, promises to buy the good at a certain date for a certain price. The bank may alternatively enter into a parallel bai'salam to exclude price risk. A parallel bai'salam is also called for if the bank does not want to commit any liquid funds for this transaction. One application of bai'salam outside agriculture where banks can play a useful role is export finance (Obaidullah 2005, pp. 95–9). Remember, though, that bai'salam is only allowed for fungible goods.

The Maliki law school in Madinah allowed trading in salam contracts in secondary markets already around the year 800. The exceptions were essential food commodities, such as wheat, barley, dates and salt, as the Prophet Muhammad had instructed his followers that food can only be sold if possessed in advance. The other three Sunni law schools do not allow resale or transfer of ownership before delivery has been made (M.F. Khan 1997, p. 37). Salam contracts allow financiers to take security or guarantee, but not to impose a penalty for late delivery (Elhiraika 2003, p. 59).

The Accounting and Auditing Organization for Islamic Financial Institutions (AAOIFI), has ruled against bai'salam for shares in a standard, Sharia Standard 21, that became effective in January 2007 (Gassner 2007b; Gibbon and Norman 2008). The reasoning appears to be that the shares cannot be described well enough for the future, as the underlying assets may change. This means that gharar is involved. But there are respected scholars who disagree and accept bai'salam for shares, on the grounds that shares are all identical and readily available on the market (Gassner 2007a).

4.2.7 *Quard hasan*

Quard hasan loans are beneficence loans, on which no interest is charged. The lender may, however, charge a commission. It is meant for those who are less well-heeled, such as farmers and other small businessmen and poor consumers. It can also be used for other ends. In Pakistan quard hasan loans, or *Qarz-e-Hasna* loans as they are called there, have been provided to science students doing advanced studies (Bokhari 1984). That means they have been used as an instrument of education policy.

A qard hasan loan is free of any rate of return, although the recipient may wish to reward the provider with a return in excess of the original amount borrowed. While banks cannot enforce the payment of additional amounts, some provide the facility to corporate borrowers in the expectation that these will return sums in excess of the original borrowing (Naughton and Naughton 2000, p. 149)

4.2.8 *Istisna*

Istisna is a contract of manufacture with progressive financing, or a contract of acquisition of goods by specification or order where the price is paid progressively in accordance with the progress of a job. Payments are made as the building or manufacturing of the object comes closer to completion.

An istisna contract concerns goods that do not yet exist, and would consequently imply gharar. However, an exception has been made by fuqaha on the basis of qiyas (analogy) and equity. The analogy is with bai'salam. A major reason for banning gharar is that one party should not take advantage of asymmetric information, that is, a lack of knowledge on the part of the other party. There is little danger of such a market imperfection under an istisna contract, where there is a party A who agrees to construct or manufacture a particular product, with predetermined specific features, and to deliver it to party B at a predetermined price (Obaidullah 2005, p. 35).

It was the Hanafi school of law that saw the need for the istisna contract. Hanafi scholars realized that some goods would never be produced if no one guaranteed their purchase. This is the case with goods produced at high cost and goods that have to be tailored to very specific tastes. Houses, ships, factory buildings and infrastructural projects come to mind. The Hanafi school furthermore allows payment to be deferred. According to some schools of law, the price has to be paid in full in advance, as under a bai'salam contract, but the Islamic Fiqh Academy of the Organization of the Islamic Conference decided in its seventh annual meeting in Jeddah in 1992 that payment in instalments or deferment of payment until completion of the object is permissible (M.F. Khan 1997, p. 38).

4.2.9 *Sukuk*

Sukuk are tradable, asset-backed, medium-term notes. The name sukuk is sometimes translated as certificates, or as Islamic bonds. Islamic bonds sounds a bit like a contradiction, and of course no predetermined interest rate is promised on these so-called bonds. Still, they may offer investors a steady stream of income. Sukuk are backed by real assets and often, but not always, they represent ownership of real assets. The first Islamic global bond issue was floated in 2002 by the Malaysian government. The lead manager of the issue was HSBC Bank Malaysia and the sukuk paid a spread over six-months LIBOR. Sukuk are mainly aimed at institutional investors, though there have been issues with a minimum value of each sukuk below the equivalent of €2000.

The Fiqh Academy of the Organization of the Islamic Conference legitimized the use of sukuk in February 1988, but it took some years before the market developed (Jobst 2007, p. 19). Sukuk are not only issued by or on behalf of governments and quasi-sovereign agencies, but also on behalf of corporations, such as the Saudi Arabian car hire firm Hanco Rent-a-car in 2004. Sukuk issues are regularly heavily oversubscribed and the volume issued shows a steep rise, from $7.2 billion in 2004 to nearly $39 billion in 2007, with more than $90 billion outstanding at the end of 2007 (Jobst et al. 2008). The restricting factor is supply, not demand. Estimates of the pool of Islamic money available for investment in sukuk exceeded $300 billion in 2006 (Soy 2006). Sukuk seem to be attractive not only to wealthy Middle Eastern investors, but to non-Muslim Western investors as well. They enter them in their books as their allocation of emerging market debt. Sukuk flotations are not restricted to Islamic issuers either. Borrowers in non-Islamic countries, from Germany to China, are also interested in tapping the Middle Eastern capital markets. The German state of Saxony-Anhalt issued a €100 million sukuk in 2004, with Citigroup as the lead manager, and the World Bank issued its first sukuk for 760 million Malaysian ringgit ($202 million) in 2005. In 2006 a US private firm, East Cameron Partners, issued a sukuk for $166 million to finance offshore gas drilling in Louisiana. In his 2007 budget, the then British Chancellor of the Exchequer, Gordon Brown, announced plans to develop London as an international centre for Islamic financial products, including a secondary market for sukuk. One measure concerned offsetting the coupon payments on the securities against the company's profits for corporation tax purposes, similar to interest on conventional bonds. The first sukuk was listed on the London Stock Exchange in July 2006.

In the cases just described, it was not the borrower itself, but a special purpose vehicle (SPV) that issued the sukuk. In Malaysia that was Malaysia Global Sukuk Inc., owned by the Ministry of Finance. The money collected was handed over to the government, in exchange for real estate which was purchased from the country's Federal Land Commissioner for a five-year duration and which was then leased to the government. The sukuk, in fact floating rate trust certificates, thus were backed by real assets. The lease rental payments from the government to the SPV match the payments payable on the trust certificates. On the expiration date, the real estate was to be sold back to the government at the face value of the sukuk, so that any rise or fall in the valuation of the underlying assets had no bearing on the sukuk issue (Horne 2002).

Sukuk come in different shapes:

1. *Ijara sukuk*. These in their turn have two forms:

    (a) the sale–leaseback construction just described;
    (b) the headlease–sublease ijarah model, in which the owner of the assets headleases them to the issuer and rents them back. This was the model used in the Saxony-Anhalt sukuk.

    Ijara sukuk can be traded on the secondary market at negotiated prices. They are not debt but evidence of ownership. But what to do when the lease period ends? One option is to issue sukuk with a fixed maturity date, as in the case of the Saxony-Anhalt sukuk. In the case of a sale–leaseback, it can further be stipulated that the issuer will buy back the real estate, as in the case of Malaysia mentioned above. If the sukuk have no fixed maturity date, the issuer might buy back the sukuk at the expiration date of the lease. The AAOIFI has issued a standard not allowing the issuer to promise to purchase ijara sukuk back at their nominal value, rather than their market value (Ali 2005, p. 31). This was repeated in a fatwa delivered in February 2008 (see below). Such a guarantee would make sukuk too much like conventional loans against interest. The terms of the original Malaysian government sukuk obviously would conflict with this standard.

2. *Mudaraba sukuk.* A company or its bank sets up a special purpose mudaraba and investors provide finance for a project in return for sukuk. The special purpose mudaraba owns the assets that are financed by the returns of the sukuk sale. The company or the bank may act as a mudarib for this special purpose mudaraba (Obaidullah 2005, p. 160). Profits should be distributed according to some pre-agreed ratio.
3. *Musharaka sukuk.* In this case, the borrower and the lender set up a joint venture of a musharaka nature, with the borrower putting in some percentage of the funds required in equity and investors supplying the rest through sukuk purchases. Profit is shared according to some formula agreed between parties, and losses and expenses are distributed according to the amount of finance contributed by each party. This is a form that is attractive, for instance, for financing toll roads, but can also be used for financing other infrastructure or real estate.
4. *Murabaha sukuk.* The SPV in this case buys a good that a company needs and resells it with a mark-up, against payment in instalments. Murabaha sukuk offer investors a steady stream of income. As murabaha sukuk are purely debt instruments, they can only be traded at their nominal value. However, in Malaysia fiqh scholars follow a more liberal interpretation of the sharia than their colleagues elsewhere, and allow trading in debt at negotiated prices (Obaidullah 2005, pp. 161–2). This means that sukuk can be traded before the date of maturity at a discount, which for all practical purposes means that interest is paid and received. In the Middle East and elsewhere this practice is anathema.
5. *Istisna sukuk.* Here the SPV representing investors becomes the seller and contractor-manufacturer of an asset to a buyer (say, the government) and uses back-to-back istisna for creation of the facility. In other words, the SPV takes upon itself the legal responsibility of getting the facilities constructed, and subcontracts the work to manufacturers or contractors. The sukuk sold to investors may have different maturities, to match the instalment plan that has been agreed upon by the two parties. Liquidity is low, as istisna sukuk are debt and can only be traded on secondary markets at their face value (Obaidullah 2005, p. 165).

This list of sukuk forms is not exhaustive, financiers are free to devise other varieties (see Obaidullah 2005 for a more detailed enumeration). One development is the convertible *sukuk*, which can be exchanged for equity. Dubai Ports, for example, issued a $3.5 billion pre-IPO convertible sukuk in January 2006.

The different forms of sukuk have different characteristics. Apart from the legal guise they adopt, sukuk can be fixed-rate or flexible-rate, in the latter case usually coupled to LIBOR or Euro Interbank Offered Rate (EURIBOR). They further differ as to liquidity. Murabaha and istisna sukuk score low on liquidity, musharaka, mudaraba and ijara sukuk are more attractive in this respect.

A sukuk flotation can be seen as a securitization of assets. Not all forms meet with universal approval of Islamic jurists. If, for instance, lease claims are securitized and sold to the public in the form of sukuk, the buyer receives a financial instrument that pays a fixed income and carries a low risk. Does this involve riba or is it a claim on a fraction of a very stable stream of profits? Opinions differ. In the same way, musharaka participations can be securitized by issuing negotiable certificates, or sukuk. This may make sense in the case of large investments, such as infrastructure projects or large industrial complexes (Khan 2002). Such securitization took off on a large scale in Malaysia after the Shafii school ruled it halal. Hanafis and most Hanbalis, by contrast, consider it haram, and Malikis deem it admissible only under very strict conditions (El-Gamal 2000, p. 6). The division goes so deep that Bahraini Islamic banks refuse to trade with Malaysian Islamic banks (*Euromoney* 2001). Other disagreements are bound to rise over the fatwa issued by the AAOIFI in February 2008 that sukuk that promise holders to be paid back the face value at maturity or in case of default are not admissible. Instead, a price based on the market value of the underlying assets is required. Otherwise, the whole construction would be very close to a conventional loan against interest, with the capital sum guaranteed.[4] AAOIFI recommendations do not have the force of law and it remains to be seen how the industry will react to it.

4.2.10 Islamic Credit Cards

Life without a credit card is hardly possible in modern economies, but credit card purchases may involve interest payments. Generally there is no problem from a Muslim point of view if card holders pay the credit card company within the grace period, so as to avoid paying interest, though not all fuqaha concur. Various sharia councils have made liberal rulings that enabled financial institutions to develop Islamic credit cards that provide credit for longer periods than the usual one-month grace period. With these cards, purchases are automatically financed over a fixed period, usually 12 months. Early payment results in a price reduction (El-Gamal 2000, p. 5).

Apparently, providers do not always see each other's product as truly Islamic. Bahrain's ABC Bank announced in June 2001 that it was to launch the first credit card conforming to strict sharia regulations.[5] Bank Islam

Malaysia Bhd in its turn claimed that its card, launched in July 2002, was the first credit card developed by the Islamic banking industry.[6] The card, both Mastercard and Visa are available, cannot be used for payments in bars, discos and night clubs, for the purchase of beers, escort and massage services or for gambling.

The characteristics of Islamic cards vary. The Bank Islam Card involves the sale of a piece of land by the bank to the customer, immediately followed by a purchase of the same piece of land by the bank at a lower price. The proceeds of the latter transaction are disbursed into an account against which the customer can redraw cash and purchase goods with the credit card. Presumably the purchase of the piece of land by the client will be paid in instalments, though the bank's website is silent on this point.[7] This construction is called *bai inah* (see Section 4.3.3). The bank's profits come not only from the difference between the purchase and sale prices of the piece of land that twice changes hand, but also from fees and profit charges, partly depending on the repayment period. One wonders whether the boundary between fee and interest has not become blurred by these 'profit' charges. The only difference with conventional cards seems to be that the 'profit' is not compounded (Obaidullah 2005, p.108). Given this minimal difference, one wonders whether the diatribes against the pernicious effects of interest that one finds in parts of the Islamic literature and on Islamic websites are not a bit overblown. Interestingly, sometimes the criticism of interest is specifically directed at compounded interest.

The Bank Islam Card is based on a disputed financing method, bai inah, and therefore fits awkwardly in this section, but that is not the case with other credit cards. The card announced by Kuwait Finance House in September 2003, to be used specifically to buy consumer durables from selected shops, was based on ijara. It was an instrument for hire purchase but was no longer available in 2007. Its *Al-Tayseer* (meaning 'ease the way') card, which can be used both as a Visa and as a Mastercard, is more like a conventional credit card in its range of applications. It requires monthly balance repayments amounting to one-third of the outstanding balance. Card holders pay an annual fee plus a fee for cash withdrawals and other transactions.

4.3 GREY AREAS

4.3.1 Introduction

Some financial instruments are clearly halal. There are no objections to buying shares in business firms, provided their activities comply with

Islamic norms (see Section 6.4). Participation in share capital in itself is not seen as speculation, but rather as co-owning physical assets, which is not unlike musharaka. But it must not be tainted by interest. Preferred stocks are not acceptable, as they provide a fixed return. This is seen as riba (Naughton and Naughton 2000, p. 150). Then we have the instruments which were reviewed in Section 4.2. They are generally, but not always universally, regarded as sharia-compliant. In this section we go further down the scale and comment upon a number of financial instruments that have been developed by the Islamic financial industry but are judged totally unacceptable by important sections of the fuqaha fraternity. First in line, however, are not the financial instruments per se, but the conditions under which they are traded, namely the trading of debt at negotiated prices. This is followed by a discussion of the most important disputed financial instruments, namely: *bai inah*, or *bai-al-einah*, repurchase by the seller; *tawarruq*, the purchase of a good on credit followed by a sale to a third party; and derivatives, in particular options, futures, bai'salam and *arbun* or *urbun*, a kind of call option.[8]

4.3.2 Trading of Debt at Negotiated Prices

The sale of debt other than at face value is generally seen as haram. Trading at other prices would boil down to paying and receiving interest. Jurists argue that gharar is involved as well, as the buyer may not know the true financial position of the debtor (Chapra 2007, p. 349). In other words, there is asymmetric information. In parentheses, if this latter argument is taken seriously, a large part of commercial activities could be branded haram and economic life might more or less come to a standstill.

In Section 4.2.9 we have seen that in Malaysia the trading of debt at negotiated prices is nevertheless allowed, provided there is an underlying real transaction. Support is provided by Chapra (2007). He finds the two arguments against the trading of debt other than at face value not convincing in the case of debts that are not created by borrowing and lending money, but as a by-product of real transactions. Selling a debt at a discount, for instance, in the case of a murabaha transaction, means that the buyer receives part of the profit margin agreed by the bank and the buyer of the good. Gharar is not involved either, as the debtor often is a well-known company with a high credit rating. Chapra would like the jurists to understand that the sale of such asset-based debt should not be considered haram. This would have at least two benefits: a secondary market would spring up and the debt could be securitized. A secondary market is important because it would give banks better opportunities for liquidity management and securitization would enable the banks to better perform their role in financial intermediation. Chapra may find a sympathetic ear in Malaysia, fiqh scholars in the Gulf States cannot but condemn his ideas.

4.3.3 *Bai inah*

A second transaction on which Malaysia and the Gulf States differ is repurchase by the seller, *bai inah*, also spelled *bai al-einah*. This may take the form of a purchase of a good on credit from a bank and selling it back to the bank at a lower price against immediate payment. Bank Islam Malaysia uses this method for its credit card. The 'real' transaction thus may involve a good that the client will never have in his possession and perhaps does not even see (Bank Islam Malaysia's piece of land). Any credit transaction can be based on this construction. One might say that this transaction formally does not involve interest, but that it is meant to provide the client with credit or a credit line and the bank with an income that economically does not differ from interest. The Shafii scholars from Malaysia and other South-East Asian countries tend to consider exclusively the formal aspects, whereas jurists from the Gulf States take intention into consideration and reject bai inah.

4.3.4 *Tawarruq*

Gulf scholars may reject bai inah, but they permit a somewhat similar transaction on the grounds of darura (necessity). This is tawarruq. Literally, tawarruq means 'monetization', that is, of the traded commodity. In a tawarruq construction someone buys a good on credit, often from a bank in the guise of a murabaha transaction, and sells it to a third party spot. The bank may charge itself with selling the good on behalf of its client. Banks may also resort to a tawarruq transaction with other banks if they need liquid funds themselves. For large transactions, platinum and aluminium, traded on the London Metal Exchange, and in Malaysia also palm oil, are used. Silver and gold cannot be used, because these are seen as equivalent to money. Consequently, a mark-up is not permissible, and banks are only interested in tawarruq transactions if they can make a profit through a mark-up.

Scholars allowing or even advocating tawarruq base themselves on Ibn Taymiyya, who ruled this transaction makruh, undesirable, but not forbidden (Gassner 2007a). The individual is free to decide for himself whether or not to engage in makruh activities. The necessity can be on the client's side, as when he needs money for a medical treatment or a marriage, or it may be on the bank's side, for instance, when regulatory constraints do not, or do not yet, allow the use of more straightforward cash management techniques. Obviously, it is hard to agree on criteria for what qualifies as 'necessity'. Like bai inah, tawarruq is seen as a case of *hiyal*, or legal stratagem. The formal requirements for an Islamic contract may be met, but the intention of the transaction is not to buy a good on credit, as in a normal murabaha transaction, but pure debt financing. No surprise then that the Fiqh Academy in Mecca rejected tawarruq, or at least organized tawarruq, in a ruling produced in 2003 (al-Suwailem 2006, pp. 103–4). The fact that many Islamic jurists reject this use, or misuse, of the murabaha contract does not seem to have had any impact on the practice, however (El-Gamal 2005a).[9] A minimum requirement for tawarruq to be acceptable for the fiqh scholars that do not reject it outright is that there is a time lag between the different transactions involved. This is to make sure that the parties are exposed to price risk and the gains from the transactions can be regarded as a reward for risk borne rather than riba (Obaidullah 2005, p. 110).

Banks do not necessarily have to organize the sale of the good underlying the tawarruq transaction. Bank clients may also buy a good on credit from a bank through a murabaha transaction and sell the good themselves. In Saudi Arabia, for instance, people are known to have bought cars on credit, only in order to resell these immediately and invest the money on the stock market (England 2007).

4.3.5 Derivatives

Derivatives have largely been anathema in Islamic finance, though the permitted bai'salam transaction is a kind of commodity future. Derivatives are seen as speculative, involving maysir and/or gharar, and often in conflict with the requirements that a contract should not cover more than one transaction and that financial instruments must be backed by real assets. Furthermore, there is a consensus that risk cannot be separated from real transactions, for that would make risk transfer a zero-sum game, which jurists see as running against the injunction in Quran 2:188, 'Do not misappropriate one another's property unjustly' (Al-Suwailem 2006, p. 83).

Derivatives come in many guises. One of these is options. Options on precious metals or foreign exchange would amount to trade in money and are categorically forbidden. Most sharia scholars, among those the jurists of the Islamic Fiqh Academy at Jeddah, see options as a promise to sell or purchase something at a specific price within a stipulated time and such a promise cannot be the subject matter of a sale or purchase, in their view. Fuqaha in Malaysia see things differently and deem any kind of benefit admissible. Since options involve a benefit for the purchaser, a right without an obligation, trading of such a benefit is judged to be permissible (Obaidullah 2005, p. 182). Others opine that only very specific kinds of options pass muster. Consider companies that provide their employees with options to buy shares of the company at a predetermined price. A rise in the share's price above the strike price is a gain to the employees and a cost to the company. However, this cost is utilized as an incentive for the employees, so the final result of the contract is a win–win outcome. The idea is that wealth created through the effort of the firm's employees compensates for the loss arising from the increase in the share's price. In the usual kind of call options, by contrast, any changes in the price of the underlying good means that one party gains and the other loses (Al-Suwailem 2006, p. 80).

There is much confusion in this area. Call options on financial instruments, for instance, would involve what fuqaha see as pure speculation, maysir, if neither the buyer nor the writer of a call holds the underlying stock, nor has any intention to hold it. This should lead to the verdict: not permissible. Stock options leave open the possibility to deliver shares at the exercise date, but this seldom happens. They are issued by an options exchange and buyers and writers use them for speculation or for hedging. Speculation is simply forbidden and hedging is considered not permissible because it is trading in risk. The case is, however, different with warrants, options to buy shares of a company at a certain price (Naughton and Naughton 2000). These options are not used for pure speculation or hedging, there is an intention to become a shareholder in a company.

An alternative to, or a variant of, call options is *urbun* (also spelled *arbun*), which is a premium paid by the buyer in order to obtain the right to decide at a later moment whether to buy or not.[10] Urbun is similar to a call option in the sense that the down payment is not returned in case the buyer decides not to buy the good or asset after all. The difference is that the premium on a call option is not returned in the case the option is exercised either, whereas the down payment on an urbun purchase is part payment for the good or asset if the sale is effectuated. This, incidentally, makes an arbun contract less attractive to the writer than a conventional call option. The Hanbali school is the most liberal in allowing arbun, other schools, in particular the Hanafi school, tend to be opposed to it (Gassner 2007b; Gibbon and Norman 2008). They argue that the retention of a down payment by the seller is akin to misappropriation of the property of others and hence is not permissible (Obaidullah 2005, pp. 182–3).

In case sharia boards ruled all call options haram, this would make not only speculation but also hedging difficult. It looks possible to devise alternative solutions. Al-Suwailem, for instance, developed the idea of hedging through not-for-profit arrangements, in particular mutual or cooperative foreign-exchange hedging funds. Mutual hedging would mean that participants credit any gains or losses on their currency operations to their account with the fund. The fund could demand initial capital from participants to provide for periods with net deficits (Al-Suwailem 2006, pp. xii, 118). Such arrangements do not yet seem to exist, however, and it might be difficult to persuade members to part with their gains. This might be circumvented by asking every participant to pay a gift into the fund commensurate with their foreign-exchange exposure.

Urbun and mutual funds are examples of (possibly) sharia-compliant forms that bankers and Muslim scholars have devised to circumvent or weaken the ban on derivatives. The need is particularly felt on the foreign-exchange market. The standard view on hedging in the foreign-exchange market is that it is haram because it involves gharar, riba and forward sales of currencies (Chapra 2007, p. 352). But, as Chapra notes, hedging reduces uncertainty and thus, if anything, reduces gharar. In favour of hedging, Chapra points to one of the important objectives of the sharia, the protection of wealth (*hifz al-mal*). Without hedging this is hardly possible under floating exchange rates. According to Chapra, we should look at the reason, *illah*, for the prohibition of forward transactions. If the prevention of speculation is the reason, hedging should be restricted to transactions related to sales and purchases of real goods and services. However, the counterparty should not be a speculator either. The question of interest could be solved if the bank that acts as counterparty invests the foreign exchange involved in a swap in a permissible way. This would mean that the funds are not invested in interest-bearing bonds, but in ijara certificates, sukuk or murabaha investments.

One way to weaken the objections of fuqaha when one wants to hedge risk on foreign-exchange markets is to use bai'salam contracts (Obaidullah 2005, p. 179). An exporter A who anticipates a cash inflow of $50 after one month and expects a depreciation of the dollar might make a bai'salam sale of $50 against rupees (with his obligation to pay $50 deferred by one month). The spot exchange rate is 1:22. Since the exporter is expecting a dollar depreciation, he may be willing to sell $50 at the rate of 1:21.5. There would be an immediate cash inflow of Rs 1075. But why would the counterparty pay rupees now for a promise to be repaid in dollars after one month? The answer is: in the expectation of making a profit. If the counterparty expects an appreciation of the dollar, say to 1:23 during the one-month period, it expects to receive Rs1150 for the Rs1075 it invested in the purchase of $50. This would of course involve speculation, but on a lesser scale than with conventional forwards. This is because the counterparty would be more restrained in trading as payment has to be made immediately, whereas under a conventional forward not only delivery but also payment is delayed. Still, a majority of fuqaha does not allow the use of bai'salam on the foreign-exchange market.

A sharia-compliant solution for hedging seems possible with the help of a swap (Obaidullah 2005, p. 198). Consider the following case. Exporter A from India has sold goods to US customers and anticipates a payment of $50 after one month, which at the current exchange rate of 22:1 would amount to Rs1100. Exporter A expects a fall in the external value of the dollar. Exporter B from the USA anticipates to receive Rs1100 after one month, but fears a fall of the rupee. A and B now can hedge their risks through a foreign-exchange swap. Exporter A borrows $50 from B and B borrows Rs1100 from A for a period of one month. After one month A repays the loan, using the $50 received from his customer, and B does the same with the proceeds of his exports to India. Both A and B can invest the borrowed sums in sharia-compliant investments, such as murabaha loans or ijara participations. If the loans are interest free, they should not meet with any objections from the fiqh specialists. Such swaps are also used by Islamic banks (Obaidullah (2005, pp. 196–7). Say an Indian bank owning dollars and a US bank owning rupees may swap these currencies and invest the money on their domestic money markets until the capital sums have to be repaid. Their investment income during this period is in their domestic currencies, which partially reduces their currency risk.

A swap involves forward transactions. These can also be used for providing credit, as an alternative for common advances in conventional banking. If a business firm, for instance, wants to have its inventory financed, the bank cannot simply provide credit against interest, but it may buy the inventory and sell it back with a mark-up on a time schedule geared to the firm's needs. The bank does not sell what it does not own and the price and the characteristics of the good are perfectly known to both parties. There is thus no gharar involved, and the margin between the bank's buying and selling prices can be labelled as profit, as the bank has to bear the risks associated with ownership and thus acts as an entrepreneur (Wigglesworth 2006).

Instead of using forward transactions in a swap, one could also hedge price risks with the help of futures. These too are generally considered to be haram, as they not only involve the sale of assets that the seller usually does not yet possess at the time the transaction is concluded, but also are in most cases not meant to result in actual delivery of goods or assets. Futures are either used for speculative purposes or for hedging, which is condemned as trading in risk. In so far as the buyer of a future contract really wants to take delivery of a good, futures contracts should meet with less disapproval. Futures trade contracts are promises to deliver or to take delivery, and these are allowed. The Maliki school furthermore allows futures contracts to be traded, like they have always done for bai'salam contracts, but the Hanafi, Shafii and Hanbali schools do not. According to them, the trader will have to wait until the delivery is made before he can resell those goods. This would at first sight preclude the development of a secondary market for futures. However, parallel transactions would solve this problem. A buyer of a futures contract would be unable to sell this contract on the secondary market, but he could sell a new futures contract and thus free his money (M.F. Khan 1997, pp. 57–9, 65).

A Malaysian authority on Islamic law, Muhammad Hashim Kamali, has made short shrift of objections against futures transactions in general on the following grounds:

1. It should not be branded as gambling (maysir), as it serves an economic purpose: it reduces price risk.
2. Futures transactions involve selling assets that the seller does not own at the time of the agreement. Such short-selling is generally seen as haram. However, the ban on short-selling in the Hadith is restricted to unique goods or assets and does not include generic (fungible) goods or assets (cf. bai'salam).
3. Possession of goods or assets prior to sale is in principle required in order to avoid deception (gharar), but this argument against futures does not hold water as delivery is guaranteed by the futures clearing house.
4. The ban of jurists on delaying both delivery and payment in a sale and the offsetting of a futures position with another finds no convincing grounds in the Quran or the Hadith.

Kamali therefore concludes that futures transactions are Islamically permissible as long as they steer clear of non-permissible commodities and of interest elements, including of course interest rate futures (Ebrahim and Rahman 2005, pp. 275–6).

There are a few Muslim countries with futures markets: Indonesia (coffee and crude palm oil), Kazakhstan (wheat), Malaysia (crude palm oil, stock index and government debt) and Turkey (currency). In addition, there is some over-the-counter trading based on bai'salam in a number of Islamic countries, including Iran (Ebrahim and Rahman 2005, pp. 277–8).[11]

Things are certainly moving in the world of Islamic derivatives. The Bahrain-based International Islamic Financial Market (IIFM, see Section 5.4.4), seeks to play a leading role. In September 2006 the IIFM signed a Memorandum of Understanding with the International Swaps and Derivatives Association, with an eye to developing a master agreement for documenting privately negotiated sharia-compliant derivatives transactions. 2008 should see the results.[12] Still, forwards and futures for financial instruments will not easily be allowed. If the AAOIFI has declared bai'salam transactions for shares inadmissible (Section 4.2.6), transactions that do not require immediate payment or do not concern instruments that represent physical goods will be seen even more as conflicting with the sharia. The industry is active in devising ways around the bans, however (see the case of the foreign-exchange swap discussed aboven).

4.4 ISLAMIC CONTRACT LAW

Islamic financial transactions are of course subject to Islamic contract law. This means that contracts have to obey the bans on riba, gharar and maysir and haram activities, but there is more. We give a quick overview of the main principles.

- Uncertainty. The ban on gharar implies, among other things, that there should be no uncertainty about the characteristics of a good, the exact price and the date of delivery. These must all be known at the time of concluding a contract. Also, a seller and/or financier first must own the goods before they can sell or lease them, which implies that the goods must exist before they can be sold. There are exceptions to this rule: istisna and bai'salam.
- Complexity in contracts. Another aspect of gharar concerns complexity in contracts. The sunna does not permit interdependent contracts (Obaidullah 2005, p. 33). A contract should not cover more than one transaction. A sales transaction and a lease agreement, for instance, cannot be combined in one contract. Also, a murabaha transaction consists of two separate transactions that should be independent of each other. They should be separately documented and the goods bought and sold should be in the risk of the financier between the purchase by the financier and the sale to the client, the ultimate buyer (*State Bank of Pakistan* 2005).
- Legal status of promises. Unlike in Western law, in Islamic law a promise is not equal to a contract. A promise to buy or sell under a murabaha contract, therefore, is a moral obligation and not a legal obligation. If the promise is not enforceable in a court of law, that may make a murabaha contract risky for a bank. Especially if prices are volatile and the client feels he can make a better deal, the bank may have bought a good that the client eventually refuses to take delivery of. The reason appears to be that sharia law does

not recognize a contract that has as its object a future thing. Ijara, bai'salam and istisna are exceptions, and only allowed if an exact description is given of the goods to be delivered, the place and time of delivery and the price to be paid (which has to be paid immediately in the case of bai'salam). All this follows from the need to steer clear of riba and gharar. Exchanges that could result in riba al-nasia (riba by way of deferment) should therefore be concluded immediately, and countervalues must be, at least in their essence, in existence and known to the contracting parties. The Islamic Fiqh Academy at Jeddah, however, has ruled that the fulfilment of promises made in commercial transactions is obligatory in the legal sense if the promises are unilateral (a unilateral promise is called *wa'd*) and the promise has caused the promisee to incur some liabilities. If the promisor then has second thoughts, the court may force him either to sell or buy the good as promised or pay damages (Deutsche Bank 2007). In conclusion, there can hardly be any overriding objections for Muslims against following Western legal practices in this respect.

- Agreement among parties. Sharia law requires that offer and acceptance must be linked and must be made during the same meeting. If acceptance of an offer is made subject to any condition, it does not count as an acceptance but as a counter-offer. If the meeting ends without the parties reaching agreement, the offer is deemed to have expired (Sinke 2007, p. 21).
- Obligations of ownership. Under Islamic law, the owner of a property pays property taxes. In the case of leased property, it is therefore not the occupier who pays the tax. The same goes for insurance. If no Islamic forms of insurance are available and the law of the land requires property to be insured, darura or necessity may be invoked by Islamic scholars as a reason to allow conventional insurance (Thomas 2001).
- Penalty clauses. As riba is forbidden, penalty interest in case of late payment is also forbidden. But this does not amount to a flat rejection of any penalty clause. In some countries, such as Bangladesh and Pakistan, a penalty provision is introduced in mark-up based contracts for late payment (Sarker 1999). There is an enormous diversity of views on this subject among fiqh scholars. At one extreme are those that allow only imprisonment to serve as a deterrent, but prohibit any monetary penalty on the defaulter and do not allow compensation to the aggrieved party, for fear that this might become equivalent to interest. Imprisonment of course only serves as a deterrent to unjustified delay in payments;

it would not offer the aggrieved party any compensation. Jurists of a more liberal bent allow the imposition of a financial penalty on the debtor who delays payment without justification. Again this would serve as a deterrent. According to some, the aggrieved party should receive this penalty only in the case that the penalty is imposed by a court. If that happens, there are again two views. In one view the aggrieved party may receive compensation both for the damage caused by late payment and for the loss of income that it may suffer. The other view only allows compensation for the actual damage but not for the loss of income. If the penalty is not determined by a court, it cannot be used for compensating the aggrieved party. It must be used for charitable objectives (Chapra 1998, 2007). The prevalent position, however, seems to be that creditors may impose penalties for late payments, which have to be donated, either by the creditor or directly by the client, to a charity, but a flat fee to be paid to the creditor as a recompense for the costs of collection is also acceptable to many fuqaha. HSBC Amanah, for instance, charges what they call an administration fee for late or partial payment and if the fee exceeds their actual expenses incurred, the surplus is donated to a public charity. Sharia scholars have agreed that conventional banks that participate in Islamically structured transactions are not bound by this rule and may be paid penalty amounts in proportion to their participation in a transaction. This regards not only murabaha contracts but also musharaka and ijara contracts (Zubair 2008).

If penalty clauses for late payment must be restricted to a compensation for the costs made by the creditor, this may mean that there is little incentive for debtors to make sure they are current on their debt service, other than that their reputation may be at stake. The Malaysian authorities try to reduce this moral-hazard risk by bringing criminal charges against borrowers who default without being forced to do so by their business situation (Bokhari 2002). This, however, is expensive and court cases may last for a long time, with an uncertain outcome. A solution found by banks themselves in the case of murabaha finance is to include a charge for late payments in the mark-up and to offer a rebate for payment on time (Pal 1999, p. 70; Kuran 2006, p. 10).

- Guarantees. Asking for guarantees is somewhat problematic. A seller in a murabaha transaction, for instance, may ask the client to find a guarantor. However, the guarantor may not ask for payment for his services other than administrative costs, as such a payment would smack of riba. There are jurists, though, who would allow

> guarantors to ask a remuneration because they would otherwise be hard to find, in particular if international trade is concerned (Oahalou and Bouissaghouane 2003, p. 62).
>
> In PLS transactions (mudaraba and musharaka), guarantees would be out of place in principle, as the financier has to bear the risks associated with entrepreneurship. In other contracts, such as ijara and murabaha, financiers can accept securities. These may take the form of a personal guarantee, guarantees from other financiers, real estate, goods (provided these are not subject to a sale contract) and pledges of physical goods. Pledges of intangibles are not admissible, because of concern over valuation and repossession (Wilson 2002).

Underlying these principles are the basic ideas which sharia law is said to represent. The first basic idea is that dealings between people should be just and equitable. There is a strong emphasis on commutative justice (Hassan 2002). Contracts where one party is duped by another are considered void. We have seen in Section 3.4.2 that the bans on gharar and maysir rest on this notion of justice. The same goes for the ban on riba. The second basic idea is liberality (ibid.). When in distress, people should be treated generously. In particular, when people are unable to repay their debts in time, they should be granted easy terms. The Quran (2:280) says: 'If the debtor is in a difficulty, grant him time till it is easy for him to repay; but if you waive the sum by way of charity it will be better for you, if you understand it.' This may be a fine principle in relationships between private persons in close-knit communities with a fair amount of social control, but in the business of banking it easily gives rise to moral-hazard problems. Debtors can be expected to take undue advantage of such leniency. Hence the problems with penalty clauses.

A fundamental difficulty with Islamic jurisprudence is that there is no homogeneous interpretation. It is not bound by precedent and if one Islamic court rules some transaction or asset halal, another one may come to the opposite conclusion. There is no ultimate authority. For instance, Malaysia has been in the forefront of developing new instruments such as sukuk, whereas Saudi Arabia initially did not allow trading in sukuk. This impedes the development of Islamic financial markets, which is why the Islamic Financial Services Board (IFBS) was inaugurated in Malaysia in 2002, with the support not only of the Islamic Development Bank (IDB) and the AAOIFI, but also the International Monetary Fund (IMF). Its aim is to develop standards for regulatory and supervisory agencies and in that way contribute to a harmonization of practices in the Islamic financial industry.

The uncertainty surrounding Islamic jurisprudence may be one reason why Islamic financial contracts often choose English law as the applicable law.[13] Alternatively, Islamic law is chosen, with a provision for commercial arbitration. This may offer the best way to apply sharia law, as national courts will not intervene as long as there are no conflicts with national law.

4.5 CONCLUSIONS

Strict adherence to sharia law restricts the range of financial instruments that can be used. Financial institutions have been extremely resourceful in developing instruments that to a greater or lesser extent mimic conventional ones. Whether they stretch the meaning of the adjective 'Islamic' too far in the process is the subject of ongoing discussions. Many seem to find any solution acceptable as long as it obeys the letter of the law, even if it in other people's opinion goes against the spirit of the law. Interpretations of the letter of sharia law moreover differ widely, and consequently financial institutions face quite an amount of uncertainty over whether instruments that have been given the stamp of approval from their own sharia board will be found acceptable by other religious boards and councils. Standard-setting bodies could help to harmonize rules and increase the size of the market for any product, which in its turn might help reduce the price of Islamic financial instruments and make them more competitive.

NOTES

1. Malley (2004) provides an overview of Sami Hamoud's role in developing Islamic banking.
2. See Gainor (2000) for a practical approach to the development of new Islamic financial products.
3. The terms 'financial lease' or 'finance lease' and 'operating lease' are not well-defined. In general, in a financial lease the lessor finances an asset but does not operate it. This does not mean that in an operating lease the lessor operates the asset. 'Operating lease' is a catch-all term for all leases that are not financial leases. One might distinguish a class of 'pure' operating leases where the lessee does not commit himself to any permanent or long-term use. Ijara wa iqtina clearly does not belong to this class. The International Accounting Standards Board denotes a lease in IAS 17 as a finance lease in the following situations:

    - The lease transfers ownership of the asset to the lessee by the end of the lease term.
    - The lessee has the option to purchase the asset at a price which is expected to be sufficiently lower than fair value at the date the option becomes exercisable that, at the inception of the lease, it is reasonably certain that the option will be exercised.
    - The lease term is for the major part of the economic life of the asset, even if title is not transferred.

- At the inception of the lease, the present value of the minimum lease payments amounts to at least substantially all of the fair value of the leased asset.
- The lease assets are of a specialized nature such that only the lessee can use them without major modifications being made.
- If the lessee is entitled to cancel the lease, the lessor's losses associated with the cancellation are borne by the lessee.
- Gains or losses from fluctuations in the fair value of the residual fall to the lessee (for example, by means of a rebate of lease payments).
- The lessee has the ability to continue to lease for a secondary period at a rent that is substantially lower than market rent.
(www.iasplus.com/standard/ias17.htm, July 2008)

It appears that ijara wa iqtina would generally qualify as a finance lease under IAS 17, given the second and fourth bullets. The first bullet only formally does not apply. This is also the case when an ijara contract is supplemented by a sales contract.

4. The fatwa is available on www.aaoifi.com/aaoifi_sb_sukuk_Feb2008_Eng.pdf. The AAOIFI sharia board is headed by Sheikh Muhammad Taqi Usmani, a name we have met earlier in this chapter and will come across again a few times.
5. www.islamic-banking.com/news/bahrain/archive/abc_card_0601.php.
6. www.islamonline.net/English/News/2002-07/25/article06.shtml.
7. See www.bankislam.com.my/Bank_Islam_Card.aspx.
8. *Bai inah* and *tawarruq* are instruments to obtain credit while nominally meeting the requirement that a financial transaction must be asset-backed. Another instrument was *'uhda*, an exchange of a cash payment for temporary custodianship and use of property, widespread in Hadramaut (Yemen) from the fourteenth through the twentieth century (Boxberger 1998). People in need of money could sell or grant custody of property, such as land or palm trees, with the right to buy it back at the same price. The buyer gained usufruct and could either use the property themself or rent it back to the seller. The 'uhda could be inherited or sold. Some authorities considered it a mortgage, others a sale.
9. See for the rejection of tawarruq, against the opposition not only of the banks but also of the government, by the Sharia Appellate Bench of the Supreme Court of Pakistan: Usmani (2000), para. 219 and 227.
10. The urbun contract is very old, it already existed at the time of the second caliph, Umar, c. 700 (Al-Suwailem 2006, p. 31).
11. The difference is that futures trading is standardized whereas forward or over-the-counter trade is not.
12. www.isda.org/press/press091206iifm.html; http://uk.reuters.com/article/electionsNews/idUKL0585255520080207.
13. See Bälz (2004) on the complexity of litigation involving Islamic contracts in non-Islamic jurisdictions.

5. Islamic banks

5.1 INTRODUCTION

In this chapter we analyse how banks have incorporated Islamic principles. There is ample evidence that these principles may lead to serious moral-hazard and information problems and we show how the banks deal with those problems. We start with a survey of the financial instruments offered by the banks, that is, the liabilities side of the bank's balance sheet. Next we discuss the specific problems thrown up by some of these liabilities. Then we discuss the problems associated with typically Islamic bank assets. Agency problems figure prominently, but that's not all. We continue with a quick overview of the practice of Islamic banking. The chapter ends with a few conclusions.

5.2 THE LIABILITIES OF ISLAMIC BANKS

5.2.1 Financial Instruments Offered by Banks

If we discuss the financial instruments offered by banks, we deal with their funding, their sources of funds. Islamic banks of course have to follow the precepts of Islamic finance. This implies that not only their lending but also their funding should make use of halal financial instruments. Islamic banks are thus free to issue shares, but not conventional interest-bearing debt. In principle they offer instruments that pay a variable return, depending on the return on their assets. In this respect deposits with Islamic banks would resemble investment funds. We shall see that, in actual practice, deposits usually offer a much more stable return. We start with an enumeration of the different financial instruments offered by Islamic banks in order to fund themselves and follow this up with a brief discussion of the various instruments.

Apart from share capital, Islamic banks attract funds by issuing or selling the following instruments:

- investment or PLS (profit-and-loss sharing) accounts
- savings accounts

- transaction accounts, or current accounts
- *quard hasan* accounts
- borrowings.

Investment or PLS accounts

Investment or PLS accounts are in principle meant as mudaraba funds, with the depositor acting as rabb al-mal, or financier, and the bank as mudarib.[1] If losses occur, these should be borne by the depositors. In practice, however, clients are not expected to share in any losses of the bank; in general there is a de facto guarantee on the capital sum of deposits. This of course is at variance with the principle that the mudarib, in this case the bank, should not shoulder any losses, but the forces of competition do not leave the banks much choice. A common practice is the smoothing of profit disbursements over time through a profit equalization reserve into which a part of a bank's profits is paid. This enables the bank to avoid low profit disbursements to its depositors in lean years, or to increase profit disbursements in order to stay competitive if conventional banks increase interest rates on deposits (Wilson 2007).

For all that, investment account holders nominally share in the losses and profits of the bank and are in that respect similar to shareholders, without the rights of shareholders. This creates a corporate-governance problem that the Islamic Financial Standards Board (IFSB) has addressed in its *Guiding Principles on Corporate Governance* (IFSB 2006; see Section 5.4.4). The guidelines aim at providing investment account holders with all relevant information. Unrestricted account holders, for instance, whose deposits are pooled with other deposits and used by the bank for investments without any prior restriction, should receive all necessary information on the calculation and allocation of profits and on the investment policies of the bank. The underlying idea is that investment account holders should be able to monitor the bank's management in order to be able to check whether the risk–return profile of the bank's investments agrees with their own preferences. Not all potential problems have been addressed by these guidelines. In particular, there are still question marks over the seniority of investment account holders' claims in case of bankruptcy (El-Gamal 2005a).

The fact that account holders do not formally have the nominal value of their deposits guaranteed may bring banks planning to offer such banking facilities in Western countries into conflict with the supervisory authorities, as the basic idea of banking regulation is that the capital sum of deposits should be guaranteed. If investment accounts could be structured as participations in an investment fund, such problems could be avoided.

Savings accounts

Islamic banks can offer savings accounts guaranteeing the nominal value of the savings deposits and even providing a return. The guarantee can be given because of the legal fiction that the client's money is placed with the bank in custody, *amanah*, or safekeeping, *wadia* (Errico and Farahbaksh 1998; Sundararajan et al. 1998). Ideally, the money should be held by the bank in the form of cash and not be re-lent, but that does not seem to be the way the banks handle these accounts. The banks of course are not allowed to pay interest on these deposits, but anybody is free to bestow gifts on anybody else, and banks are no exception. They thus may pay depositors a gift, *hiba*, depending on their profitability. This is not a form of interest, or riba, because there is no promise of a predetermined payment. The Bahrain Islamic Bank, for example, offers savings account holders 'an annual rate of return based on what Allah has granted in the form of profits' (Raphaeli 2006).

In Iran even less effort is made to hide the similarity to conventional interest. The central bank requires the banks to pay their depositors a certain minimum 'profit' rate. It publishes provisional deposit rates for time deposits up until five-year deposits with public banks, either one rate or a range (for instance, 13–17 per cent). Depositors have near-certainty that their share in realized profits will not substantially differ from these provisional rates. The measure was taken for government-owned banks, not private banks and non-bank credit institutions, apparently in order to ensure the attractiveness of deposits held in state banks. The rate on foreign deposits in the domestic banking system, moreover, is LIBOR, which is openly and unashamedly an interest rate (Kia 2006).

Transaction accounts, or current accounts

Transaction or current accounts pay no interest, but the nominal value of deposits is officially guaranteed. Again, this is under the flag of amanah or wadia. In cases where conventional banks might pay interest, Islamic banks can offer free services. HSBC Amanah, for instance, offers depositors free payment services, provided their total deposits exceed some minimal value. In that case, clients also receive discounts on such things as the hire of a safe deposit box. Lloyds TSB assures its Muslim clients in the UK that the money they hold in their current account or in their so-called Islamic business account will be used by the bank in a sharia-compliant way. Overdrafts are not allowed, and if it proves impossible to intercept an electronic payment and a negative balance ensues, the bank will not demand interest but charge a fixed fee. On Lloyds TSB's Islamic student account overdrafts are allowed, but no interest is charged. Presumably a fixed fee does the trick.

Quard hasan accounts
Quard hasan accounts pay no interest and are meant to provide funds that the bank in its turn uses to grant quard hasan loans.

Borrowings
Conventional banks hardly ever do without fixed-income liabilities. The closest Islamic equivalents are surely sukuk and Islamic banks are starting to use these for their own funding. The pioneer was Malaysian Banking Berhad (Maybank), which issued a $300 million (RM 1.03 billion) subordinated Sukuk in 2006 in order to strengthen the tier 2 capital of the bank.[2]

5.2.2 Problems of PLS Funding

Profit-and-loss-sharing arrangements throw up problems in the relationship between a bank and its depositors. A bank's assets are not quoted on stock exchanges and its profits and losses are consequently difficult to ascertain. It is well-nigh impossible for depositors to assess the quality of a bank's outstanding loans. A predetermined rate of interest on deposits saves on information costs in such circumstances. For its part, it gives the bank, like its clients, a stronger incentive to try and allocate funds in the most profitable way (see Goodhart 1995). There is a moral-hazard problem. PLS modes of finance may offer the banks an incentive for risk taking, and for operating with very little own funds. Depositors will have to take the brunt if investments go sour, just like equity investors in a conventional investment company, only they have no say in the appointment of the managers. The only thing they can do is shift their funds to other banks, but they may not always have sufficient information to do so in time. Indeed, this moral-hazard problem was cited as one reason by the Rector of Al-Azhar University in Cairo in his 2002 fatwa for declaring interest-bearing bank deposits halal (see Section 3.3.1). It does not come as a surprise, then, that depositors appear to find PLS accounts less attractive than conventional time and savings deposits, and often prefer to hold their money in (guaranteed) transaction accounts if those conventional instruments are not available.

5.3 PROBLEMS WITH ISLAMIC ASSETS

5.3.1 Capital Adequacy Standards

Islamic banks may invest their funds in any of the halal instruments. These have been discussed in Chapter 4. An Islamic bank's balance sheet would

Table 5.1 Balance sheet of an Islamic bank

Assets	Liabilities
cash	investment accounts
mudaraba participations	savings accounts
musharaka participations	transaction accounts
murabaha advances	quard hasan accounts
investments (ijara, sukuk)	borrowings (sukuk)
	own funds

mainly look as depicted in Table 5.1. Islamic banks face problems that their conventional competitors do not have to cope with. One thing is that specifically Islamic financial assets, first of all PLS participations, but also murabaha credit, do not always sit easily with the norms imposed by bank supervisors or recommended by international agencies. Capital adequacy standards in particular do not favour PLS participations.

The Basel Committee of Banking Supervision (BCBS) takes the stand that banks should not hold significant equity positions in companies that are also their counterparties. This is based on the idea that a bank faces increased risk when ownership and the provision of debt funding are in the same hands. Mudaraba and musharaka participations are, from a risk perspective, similar to equity holdings. They are not held in a bank's trade book, that is, they are not held with the intent of trading and under both the Basel II and the IFSB norms, which generally follow Basel II, this means they carry a 400 per cent risk weight (Schoon 2007). PLS arrangements thus are expensive for the banks. They will try to get compensated by demanding a relatively high share of any profits earned with the money they make available to clients. This in turn makes PLS funding unattractive to the banks' clients as well.

With murabaha, there is a related problem. A bank offering murabaha finance becomes owner of the assets it finances, however briefly. Some countries prohibit banks investing in moveable or immoveable assets for business purposes (Grais and Pellegrini 2006b, p. 13). If it is allowed, the required capital–asset ratio will be very high again.

5.3.2 Agency Problems

PLS arrangements bring specific agency problems with them. Any financing activity may run into agency problems, but in mudaraba and musharaka finance they are particularly prominent. This will become clear if we look more closely at what bankers actually do during a loan cycle. They go through three stages: screening, monitoring and enforcement.

1. Screening. Banks have to closely screen potential borrowers in order to find out whether they are trustworthy and their projects are promising. Fantasizers and swindlers should be kept at a distance. This screening serves to mitigate the problem of asymmetric information and in that way to avoid adverse selection, that is, a poor choice of borrowers and projects. There is asymmetric information in that the prospective client has information about his own person or firm and on the projects to be financed that they are not always willing to share with the financier. The financier thus has to spend time and money to find out whether the potential borrower can reasonably be expected to be as good as his word and his projects are not pipe dreams.
2. Monitoring. After a loan contract has been concluded, the bank has to monitor the borrower in order to make sure that the funds provided are used for the ends for which they have been made available. This monitoring serves to minimize moral hazard, that is, behaviour by the borrower, once he has received the funds, that is detrimental to the interests of the financier.
3. Enforcement. If things go awry and the borrower defaults, or if there is serious danger that he will do so, the financier will try to force the counterparty to observe the terms of the contract. This enforcement may ultimately lead to the bankruptcy of the borrower. That can be prevented to a large extent if the borrower provides security. Some projects are less risky than others in this respect. Trade finance, for instance, is relatively risk free, as the lender can obtain title to the goods financed and sell them if the borrower defaults. In other cases the borrower may provide collateral or conclude a covenant with the lender to lower the risks. Penalty clauses may also act as an incentive to make the borrower observe the terms of the contract.

The interesting question now is whether the agency problems facing Islamic banks differ from those facing conventional banks, and if so, what the implications are for screening, monitoring and enforcement. It seems that Islamic finance, especially under mudaraba and musharaka contracts, but to a lesser degree also under other contracts, indeed differs substantially from conventional banking in this respect. The problems peculiar to musharaka and mudaraba will be discussed in fuller detail, but there are also some general problems. As we saw in Section 4.4, an efficient and reliable sharia litigation system is wanting, guarantees cannot always be demanded and penalty clauses will be of limited value to creditors. As enforcement thus is appreciably more difficult under Islamic banking than under conventional banking, screening becomes doubly important. It must be said that with murabaha and ijara the risks for the financier are lower than with mudaraba and musharaka. Under an ijara contract, the financier retains title to the goods and with murabaha he may retain title to the goods, though transfer of ownership may also take place before the loan has been repaid.

5.3.3 More on Monitoring under PLS

PLS financing, or mudaraba and musharaka, creates particular information and moral-hazard problems that require intensive monitoring. First, there is an information problem. The bank or financier needs more information than under conventional banking. Under conventional bank lending, the borrower pays a predetermined interest rate. Under musharaka and mudaraba contracts, profits are shared between borrower and lender, and the financier also shoulders part or all of the losses. Thus the lender and the borrower first have to agree on the accounting system to be adopted, in order to avoid quarrels on the determination of profits, and in addition the lender has to monitor the borrower in order to avoid being cheated. The borrower, after all, has an interest in reporting low profits. The financier must keep close tabs on the borrower in order to receive the required information, but borrowers are often reluctant to open their books to the banks, not only in order to minimize the sums to be paid to the bank but also for fear that information will be leaked to the tax collector. In some countries smaller businesses don't even have any books to open. The economic anthropologist Professor Willem Wolters mentions an Islamic bank in Yogyakarta, Java, that lent money to small traders under mudaraba contracts. As those traders kept no books at all, finding out how large profits were was a cumbersome and time-consuming process. The bank had to send surveyors to the market to make an estimated guess of the traders' sales and profit margins (Wolters 2005).

Monitoring under PLS finance has to deal with a second problem that figures much less prominenty in conventional banking. This is the moral-hazard problem. Under a mudaraba contract, the financier alone bears any losses. This makes mudaraba financing especially attractive for all kinds of visionaries and gamblers. As the more average type of borrower is concerned, they will hardly feel tempted to pull out all stops. Why toil from dawn to dusk or burn the midnight oil if in case of failure the loss is borne by others? This is peculiar to the mudaraba contract. Another factor that serves to reduce the drive of the borrower to do his utmost to make a success of a project and to maximize profits is the sharing of profits between the borrower or entrepreneur and the financier. This regards both mudaraba and musharaka. What is the mechanism? Under conventional banking, the borrower pays a predetermined rate of interest and all returns

Table 5.2 Yields for the debtor and the bank under conventional banking with a 10 per cent interest rate and Islamic banking with 50:50 profit sharing

Return on the project	Yield for the borrower		Yield for the bank	
	conventional banking	Islamic banking	conventional	Islamic
0%	−10	0	10	0
5%	−5	2.5	10	2.5
10%	0	5	10	5
15%	5	7.5	10	7.5
20%	10	10	10	10
25%	15	12.5	10	12.5
30%	20	15	10	15

above that rate, abstracting from taxes, will be retained by the borrower. He thus has an incentive to go for high returns. Under PLS, only part of the profits is for the borrower, but even low returns do leave a positive net result for the borrower. Under conventional banking, by contrast, the yield for the borrower is negative if returns on a project are lower than the interest rate paid to the bank. Table 5.2 gives a numerical example illustrating the difference. We see that with a 50:50 distribution of profits between the borrower and the financier and a 10 per cent interest rate on bank loans, the borrower would earn a yield of 2.5 per cent when the return of a project is 5 per cent, whereas with a conventional bank loan this yield is only earned when the return is 12.5 per cent. The borrower is likely to be content with a lower return than under conventional banking. The upshot is that the financier goes home with a lower yield on his capital and that society is saddled with a less efficient use of its resources and thus with a lower per capita income than would be attained under conventional bank loans.

An additional problem with mudaraba that makes monitoring even more difficult is that there is no recognizable default on the part of the agent-entrepreneur until the contract expires, and the financier cannot, as under a musharaka contract, himself actively take part in managing the project. Under a mudaraba contract, the borrower, or user of funds, does not bring in any funds himself. He need not be an entrepreneur but may be a mere manager. Shirking and spending money on other things than improving efficiency are difficult to prevent and it appears that Presley and Sessions (1994; see also Mills and Presley 1999, ch. 4) are unduly optimistic when they expect mudaraba contracts to provide such good incentives to managers as to make monitoring superfluous. They too easily assume that managerial effort is an increasing function of expected yield, not only at low rates but also at high rates of marginal expected yield. If leisure, honorary positions and spending on luxuries compete in a manager's utility function with income, the principle of utility maximization would predict lower effort than under conventional bank loans, provided relatively low returns go unpunished.

Close monitoring thus is required under PLS forms of finance. This can become quite expensive, like in the case of the surveyors sent into the field by the Yogyakarta bank mentioned above. Monitoring under PLS can hardly be done by simply looking at some balance sheet ratios. Clients will have to be visited on the spot. Standardizing the monitoring process consequently is hardly possible, which puts larger banks in particular at a disadvantage (Čihák and Hesse 2008).

The danger of moral hazard can be mitigated by demanding collateral or security. This would protect the bank against losses. We have seen that sharia law does not allow collateral or security in the case of PLS modes of finance, as the financier should participate in the risk of the business he finances (Saleh 1986, p. 106). Under PLS, any loss is to be borne partly or wholly by the provider of funds, except if the loss is due to misconduct, negligence or violation of the conditions of the contract. However, loan covenants and other such constraints on the behaviour of borrowers are allowed (Suleiman 2005). The rules are not always strictly applied. Indonesia's Bank Muamalat, for instance, includes collateral data in its list of requirements for a musharaka or mudaraba application and Sadr and Iqbal (2002) report that the Agricultural Bank of Iran routinely asks for a third-party guarantee in the case of smaller musharaka participations, and for real estate as collateral in the case of larger musharaka participations. It thus seems that in the case of misharaka and mudaraba, collateral is sometimes allowed by the fuqaha in order to protect the Islamic bank from any misconduct by its clients (Karim 2002, p. 98).

5.3.4 More on the Downside of Islamic Forms of Finance

It has been noted that PLS banking calls for careful screening because of the danger of adverse selection, and careful monitoring because of the dangers of asymmetric information and moral hazard. One factor contributing to adverse selection is that in a mixed financial system with both Islamic and conventional banks, entrepreneurs may not like the idea of profit sharing if they have rosy expectations of the success of their ventures whereas they may prefer profit-sharing finance from Islamic banks if they are less sure of a positive outcome. This might burden Islamic banks with a disproportional share of bad debts, which can only reinforce their preference for other forms than PLS. Empirical research provides support for this idea. In a survey among 385 small business firms in Sydney it was found that they were more likely to apply for PLS methods of finance with Islamic banks the higher the levels of business risk. Not unnaturally, high interest rates also made them more inclined to ask for PLS funds. Less understandably, high expected rates of return had similar effects. Perhaps these were positively correlated with business risks. What the entrepreneurs did not like was the close monitoring, which could result in management intervention on a day-to-day basis, that went with PLS finance.[3]

It is not only potential clients, but also the banks that have reservations about PLS finance. One contributing factor is of course the fact that a disproportionally high share of applicants may turn out high-risk debtors, translating into uncertain and variable returns. Another is the fear of incomplete information, or even deliberate misreporting. All this adds to the need for close, and consequently expensive, monitoring. Not surprisingly, then, it was found in a survey among Islamic banks that reputation and the experience of the entrepreneur (mudarib) were the most important factors for financiers in deciding whether or not to enter into a mudaraba contract (Khalil et al. 2002).

Banks and the authorities have sought ways to mitigate the moral-hazard problem. The line followed in Iran is that the entrepreneur entering into a musharaka contract is to a great extent treated as a borrower who must repay his debt, even if he suffers losses (Yasseri 2002). The central bank publishes 'expected rates of return on facilities', that is, for loans, differentiated over industries. These rates of return apparently have to function as benchmarks for the profit rates that a competent entrepreneur should be able to make. The Iranian approach of course is totally at odds with the basic idea of the financier participating in the risks of the business it finances. Apparently, the more Islamic a government claims to be, the more it can take liberties with the fundamental tenets of Islamic finance.

All this does not mean that murabaha or ijara are free from moral hazard. In so far as ownership remains with the financier, this provides some security. Possession, however, is with the borrower, and there is a risk that he will not treat the good in question with the utmost care. This, though, is a universal agency problem that conventional bankers also have to face. Peculiar to Islamic finance is that the financier, if formally the owner, is vulnerable because he may be liable for any damage from the use of the asset financed, such as injury caused by equipment or environmental damage caused by oil spillage. It is, consequently, the formal owner that has to take care of insurance. We have, furthermore, seen in Section 4.4 that late payments pose special problems, as the scope for applying penalty clauses is rather limited. Banks may therefore be inclined to find compensation in higher mark-ups and ijara rates. There are, indeed, strong indications that murabaha finance is more expensive than comparable conventional loans (Dar 2007). Other forms of Islamic finance are probably little better in this respect (see Sections 6.3.6 and 8.2.2).

5.3.5 Potential Benefits for Banks of PLS Finance

We have been discussing all kinds of problems associated with the assets of Islamic banks. There are also potential benefits for the banks, however. If Islamic banking is confronted with higher screening and especially higher monitoring costs than conventional banking, the danger of insolvency is lower, provided PLS principles are applied rigorously. Conventional banks run an interest risk. If interest rates fall and debit rates are adjusted faster than credit rates, or if interest rates rise and banks borrow short but lend long, profits are squeezed. Also cyclical downturns may hit them hard. Borrowers default and income on loans falls, but interest on deposits and bonds must continue to be paid. If PLS principles are applied, a lower income on outstanding loans and participations goes hand in hand with lower payments to depositors and the bank's solvency is not endangered. In practice, however, the losses of Islamic banks are not shared with depositors and often a minimum yield on deposits is guaranteed. As a result, the potential benefts of PLS finance cannot be realized.

Still, if Islamic banks rise to the challenge of an increased degree of moral hazard, PLS finance may play a useful role. If they not only monitor financial transactions, but also cooperate closely with their clients in their daily activities, including the timing of purchases of raw materials, keeping an eye on prices and quantities, a reduction of bad debts may be the result. This is claimed to have been the case in Sudan, where Faisal Islamic Bank and Sudanese Islamic Bank, the latter with farmers as its partners, entered into musharaka contracts and essentially acted as venture capitalists, providing not only financial assistance but also expertise in a broad field of business management (Van Dooren and Kerkhoven 1987; Lewis and Algaoud 2001, p. 105). Later studies, however, give the impression that it was not an overall success and Elhiraika (2003) paints a much less rosy picture of Sudanese agricultural finance during the 1990s. Nevertheless, it seems that the natural role of PLS finance, in particular musharaka, is to provide venture capital.

An additional plus of Islamic banking, much trumpeted by its advocates, is that it is less likely to suffer from banking crises such as the 2007–08 credit crisis. As Islamic banks are not allowed to invest in financial instruments that are not asset-backed, problems with esoteric collaterized debt products, for instance, will not directly hurt them. Note, however, that this is no guarantee that they won't burn their fingers on real-estate finance, as they are free to invest in shares or certificates of property developers and lease firms (provided these are sharia-compliant, of course). Further, if they do not share in the downside of trade in all kinds of credit instruments, the benefits pass them by as well. Occasional excesses should not mask the fact that many economic agents can only hedge risks thanks to the availability of a rich menu of interest-based instruments. It's like flying. Revealed preference shows that the occasional crash does not outweigh the great benefits fast air travel brings. It must be conceded, however, that Islamic banks are less likely to succumb to the usual herd instinct of bankers when some debt-based bubble promises high profits and the eventual crash lies outside their horizon.

5.3.6 Liquidity and Risk Management

Islamic banks labour under a number of handicaps. The ban on riba makes liquidity management difficult, as it precludes Islamic banks operating in the conventional money market. Investing in time deposits and certificates of deposit is not acceptable, and floating-rate notes, even though not offering a fixed interest rate, are not usually seen as sharia-compatible either. Borrowing on the money market is likewise not acceptable. One solution found by Islamic banks is to invest liquid funds in the London Metal Exchange, which ensures that the investments are backed by real assets (*Euromoney* 2001). New asset-backed money-market instruments may further ease the plight of Islamic banks' CFOs in the future (see Section 7.3).

Risk management is also much more difficult than under conventional banking. Even if the industry is extremely ingenious in devising new products that succeed in receiving the stamp of approval of sharia boards, opportunities to hedge against all kinds of market risks are still restricted, as derivatives are much less widely available to Islamic banks than to their conventional competitors.

5.4 THE PRACTICE OF ISLAMIC BANKING

5.4.1 Introduction

We first look at the uses of funds of Islamic banks, or, what kinds of credit they actually provide, and then provide a sketch of the development of Islamic banking and of issues associated with the Islamic character of those banks. We also point to financing needs that are not satisfactorily met by Islamic financial institutions, in particular the need for working capital, especially in small- and medium-sized enterprises (SMEs), touch on the efficiency of Islamic banks and conclude with a summary of the positive and negative contributions of Islamic banking.

5.4.2 Uses of Funds

What kinds of financing do Islamic banks offer in practice? It has been suggested that genuine profit-sharing forms, with their informational and moral-hazard problems, generally are less attractive to the banks than financial products that more closely resemble conventional interest-bearing debt. The empirical evidence confirms this conjecture; the available figures show that profit-sharing and profit-and-loss-sharing arrangements are far from dominant. Iqbal (1997, p. 40) estimated that in the mid-1990s murabaha contracts made up some three-quarters of Islamic bank financing and ijara contracts some 10 per cent. These two categories averaged 95.3 per cent of new financing by Bank Islam Malaysia over the 1983–94 period (Aggarwal and Yousef 2000, p. 103). In Iran instalment sales, the Iranian version of murabaha, rose from 34 per cent of the outstanding facilities of Islamic banks extended to the non-public sector in 1984–85 to 49 per cent in 1990–91, falling to 43.4 per cent in 1996–97. Mudaraba financing steadily declined from 18.5 per cent in 1984–85 to 6.7 per cent in 1996–97 but musharaka participations started at 18.6 per cent and ended up at 23.4 per cent (Sadr and Iqbal 2002; Yasseri 2002). Even the IDB, set up by governments to promote the use of Islamic financial instruments, saw the share of musharaka and mudaraba financing in its asset portfolio fall from 55 per cent in 1975 to a very meagre 1 per cent in 1986, whereas murabaha rose from nil to over 80 per cent, the rest largely taken up by ijara (Kuran 2006, p. 11). The Indonesian Bank Muamalat reported that 39 per cent of finance was provided in PLS forms and 56 per cent as murabaha loans in 2003 (Wolters 2005, p. 13). In Sudan musharaka took up between 23 and 32 per cent of banks' financing in 2002–04 and mudaraba between 4.6 and 5.7 per cent (El-Hawary et al. 2007). The figures may even paint too rosy a picture of the share of PLS arrangements. It has been documented, for instance, that state banks in Pakistan have set target returns on musharaka and mudaraba credit, promising to return any 'excess profit' to the entrepreneur (Kuran 2006, p. 9). Arrangements parading as musharaka and mudaraba in the statistics thus were in fact based on a fixed rate of interest.

5.4.3 The Development of Islamic Banks

We now give a short history of Islamic banking. Interest-free banking seems to have been tried first in the 1930s in India, but those attempts came to nought (Kuran 2006, p. 14). In 1956 Tabung Hajji, or the Pilgrims' Administration and Fund, was set up in Kuala Lumpur on the initiative of the Malaysian government. It collects savings for hajj, the pilgrimage to Mecca, and invests its funds in real estate, manufacturing industry and agriculture in sharia-compliant ways. Tabung Hajji had little impact on the discussion and development elsewhere in the Islamic world. It seems to have been unknown to Islamic bankers and economists, at least in the Middle East, until it came up in discussions at the IDB in 1981 (Kahf 2004). Another isolated initiative was the Mit Ghamr Savings Bank, established by Ahmad al-Najjar in 1963 at Mit-Ghamr in Egypt and based on profit sharing. Initially, it did well. Mr al-Najjar set up a number of similar institutions in other small towns. They were, however, closed down in 1967. This was for political reasons, as the banks had become associated with the Muslim Brotherhood, even if Ahmad al-Najjar himself was not affiliated with them. It has been suggested that the government cracked down on the banks because Muslim Brotherhood members had infiltrated as clients, depositors and employees, though the official reasons given were of a technical nature, such as non-observance of regulations (ibid.).[4] In the 1970s the climate in Egypt and the Islamic world at large changed and banks could openly label themselves as Islamic (Ariff 2001). Private banking following Islamic principles started in 1975 with the foundation of the Dubai Islamic Bank, followed by the Faisal Islamic Bank in Egypt and the Sudan in 1977.

Islamic banking really got on the agenda after the Third Islamic Conference of Foreign Ministers, held in Jeddah in 1972. The finance ministers of 18 countries presented a plan to introduce sharia principles in the financial and banking system and in the wake of the conference several countries took steps in this direction (Lewis and Algaoud 2001, p. 120). Then in December 1973 the Conference of Finance Ministers of Muslim Countries, again held in Jeddah, issued a Declaration of Intent to establish an IDB, which duly started operations in 1975. The purpose of the bank is to foster economic development and social progress of member countries and Muslim communities in accordance with sharia principles, through participation in equity capital and providing loans. More recently, the IDB launched a venture capital fund targeting high-tech ventures in Muslim countries (Al-Rifai and Khan 2000).

The first oil crisis in 1973–74 suddenly provided the Middle Eastern world, Arab countries in particular, with enormous amounts of money, which gave a strong impetus to the development of Islamic financial institutions. Increased self-confidence in the aftermath of the oil crisis among Arabs may have helped in their efforts to develop a financial system of their own invention.

Iran and Sudan claim to have fully Islamized banking systems.[5] Pakistan has a long history of attempts and setbacks (see Section 1.3), but also has a largely Islamized financial system. Other countries, such as Malaysia, Egypt, Jordan, Turkey, Bahrain and Indonesia, operate mixed systems, with both Islamic and conventional banks. Islamic banking made a start in Morocco in 2007. Islamic banks also operate in Western countries. In Europe such banks have been, or were, found in Denmark, Luxembourg and Switzerland, but the UK is the only European country where Islamic banking has really taken off. It is hardly possible for Islamic banks to operate as fully-fledged commercial banks in Western countries without making some concessions to the prevailing monetary system. Interest-based operations cannot be fully avoided, as central banks require commercial banks to deposit or borrow funds against interest. Setting up as a secondary bank instead of as a clearing bank would be a way to circumvent this problem.

Islamic banking products are not only offered by fully Islamic firms, but also by non-Islamic banks. Western banks, such as HSBC, Citibank, Deutsche Bank, Standard Chartered and BNP Paribas, are among the many institutions active in this field. In Muslim countries they cater for both the wholesale and the retail markets, but elsewhere they tend to restrict themselves to the wholesale market. HSBC and Lloyds TSB, however, also tap the retail market in the UK, along with specialized Islamic firms. Penetration is increasing in other parts of the world as well. In South Africa, for instance, one of the leading banks, ABSA, offers Islamic banking facilities to both business firms and consumers. Usually a separate legal entity is set up for this purpose. However, this does not seem strictly necessary, as long as all money streams, including the funding of Islamic activities, is strictly separated from the bank's conventional business (Yaqubi 2000).

5.4.4 Standard-setting Organizations

Islamic banks, being a comparatively recent invention, saw themselves confronted with a host of problems which are easier to solve with the help of collective action. The information problems that are typical of Islamic banking, for instance, call for uniform norms for financial accounting. The AAOIFI, the Accounting and Auditing Organization for Islamic Financial Institutions, which was established in Algiers in 1990 (initially called Financial Accounting Organization for Islamic Banks and Financial Institutions) and later moved to Bahrain, tries to fill the gap. It has been publishing norms for accounting, auditing and solvability since 1993 and, more recently, also for the application of the sharia. The need for such norms, to a great deal consisting of adjustments of the IAS, became especially pressing after the collapse of the Bank of Credit and Commerce International (BCCI) from Abu Dhabi in 1991. The failure of BCCI led to substantial losses for a number of Islamic banks and undermined trust in them. AAOIFI standards are, however, not universally applied. Still, they have been made mandatory in Bahrain, Sudan and Jordan and are being implemented as guidelines by the Saudi Arabian Monetary Agency (SAMA). They underlie accounting standards in Indonesia and Qatar, and Malaysia seeks to harmonize banking supervision across countries on the base of these standards (Sundararajan and Errico 2002, p. 16). The AAOIFI was set up by the industry itself. It has no power of enforcement and it is a very small outfit, with a permanent staff of some 15 persons plus around 40 outside consultants (Khalaf 2007). One of the AAOIFI's directives is that the profits of transactions that conflict with sharia have to be given to charities, but cannot be deducted from zakat obligations.

Another international organization, the Islamic Financial Services Board (IFSB), issues standards for the supervision and regulation of Islamic financial institutions. It was founded in Kuala Lumpur in November 2002 with technical assistance from the IMF and grew out of an initiative by the central bank governors of ten Muslim countries and officials from the IDB and the AAOIFI earlier that year when they met in Washington at the IMF/World Bank spring meeting. It started operations in March 2003. Membership is made up of the supervisory and regulatory authorities of a number of Islamic countries plus Singapore, the IDB, the IMF, the World Bank, the Bank for International Settlements, the Asian Development Bank and over 100 market players and professional firms. It has set itself the task of complementing the work of the Basel Committee on Banking Supervision, the International Organization of Securities Commissions and the International Association of Insurance Supervisors (see www.ifsb.org). It also provides research, training and technical assistance and aims to develop into a kind of Bank for International Settlements for Islamic Banks (Sundararajan and Marston 2002, p. 157; *New Horizon* 2003, pp. 2–5). There is some overlap with the activities of the AAOIFI, as both busy themselves with capital adequacy norms and corporate governance.

Also in 2002 the monetary authorities of Bahrain, Brunei, Indonesia, Malaysia and Sudan, jointly with the IDB based in Saudi Arabia, set up the IIFM in Bahrain in 2002, with an eye to fostering the development and self-regulation of an Islamic capital and money market, among other things through standardization of Islamic financial instruments and the issuance of guidelines (Sundararajan and Errico 2002, p. 15; www.iifm.net/profile.php). In April 2008 they were reported to be in the final stages of developing the first standardized Master Agreement for Islamic financial products, the Master Agreement for Treasury Placement (www.albawaba.com/en/countries/Bahrain/225108). They are also working on the development of other Master Agreements (see Section 4.3.5).

Finally there is the the Islamic International Rating Agency (IIRA) in Bahrain, which started operations in July 2005. It rates creditworthiness, sharia compliance and corporate governance of financial institutions, and also insurers' financial strength. It has to compete with the large international rating agencies (Haladjian 2006).

5.4.5 Safeguarding the Banks' Islamic Character

The first thing a bank observing Islamic principles has to do is to make sure that their activities are sharia-compliant. Firms offering Islamic financial products therefore have instituted sharia boards. There is nobody in a position to set formal requirements, but a fatwa by a qualified scholar declaring that the products tauted as Islamic pass muster is the bare minimum, and a fully-fledged sharia board made up of at least three members is generally deemed desirable. Some of these boards may be composed of people who don't find it below them to receive bribes or favour their connections (Scheepens 1996), but the more serious institutions appoint experts. Still, even without bribes sharia boards tend to be rather liberal in their interpretations of the fiqh. Whenever minimum formal requirements are satisfied, they tend to give the seal of approval. Nienhaus (2007) sees two causes of this permissive attitude. First, board members realize that banks have to innovate in order not to be left in the slow lane vis-à-vis their competitors. Second, sharia board members of any particular bank have little reason to be more strict than members of boards of other banks. That would make life for their bank harder and might jeopardize their reappointment.

Religious scholars with expert knowledge of financial markets and products are in short supply and one sees the same names cropping up in different places.[6] One author estimates that the number of religious experts with sufficient knowledge of finance does not exceed 60 worldwide (Devi 2008). Top scholars are said to receive up to $250,000 or $300,000 for a capital-markets deal involving a sizeable amount of paperwork (Tett 2006; Devi 2008). Costs of Islamic finance and uncertainty about what is acceptable where would fall with harmonization or centralization of decision making. Adopting AAOIFI standards would help, but these are not universally welcomed by sharia boards, as they sometimes feel their wings are clipped by these standards. In Malaysia the government has imposed uniformity by setting up a national sharia board overseen by the central bank.

Banks in Iran can do without a sharia board, as haram activities are simply forbidden and it is not deemed necessary for banks to ask Islamic scholars advice over whether some venture by their clients is sharia-compliant.

As the whole idea of Islamic banking was born in the bosom of salafi reformists, it is no surprise that some Islamic banks dislike the idea of men and women rubbing shoulders in their premises, God forbid (and God forbids, they are convinced). This has led to the provision of special desks for women. In Saudi Arabia, of course, this is about the only way to tap the potentially vast female market segment, but in other countries, too, the practice is spreading. The National Bank of Sharjah, UAE, which completed a shift to Islamic banking in July 2002, opened 'Ladies Only' offices, in order to 'provide privacy to women', that is, to separate the sexes. Dubai Islamic Bank did the same in mid-2002, in order to take account of 'the social needs of present-day Islamic culture', and it already has separate for-women-only parts in existing offices. In 2007 the Emirates Islamic Bank launched Al Reem, a women's banking service with an exclusively female staff (Kinninmont 2007).

5.4.6 How to Provide Working Capital

There can for all practical purposes be no question of overdraft facilities with an Islamic bank, even if ingenious solutions have been tried.[7] Business firms, in particular SMEs, consequently may find it difficult to find working capital in an Islamic financial system. The usual PLS forms of finance are often unattractive for both bank and client, and do not meet fluctuating financial needs. Moreover, bai'salam is at best only available for fungible goods. One solution was tried out by Indonesia's Bank Muamalat, namely short-term profit sharing by job order (Karim 2002). This worked as follows. An entrepreneur receives an order for a certain project and the bank provides working capital on a profit-sharing basis (mudaraba or musharaka). The credit risk is borne by the bank. This is possible because it has opportunities to check the financial solidity of the business firm's customer through bank-checking mechanisms provided by the central bank. For terms up to two years, a similar solution was devised for small firms that acted as subcontractors for bigger firms. Profit-sharing financing was offered related to the payment schedule agreed between the bank's client and the big firm. All this was tried out in a pilot project that started in 1998, but ten years later Bank Muamalat's website provided no information on such facilities, other than very brief references to musharaka and mudaraba finance and long lists of requirements that must be met before one is eligible for a profit-sharing participation.

More, though apparently still only limited, success has been shown by another method, Islamic factoring. The factor in this case does not discount its client's receivables, but acts as an intermediary between a firm selling goods and the buyer of the goods. It buys the goods from the firm against immediate payment and resells them on credit. The selling firm will act as the financier's agent in this murabaha transaction. Specialized companies, which may be bank-affiliated, are better placed to provide these services than banks themselves, due to the restrictions placed on trading real goods by banks.

5.4.7 The Efficiency of Islamic Banks

Sharia norms impose costly procedures on banks. First, there is the expense of having to ask a sharia board for a fatwa each time a new product is launched. Next, Islamic banks may be expected to face higher costs of monitoring than conventional banks. Furthermore, more separate contracts are required under sharia law than under conventional legal systems. This leads to higher costs. But that is not all. Other operating costs will be higher as well. In the case of the prevalent murabaha finance, in particular, the bank is required to purchase a good and resell it to its client, which surely takes up more labour time than the equivalent single loan transaction at a conventional bank and requires additional expense on insurance, storage and so on. High required capital–asset ratios further add to the costs.

Conclusive empirical evidence on costs is not yet available (see Brown et al. 2007). One complicating factor is that Islamic banks started on a small scale and may have had fewer opportunities than conventional banks to exploit economies of scale. Research among 18 Islamic banks by Yudistira (2004) supports this conjecture, at least for the smaller banks.

5.5 CONCLUSIONS

Islamic banking works under a number of restrictions to which their conventional competitors are not subject. These give them their special character, but may also act as handicaps. For one thing, Islamic banking products will often be more expensive than conventional products. This is so for several reasons. PLS modes of finance suffer from moral hazard and informational problems that make for substantial costs of monitoring. Murabaha requires more work than conventional credit, and it carries the additional burden for the banks of temporary ownership of the goods financed, however briefly. This implies storage costs, costs of insurance and relatively high capital–asset ratios, which all eat into a bank's profits. Further, Islamic contract law says that each transaction requires a separate contract, which is costly. If shareholders and depositors then want a similar return on their money as conventional banks provide, Islamic banks will have to demand high profit shares, charge higher fees or work with higher margins, to the extent that market conditions allow them to do so, that is, to such an extent that clients just do not yet run away to the Islamic banks' conventional competitors.

Another point is that the range of products and services offered by Islamic banks is narrower. It is especially difficult for them to meet SMEs' need for working capital. They also have less opportunity than conventional banks to meet their clients' need for hedging facilities.

It is not only the banks' clients that have to cope with various restrictions, the banks themselves have less scope for hedging their risks and managing their liquidity as well. A factor directly adding to the cost of doing business the Islamic way is the need to have a sharia board, made more expensive as the scarcity of sharia scholars with enough knowledge of finance to serve on such boards drives their price up.

Against these minus points, there are a few pluses. First, if PLS principles are strictly applied, the solvability of banks is insulated from interest rate risk, and also from credit risk, as poor performance of borrowers is compensated by low profit disbursements to depositors. This would be fine for the banks, but only shifts business risks to their customers. In actual practice, PLS principles are hardly strictly applied. Depositors often receive a guaranteed minimum return. Another potential plus is the fact that Islamic finance is bound to restrict itself to asset-backed operations may help Islamic banks escape credit crises. By the same token, however, this makes them miss out on the benefits of pure interest-based instruments.

One is led to the conclusion that Islamic banks and their clients have to pay a price for their principles. Probably this price is higher in the retail sector than in wholesale activities. The additional costs involved in a murabaha transaction of a couple of thousand euros, dollars or ringits will weigh more heavily as a percentage of the value of the transaction than the extra expense of ijara or murabaha financing of, say, the purchase of airliners for a few hundred or thousand millions.

NOTES

1. Interestingly, similar forms of deposit were found in Europe in the Middle Ages (Lewis 2007, pp. 73–4).

2. Tier 2 capital includes undisclosed reserves, revaluation reserves, general provisions, hybrid instruments and subordinated term debt. It is the second line of defence for meeting unexpected losses, after tier 1 capital, the bank's equity capital plus retained earnings and often also irredeemable and non-cumulative preferred stock.
3. A. Jalaluddin and M. Metwally (1999), 'Profit/loss sharing: an alternative method of financing small businesses in Australia', *The Middle East Business and Economic Review*, **11** (1), pp. 8–14; cited in Gait and Worthington (2007).
4. Kahf (2004) notes that the Mit Ghamr Bank and its siblings induced higher savings among the poor and stimulated small-scale entrepreneurship, but that Ahmed al Najjar never published any figures on the activities of his banks.
5. In August 1983 the Iranian parliament passed the Usury-Free Islamic Banking Law, which banned fixed interest on most borrowing and lending operations. The banks got 14 months for the transition, starting in January 1984 (Gafoor 1996, p. 40).

   In 1984 President Numairy of Sudan decided that the banking system should forthwith be run according to Islamic principles. The banks got a full two months to bring the transition about. This of course led to some window dressing in that 'interest' in loans contracts was replaced by 'profit', so that murabaha contracts suddenly predominated. In 1990 further steps were taken to create a fully-fledged Islamic financial system, including setting up a training programme for bank staff and the obligation for all banks to appoint religious researchers who had to keep an eye on daily operations to see to it that they complied with the sharia.
6. One name that will be familiar to frequent readers of Islamic financial news is that of Muhammad Taqi Usmani. Sheikh Usmani is a retired judge of the Federal Sharia Court of Pakistan and of the Sharia Appellate Bench of the Supreme Court of Pakistan. He is said to have close ties with Maududi's Jamaat-e-Islami (El-Gamal 2003b, p. 6). Sheikh Usmani sits on the sharia boards of numerous financial institutions, including HSBC Amanah, Citi-Islamic, Abu Dhabi Islamic Bank, Bahrain Islamic Bank and Dow Jones Islamic Index. Further, he is a member of the Bahrain Monetary Agency sharia board, heads the AAOIFI sharia council and sits on the newly formed IRA's sharia council (Euromoney 2007a; Khalaf 2008).

   Sheikh Nizam Yaquby (or Jacubi) is another well-known name. He is not only an adviser to Abu Dhabi and Bahrain Islamic banks but also to Dow Jones Islamic Index and to Shariah Funds Inc., a division of Meyer Capital Partners, which launched an Islamic fund of hedge funds in 2004. His name further appears on Lloyds TSB's sharia committee.

   A third ubiquitous name is Sheikh Hussein Hamid Hassan, a graduate of both New York University and al-Azhar, who helped found Dubai Islamic Bank in 1975 and became its leading sharia adviser, whose advice is also sought by many other financial firms. In 2007 he chaired the sharia boards of at least 15 Islamic banks and other financial institutions (*The Economist*, 9 June 2007).
7. A quite complicated overdraft facility was developed in 2007 by Abu Dhabi Commercial Bank (ADCB) for one of its clients, Abu Dhabi Investment House (ADIH). The agreement was based on a mudaraba relationship between the bank and ADIH and required ADIH to pay ADCB a profit rate of not less than three-month EIBOR (Emirates Interbank Offered Rate) plus 150 basis points over the 12-month tenor of the overdraft (*Euromoney* 2007b). ADIH received a bonus if the share of the profits of ADCB in the activities funded by the overdraft exceeded a certain threshold, but if profits were lower than forecast ADIH promised to pay ADCB compensation. Obviously, this is not a model fit for providing overdraft facilities to SMEs. Apart from the moral-hazard risks associated with mudaraba, how could one ever establish the profits made specifically with the money borrowed under such an arrangement? One way out might be to assume that the profit rate equalled the profit rate on the whole business, but even then the moral-hazard risk would remain.

6. Special sectors

6.1 INTRODUCTION

Apart from banks there are specialized financial institutions active in various fields of Islamic finance, in particular insurance, home finance and investment. Banks may also engage in these activities, and in so far as they do, the discussion in this chapter is relevant for them as well. Home finance may even be a major product line for them. This chapter discusses the restrictions sharia imposes on activities in the three areas and the ways financial institutions have found to cope with them.

6.2 INSURANCE

6.2.1 Arguments for Rejecting Conventional Insurance

The advocates of Islamic finance feel that there is a need for Islamic forms of insurance because in their eyes conventional insurance is tainted with riba and gharar and is therefore to be rejected. Maulana Maududi (1999, p. 288) argued that there are three basic objections to conventional insurance. First, premiums are to a large part invested in interest-bearing assets. Second, paying premiums in order to receive a sum of money in the event of death or a mishap must be seen as a sort of gamble and therefore gharar is involved. Modern scholars use similar arguments (El-Gamal 2002). Maududi's third argument concerns life policies. A sum paid at the death of a policy holder, so his argument goes, is a bequest that should be distributed among his legal heirs and not be paid only to the beneficiaries designated in the policy. Conventional life insurance was already declared unacceptable in 1903 by some prominent Islamic scholars in the Arab countries. This was followed in 1978 by a resolution of the Fiqh Council of the World Muslim League and in 1985 by one from the Fiqh Council of the Organization of the Islamic Conference declaring that conventional insurance as presently practised is haram (O.C. Fisher 2001).

Though many fuqaha reject conventional insurance, views among Muslim scholars differ, on insurance no less than on other subjects. Hardliners reject conventional insurance in no uncertain terms. Sheikh

Omar Bakri Muhammad, who served for a number of years as Principal lecturer at the London School of Sharia, called it 'just one of the filthy and rotten schemes of the Capitalist system' (Bakri Muhammad n.d.).[1] Others accept that if Islamic forms of insurance are not available Muslims may buy conventional insurance, following the principle of darura, or necessity. Many Muslim jurists accept the principle of darura in case insurance is enforced by law. A much more positive attitude, however, can also be found, even among highly respected Islamic scholars. The Syrian Islamic scholar Professor Mustafa Al-Zarqa (1904–99), for instance, argued that insurance companies gather together the risks of a large number of people and redistribute them in a manner that makes them bearable.[2] This is a form of lawful cooperation that is compatible with the general objectives of the sharia. Taking the theory of probability into consideration, a conventional insurance contract does not contain any unbearable amount of ambiguity or undue uncertainty. In this view all kinds of insurance, including life, health and property insurance, are permissible. The usual conditions have to be fulfilled, of course. The contract must not contain any riba element and the object of insurance must be permissible in the sharia. A casino, for instance, would not be a legitimate object to insure. Mr Al-Zarqa is not alone in his acceptance of conventional insurance (see for Europe, for instance, Fatwa Bank 2000). This does not mean that Muslims should feel free to buy policies from just any conventional insurance firm, if only because these firms usually have a large volume of interest-bearing financial instruments on their balance sheets. Among non-Islamic insurance companies, cooperative or mutual companies would be preferred (Fatwa Bank 2001).

It would appear that those who reject conventional insurance do not follow Frank H. Knight when he made a distinction between risk and uncertainty. In the case of insurable risks the probability distribution of damages and claims is known to a lesser or greater degree. The outcome for the policy holder, and even more so for the insurer, is thus much more predictable than in the case of Knightian uncertainty. Arguably, the concept of gharar could be restricted to the class of uncertainty. Scholars such as Mr Al-Zarqa seem to accept that risk can be seen as free from gharar.

Muslim scholars opposed to conventional insurance maintain that security or insurance itself cannot be the object of a sale, because that would amount to gharar (El-Gamal 2000, p. 7). Even those that do not share this view will be able to understand the point. Other religious arguments on whether some forms of insurance policies are admissible or not, may strike the non-Muslim as rather arcane at times, however. Billah, for instance, notes that some insurers (even Islamic firms) charge lower premiums for life insurance policies for women than for men, as women have a higher life expectancy. He doubts whether such sex discrimination is justified by sharia principles, as the life expectancy of human beings is determined only by Allah 'regardless of the sex of the creature and, therefore, no creature should overrule the power of Allah' (Billah 2002). One is tempted to retort that Allah's plans may be unknown to man, but that actuarial differences between various groups as regards life expectancy are there for all to see (but of course, as with investment yields, results in the past do not provide any guarantee as to the future).

6.2.2 The Islamic Solution: *Takaful*

The salafi reformists (see Section 2.4) who reopened the debate on insurance had no clear idea how to shape Islamic forms of insurance. Maulana Maududi proposed that a body of experts should try and find out how insurance could be provided on an Islamic basis (Maududi 1999, p. 289) and Qureshi (1991, p. 214) advocated a nationalized form of insurance. In the course of time, Islamic solutions have been found. The Fiqh Councils of the World Muslim League and the Islamic Conference resolved in 1978 and 1985, respectively, that conventional insurance in its existing form is haram, but *takaful*, that is, cooperative or mutual insurance, was declared permissible (O.C. Fisher 2001). The word 'takaful' derives from the verb *kafala*, meaning to help or to take care of one's needs (Billah 2007, p. 403). It was not until the late 1970s that takaful was put into practice. The Islamic Insurance Company of Sudan, established in 1979, seems to have been the pioneer. In Europe, outside Britain, success has so far been elusive. A Luxembourg-based firm, Takafol S.A., owned by Dar Al-Maal Al-Islami Trust, started offering Islamic insurance in 1983 and also made feeble attempts to market their products in other countries, including the Netherlands. In 2003 they were taken over by a Bahrain-based company, Solidarity Company BSC, which signalled the end of their activities as an insurer. It is only in Malaysia and the Arab countries that takaful took off, and even there it has captured no more than a relatively small slice of the market, as far as can be inferred from the scant data (in Malaysia so far much below 20 per cent of the market). In 2006 takaful premium income totalled some $170 million in Malaysia (Bjelanovic and Willis 2007). For 2001, premium income in Malaysia was $143 million, so growth has hardly been breathtaking, and in the Arab world it amounted to $340 million; the two took up 90 per cent of a global total of $538 million.[3]

Islamic insurance, or takaful, differs from commercial insurance in that it is a cooperative form of insurance, though the actual business operations may be left to commercial firms, who act as managers, or agents, with the policy holders as their principals. It should be noted that the ideal of mutuality is hardly ever realized in the real world and insurance firms seldom act as a pure agent, a *wakil*, that contents itself with a fee for its services. Instead of following this *wakala* model, insurance firms often act as a mudarib, sharing in the profits but not the losses of the principals, the policy holders. Of course, a sharia supervisory council must be in place before a company can start offering takaful products.

One might wonder whether takaful insurance does not imply gharar too, just like conventional insurance. After all, under takaful insurance the insured party may receive a large sum after having paid a low sum in the form of premiums, or receive nothing, though having paid large amounts of premium. Indeed, one commentator brands it as riba al-fadl, unequal exchange (Fatwa Bank 2001). However, takaful insurance is propagated as a form of mutual cooperation, solidarity and brotherhood in the face of unpredicted risk or catastrophes and insurance premiums are not seen as payments made to reduce insecurity, but as *tabarru*, voluntary contributions made for the good of brothers and sisters that suffer mishaps. Takaful is based on the principle of *ta'awon*, mutual assistance. Premiums thus can be seen as gifts and donations and there is no purchase and sale transaction (Fatwa Bank 2000). Payments of claims to the policy holders may also be tagged as tabarru (El-Gamal 2005b).

Under a family (life) takaful policy, contributions are partly put into an investment account and partly into a *waqf*, a charitable trust. The contribution put into the waqf is a donation, and can be used for assisting policy holders who need assistance. Property and casualty insurance have no need for an investment account, a waqf suffices. Profits, or surpluses, are returned to participants, the policy holders, but the operator or agent, the insurance firm, also receives a share if a mudaraba construction has been chosen. If all profits are distributed among policy holders, no reserves are built up. In case claims exceed contributions over any financial year and funds are insufficient to fully honour them, compensation of damages will be reduced below the full 100 per cent (Al-Suwailem 2006, p. 117). The insurance firm, as agent or mudarib, is after all not obliged to shoulder any part of a loss (Billah 2007). Policy holders themselves may make good the deficit and the insurance firm may help them out by providing a loan. This should of course be interest free, but presumably the firm may demand a fee. Voluntary contributions, or gifts, can be donated as well. Some insurance companies at least seem to make binding promises to do so (El-Gamal 2005b). The absence of reserves is not mandatory, policy holders are free to decide to leave part of any surplus in the waqf (Ismail n.d.).

It has been argued by fiqh scholars that the commercial risks for the insurer under commercial forms of insurance are higher than under a takaful construction. This is because a commercial insurer is obliged to pay claims even if these exceed total premium income. Many would label this as gharar. The flip side of the coin of course is that policy holders face increased uncertainty, but that problem is hardly taken seriously in the Islamic literature. On the contrary, it is seen as an incentive to monitor and discipline policy holders not to exploit the system, which, it is piously added, should reduce moral-hazard problems (Al-Suwailem 2006, p. 117).

One factor inhibiting the spread of takaful is the dearth of takaful reinsurance, or *retakaful*, companies. There seem to be five such companies, among which two are from Malaysia. In line with darura principles, takaful companies have received dispensation from sharia scholars allowing them to make use of the services of conventional reinsurers, even if not everybody agrees with this leniency (see Billah 2002).

6.3 HOME FINANCE

6.3.1 Introduction

The Islamic character of Islamic home finance is found in the absence of interest payments. Of course, not all Muslims agree that their faith requires them to eschew interest, but even among those that do, there are people who find interest-based home finance for Muslims living in non-Muslim countries acceptable, in particular fuqaha who follow the Hanafi madhhab. The European Council for Research and Fatwas and the League of Scholars of Sharia in the USA have pronounced fatwas allowing interest-based borrowing from banks for financing homes, on the basis of darura (necessity), in agreement with the Hanafi view (Ramadan 2004, p. 190). Nevertheless, many Muslims in North America and Europe do not seem to be completely happy with such loans, certainly not Ramadan's salafists of different stripes, nor many of his Scholastic traditionalists. Dutch Muslims with a traditional Moroccan background have been cited as saying that an aversion to riba is what keeps them from buying a home (*Kiezen voor de stad* 2007, p. 41). Financial institutions, both Muslim and conventional, have been developing sharia-compliant home finance products in response to the demand, or perceived demand, from this segment of the market. These products are available in four forms:

- *murabaha*
- *ijara wa iqtina*
- *musharaka mutanaqisah*
- *istisna* (only during the construction period).

These are discussed successively and the legal hurdles and other disadvantages that may stand in the way of capturing a large share of the market are explained. The section concludes with a recapitulation of the problems common to the various Islamic forms of home finance.

6.3.2 *Murabaha*

Under murabaha finance the home buyer finds a home and approaches the financier, asking him to buy the house and promising to buy it subsequently from the financier. The financier buys the house and resells it to the ultimate buyer with a mark-up against periodic payments. In the UK, for instance, Ahli United Bank (earlier UBK or United Bank of Kuwait) has been offering murabaha finance since 1998. Its customers pay the bank a fixed monthly instalment over a period of 10 to 15 years (www.ihilal.com). The mark-up, or profit margin, included in the purchase price takes the place of periodic interest payments under a conventional mortgage contract. Indeed the mark-up usually equals the present value of future interest payments under such a conventional mortgage. Muslims may be averse to charging or paying interest, there are no objections to using conventional interest as a benchmark. Calculations are often based on LIBOR, but EURIBOR or other rates may figure as well. Ownership first passes to the financier and may then pass immediately to the home buyer. The client makes a down payment and the balance due under the murabaha agreement is secured by a first mortgage.[4] Transfer of ownership may also wait, possibly until the last instalment has been made.

Murabaha home finance looks simple and straightforward at first sight. However, murabaha is a form of trade finance in the first place and its suitability for home finance may be questioned. Anyone considering murabaha home finance should realize the following points:

- First of all, murabaha replaces interest payments with a mark-up, which puts murabaha finance, like all Islamic forms of home finance, at a disadvantage vis-à-vis conventional interest-based finance in jurisdictions where interest payments on home finance are deductible for income tax purposes.
- Murabaha requires two transfers of property against one in conventional home finance, which brings higher costs with it. The house is first bought by the financier and later resold to the client, the ultimate buyer. Stamp tax or stamp duty must be paid twice, as must registry and solicitor or public notary fees.[5] On top of that, the inclusion of the mark-up in the price of the home makes for a substantial price increase at the second sales transaction and a proportional increase

in stamp tax. The following numerical example gives an impression of the order of magnitude of the increase.[6] Consider someone buying a house costing £150 000 with a down payment of £50 000. The financier supplies £100 000 and charges £61 789.09 for a loan period of 15 years. The price paid by the ultimate buyer therefore is £211 789.09, an increase of more than 40 per cent over the original price. The margin above the amount borrowed is more than 60 per cent, and with longer loan periods this percentage would only increase.

In the UK the authorities, in particular the Governor of the Bank of England, Sir Edward George, the Chairman of the Financial Services Authority, Mr Howard Davies, and the Chancellor of the Exchequer at that time, Gordon Brown, were keen to develop an Islamic financial market and they saw to it that the hurdle of double stamp duty was removed (George 2003). Gordon Brown was willing to regard the two sales as part of one financing agreement instead of two unrelated sales and the 2003 Stamp Duty Land Tax requires payment of stamp duty only once.[7] In the Netherlands no double payment of stamp duty is required if a house is resold within a period of six months. It should be noted that the sharia only requires that ownership should rest with the financier for some period, in order for him to run the risks associated with ownership (such as fire, theft and decay), without stipulating anything about the length of that period.

- Murabaha finance proves extremely inflexible in the sense that selling before the end of the loan period may prove prohibitively expensive. If the buyer/borrower from our numerical example, who was charged with a mark-up of £61 789.09, decides to move house after, say, one year, they are not entitled to a discount on the mark-up and would have to repay the outstanding balance of the loan. This plus the monthly payments made over that year would amount to the full £161 789.09. Whether one keeps the house for one year or for 15 years, the full amount of the loan including the mark-up has to be repaid. In most cases this will come down to a considerable loss to the home owner and they might well be unable to repay the loan. Under a conventional loan one would have repaid the principal in addition to one year's interest only, in total say £105 000 or £106 000. The Islamic financier is free to give a rebate on the mark-up, but this cannot be but a gift and the financier cannot promise beforehand to grant it, as that would imply a time-dependent mark-up, which is tantamount to riba. Moreover, even if the financier might be willing to give a discount, if he goes bankrupt or is taken over by another firm, the receivers or the new owners will hardly be inclined to show the same leniency.

- Another problem with murabaha finance is that the loan period cannot be lengthened. The good has been bought and cannot be used again to obtain finance from the financier. This also precludes finance for alterations and reparations (Kranenborg and Talal 2007).
- A feature that makes murabaha home finance unattractive to the financier is that it cannot be securitized. Debt may only be traded at par, otherwise interest and *riba al-fadl* would be involved. A portfolio of murabaha loans therefore is very illiquid.

6.3.3 *Ijara wa iqtina*

Murabaha home finance has some unattractive features. Not surprisingly, therefore, some financiers that started out offering murabaha finance later switched to other forms. The first 'Islamic mortgage' written by the Pasadena-based American Finance House – Lariba, for instance, in 1987, was a murabaha mortgage, but they later moved over to ijara wa iqtina, lease purchase. Under ijara wa iqtina, the client finds a home and asks the financier to buy it. The financier then sells the house to the client against deferred payment, possibly at the same price, but retains title until the last payment has been made. At the same time, parties enter into a lease agreement. This is an agreement separate from the purchase agreement, as the sharia requires a separate contract for each individual transaction. A monthly payment is agreed that includes both rent and amortization of the principal. These monthly lease payments are usually geared to an interest rate and will be periodically revised. Ahli United, for instance, leases a house to its customer for a period of up to 25 years against a monthly instalment which is reviewed every year, using LIBOR as a benchmark. It thus charges a fixed implicit interest within each April–April period, though officially no interest is involved. It is also possible that the house is leased and that the lessor in a separate document unilaterally promises to sell it at the end of the lease period for a nominal amount. This would meet the objections of those who don't feel comfortable with a sale–purchase agreement to be executed at a future date, as this might reek too much of a forward transaction.

Some Muslim scholars are less than happy with the whole phenomenon of ijara wa iqtina, for that matter. El Diwany, noted for his strident criticisms of the existing financial system, including the Islamic variants, notes two dubious points (El Diwany 2003a). First, if rental levels are revised yearly, this introduces uncertainty which might be labelled gharar. Second, under the Ahli United model the client bears the risk of a fall in the price of the house. In particular, if the client is no longer able to pay the monthly instalments and the house has to be sold in order to repay the loan, he is saddled with a loss if house prices have fallen in the meantime. But bearing such risks if you are not the owner (the lessor remains the owner) can hardly be called fair. Ijara wa iqtina is neither a full sale nor a full rental, but a mixture that is not necessarily sharia-compliant, according to El Diwany. Sharia boards don't share his negative views however.

Like murabaha finance, ijara wa iqtina is at a disadvantage vis-à-vis conventional home finance in that two sales transactions and two transports of title are involved, with the associated expenses on taxes and fees. For the financier, ijara wa iqtina is, however, much more attractive than murabaha because securitization is possible and ijara wa iqtina loans therefore are not illiquid (Thomas 2001). After all, ijara implies ownership of property, which can be sold to others. In the USA Fannie Mae and Freddie Mac, the institutions that provide a secondary market for mortgage loans, have been buying ijara wa iqtina loans from Lariba since 2001 (Maurer 2003; Smith 2005). The downside is that the financier formally owns the house and, if a bank, under the Basel capital adequacy standards has to set aside a higher percentage of own capital than for a mortgage-secured loan (El Diwany 2003a; George 2003). Under both Basel I and Basel II, conventional mortgages and murabaha mortgages carry a risk weighting of 50 per cent, but ijara mortgages carry a 100 per cent rate. Ijara is a lease, with the house treated as a fixed asset on the bank's balance sheet. Ijara finance would then be relatively costly for a bank. The European Union's 2006 Capital Requirements Directive, however, allows ijara to be risk-weighted in the same way as conventional mortgages (Ainley et al. 2007).

If the financier retains title to the home, unfortunate consequences for the buyer may follow if the financier fails before title is transferred. The buyer is left with empty hands: they are just an ordinary creditor and the property is part of the bankrupt's estate. Also if the buyer is behind on their payments, the financier may decide to sell the home. Websites of UK financiers sport grave warnings like 'Your home is at risk if you do not keep up monthly payments on your home purchase plan' (on Ahli United's website www.iibu.com/).

Selling the home before the end of the financing period should be easier than in the case of murabaha finance. Still, the financier must agree, as Islamic contracts cannot be one-sidedly ended. In actual practice this does not seem to be a hurdle; Ahli United adds a standard provision to contracts to the effect that 'You may purchase the property from AUB UK (Ahli United Bank UK) at any time by paying us the balance of the purchase price.' And if you buy the property, you are free to sell it. The only thing required is a tide-me-over loan.

6.3.4 *Musharaka mutanaqisah*

Musharaka mutanaqisah is diminishing musharaka. A home buyer and a financier jointly own a home and over time the financier's share diminishes continuously as the home buyer's share increases. Usually, musharaka mutanaqisah is combined with ijara. In Lariba's home buying scheme, for instance, the client leases the financier's share in the property and agrees to buy that share over a period of up to 30 years. Often, the client buys the home as the financier's agent from the vendor and registers it directly into their own name (Smith 2005). In the UK, however, HSBC Amanah only transfers ownership at the end of the agreed period.[8]

A special case of musharaka mutanaqisah is the cooperative housing finance that was offered in Canada for a number of years by the Islamic Co-operative Housing Corporation Limited in Mississauga, Ontario and was later introduced in the UK by Ansar Housing Ltd.[9] Prospective clients have to purchase shares and the organization in this way collects funds that are used to finance houses. The bank buys the house and enters into a partnership with the buyer, who occupies the house. The buyer transfers the value of his shares to the partnership and pays rent to the partnership. The rent is distributed among the shareholders in the partnership, that is, the bank and the buyer. In the course of time, the buyer buys the bank's shares in the partnership with the portion of their periodic payments that is meant for amortization, until they own all the shares in the partnership. Finally, title in the property is transferred from the partnership to the buyer, possibly after the buyer has made a special payment reflecting the rise in the value of the house. This payment is made for the benefit of the shareholders of the bank. Instead of a musharaka contract, a mudaraba contract would also be possible.

The attractiveness of musharaka mutanaqisah varies, depending on the legal environment. In the UK there seem to be fewer obstacles than in some other countries, because it is quite easy to set up a limited company for musharaka in a particular project. In other countries musharaka mutanaqisah would probably require setting up a joint venture, which may be relatively expensive. After the Finance Act 2003 replaced stamp duty by the Stamp Duty Land Tax in December 2003, in the UK ownership may pass from the financier to the home buyer in steps without recourse to a notary public and without having to pay stamp duty, if ownership resides with a Third Party Trust. In other countries, such as the Netherlands, every transport of ownership of part of a home requires the services of a notary public, plus payment of stamp duty.

In countries where interest paid on mortgage loans is deductible for income tax purposes, musharaka mutanaqisah, like other Islamic forms of finance, is at a disadvantage. Selling the home before the end of the agreed financing period, however, should not throw up any particular problems.

6.3.5 *Istisna*

The fourth type of Islamic home finance contract is istisna. This is a contract under which the bank finances the construction of a house. The customer approaches a contractor and agrees the terms and conditions including costs. The customer then approaches a bank for the financing of the construction. The bank enters into an istisna contract with the customer and adds a profit margin over the cost. It enters into another istisna contract with the contractor to construct the house and will make periodical payments to the contractor as the construction proceeds. The ultimate house buyer, the client of the financier, may act as the financier's agent to monitor the progress of the construction. When completed, the house will be delivered to the client and if the client is unable to fully pay the price of the home, the financier will provide funds under one of the forms discussed above (www.ihilal.com).

6.3.6 Costs and Other Problems

Not much is known about the costs of Islamic home finance, but the few data available suggest that it is more expensive that conventional home finance, quite apart from the question of tax deductibility of interest payments on mortgage loans. Islamic home finance is more complicated that conventional finance and more labour intensive. According to one source, Islamic home finance is 100 to 300 basis points more expensive than conventional finance in Canada, and 40 to 100 basis points more expensive in the USA (*Executive News* 2007, no. 25, IslamicFinance.de). Low transactions volumes possibly play a role and cost differences may diminish when Islamic home finance takes hold and scale economies can be exploited. Still, in many cases there will be the complication of two sales transactions, as the financier has to own the property for a time. This may bring with it not only additional expenses for the services of a notary public, but also double payment of stamp duty, at least outside the UK.

Then there is the question of deductibility of interest on mortgage loans for tax purposes. If no comparable deduction is available for Islamic home finance in countries with such deductibility, it can hardly compete. Introducing tax deductibility of home finance-related costs for Islamic home finance often may be very complicated, as it might require far-reaching reforms of the tax system and of real-estate law (see for the Dutch situation Israël 2006; Kranenborg and Talal 2007). If, for instance, title of ownership remains with the financier until the end of the contract period, there may be formal objections to claims to tax deductability for borrowers. For another thing, in the Netherlands the law requires hire or lease purchase contracts to explicitly state which part of regular payments is amortization and which part interest (Israël 2006). The Islamic character of a contract then may be in doubt and Islamic home buyers themselves may have second thoughts (Visser 2007). Still, these difficulties are not always insurmountable. Tax authorities in the USA, for instance, accept deductibility of interest-like costs for consumers (Thomas 2001).

Nor is this all. Other legal obstacles abound. For instance, if the financier buys the property, occupiers may be ineligible for public sector home ownership schemes (sale of council houses). For another thing, Islamic home finance implies that financiers hold real estate for their own account, however briefly in each individual case, and this may lead to higher capital requirements (see Section 6.3.3 for the case of ijara) or it may be discouraged by prevalent regulations. In the USA, for instance, banks are restricted from owning real estate property, unless it is related to foreclosure activities or the operations of the bank itself. The rationale is that banks should not become involved in speculative real estate investments. US regulators, in particular the Office of the Comptroller of the Currency (OCC), however, tend to focus on the economic substance of Islamic home finance transactions, rather than the form, and to easily approve applications for licenses to offer Islamic home finance (Shayesteh 2007).

6.4 INVESTMENT

6.4.1 Conditions for Islamic Investments

Fully-fledged Islamic commercial banking may come up against all kinds of practical difficulties, especially in Western countries where the interest-based institutional set-up cannot be fully reconciled with Islamic tenets, but no such impediments stand in the way of Islamic investment. It does not differ markedly from conventional investment, except that the range of admissible assets is more narrow. One site providing information for Islamic investors proudly pronounced: 'Our goal, in simple terms, can be summarized as: To help Muslims help themselves and each other by getting rich in an Islamically Correct® way.' This was perhaps a bit too brazen, for a few years later the motto was couched in more suave management talk: 'Our vision is to help Muslims help themselves, help each other and help others by growing their wealth, and serving their financial needs in an

Islamically Correct® way'.[10] Anyhow, Islamic investment apparently is not a totally different world from conventional investment.

Investment in common stocks makes the investor share in the profits and losses of a firm, it is akin to PLS arrangements. The Council of the Islamic Fiqh Academy at its seventh meeting in 1993 explicitly gave its blessing to investments in shares, provided, of course, that these meet the standards of the sharia. This means that Muslims should not invest in firms that produce, or trade in, forbidden goods and services, such as alcoholic drinks and pork-related products. Investments in entertainment, including not only gambling and pornography, but also movies and music, and even hotels, are seen as haram too. Investments in tobacco and often defence and weapons companies are likewise not admissible. Conventional financial services do not pass muster either, because a large part of income in the financial service sector derives from interest. The same goes for shares in companies whose business practices are considered unethical, such as biotechnology companies that use aborted embryos and resort to human cloning. Muslims can, by contrast, safely invest in industries such as telecommunications, technology and temp agencies. There is no requirement that firms whose shares are bought are of a special Islamic character. It goes without saying that investments in conventional bonds are ruled out. Preferred shares and warrants that promise a definite return to its holder, for instance, during years with poor results, are not acceptable either, as those returns would resemble interest (Ali 2005, p. 24).

The investor should fully share in the profits and losses of the firm. Along with investment in shares, investment in investment funds is considered halal, not only in equity funds, but also in real estate and property funds, Murabaha funds commodity funds and leasing funds.

The restrictions on Islamic investment, if strictly applied, would severely limit the number of shares acceptable for Islamic investment. In countries where the economy is not fully organized according to Islamic principles, there are precious few firms that never borrow money against a predetermined rate of interest, never deposit money at a predetermined rate of interest or never invest in bonds. It seems that the larger Islamic banks saw a huge market and have prodded Islamic scholars to come up with a practical solution, relaxing some of the requirements (McBride 2000). Dow Jones's Sharia Supervisory Board, with heavyweights such as Sheikh Muhammad Taqi Usmani and Sheikh Nizam Yaquby, has developed screens that seem to function as the standard for the investment industry.[11] These are quite lenient. Excluded are companies whose:

- Total debt divided by trailing 12-month average market capitalization is 33 per cent or more.

- Cash plus interest-bearing securities divided by trailing 12-month average market capitalization is 33 per cent or more.
- Accounts receivable divided by 12-month average market capitalization is 33 per cent or more.

The criteria appear to be rather arbitrary, it would be difficult to base them on the sunna. The returns on the shares and funds that have received the stamp of approval of sharia boards thus includes interest income. It is a moot point whether this 'impure' or 'contaminated' income should be 'cleansed' or 'purified', that is, be given to a charity. Most scholars allow purification, but some find it unnecessary, as it would be difficult to identify the contribution of a firm's interest payments and receipts to the return on its equities. Purification is either done by a fund manager or by investors themselves, on the basis of information provided by the fund manager (Girard and Hassan 2006). Zakat calculation on investment profits, however, is still controversial.

As in stock investment, the criteria are not too strict in real estate investment either. In the guidelines for Islamic Real Estate Investment Trusts (REITs) issued by the Malaysian government in November 2005 and approved by the Syariah Advisory Council of Malaysia's Securities Commission, up to 20 per cent of the rental incomes that provide the income from the properties in a fund may have been earned on haram activities. One of these REITs is the first Islamic health care REIT in the world, launched in 2006, with its income consisting of rental income from hospitals.

There are people who have a gnawing suspicion that investment in shares, and even more investment in funds, is a form of maysir, gambling. Others may yearn for a stable income stream such as provided by bonds. A solution for such investors is available in the guise of ijara funds. A financial institution in this case sets up a lease company and sells shares of the company to investors. Like money market funds, not an alternative for devout Muslims, these provide a reasonably stable income. In addition, they provide a hedge against inflation. Another way out for those investors is investment in sukuk, which are often themselves based on ijara contracts.

The ban on riba not only restricts the gamut of financial assets that can be included in halal portfolios, but also the way of acquiring them. Margin trading, of course, is out of the question. It is no surprise that the Council of the Islamic Fiqh Academy ruled in 1993 that one may not borrow money against interest with a stockbroker or any other party to buy shares and to deposit them as security for the loan. However, if the purchase of shares can be done without riba being involved the picture changes. One way is provided by Bank Islam Malaysia Berhad, which offers share financing through mudaraba profit sharing contracts (Naughton and Naughton 2000, p. 153).

6.4.2 Performance of Islamic Funds

In 2007 there were said to be more than 250 sharia-compliant mutual funds, managing an estimated $300 billion (Akhtar Aziz 2007). This is up from some $800 million in 1996 and between $5 billion and $7 billion in 2001 (Gainor 2000). In between, negative stock market developments reduced investments to no more than some $3.5 billion in 2002, managed by roughly 105 Islamic mutual funds (Iley and Megalli 2002).

Various Islamic indexes are available to give the investor guidance. The first one was launched by RHB Unit Trust Management Bhd. in May 1996 in Malaysia. Financial Times – Stock Exchange (FTSE), in collaboration with International Investor, an Islamic investment bank, launched FTSE Global Islamic Index Series (GIIS) at the end of December 1998. Dow Jones Islamic Market Index (DJI) followed in February 1999 and Kuala Lumpur Shariah Index (KLSI) in April 1999.[12]

The screens applied by Dow Jones's Sharia Supervisory Board and similar bodies favour investments in newer companies that raise money on equity markets rather than through banks. Technology and IT funds have been quite popular. They took a beating around 2000, but seen over longer periods Islamic funds by and large do not seem to perform systematically worse than conventional indexes. Hakim and Rashidian (2002) compared the risk–return profile of the DJI with those of another index, the Wilshire 5000 index, which tracks the performance of the shares of the largest 5000 US companies. They found that, between 12 April 1999 and 4 October 2002, DJI is correlated with neither the Wilshire 5000 index nor the three-month treasury bill (as a proxy for the risk-free interest rate), but they also found that an Islamic basket of stocks, which leaves out many stocks as haram, performed not worse than a much larger basket of stocks. In a more recent paper (Hakim and Rashidian 2004), they compared the performance of DJI with that of the Dow Jones World Index (DJW) and of a socially responsible index, the Dow Jones Sustainability World Index (DJS). DJS is the closest substitute for DJI, as it does not invest in stock of companies engaged in gambling, alcohol, tobacco or weaponry. It does not, however, shun interest- or pork-related investments. DJI and DJS are both subsets of DJW and thus, inevitably, less diversified. DJI faces more restrictions than DJS and is consequently also less diversified than DJS. The sample was made up of weekly observations over the 5 January 2000 and 30 August 2004 period. DJI showed a somewhat lower return than

DJS and nearly double its systematic risk (beta). DJW had the highest average return, a full 3 per cent higher than DJI (or rather a full 3 per cent less negative than DJI). Surprisingly, given that it is a subset of DJW, DJI had somewhat lower volatility (beta < 1, with DJW functioning as the market index). Hakim and Rashidian's conclusion that 'we find no evidence that the compliance to sharia, as interpreted by the DJI, has resulted in any discernible costs to investors' is, however, only true in comparison with DJS. Girard and Hassan (2006) found that the Dow Jones Islamic indices outperform their conventional counterparts from 1996 to 2000, underperforming them from 2001 to 2005. Overall, diversification benefits and reward to risk were similar.

Real-world mutual funds do not always track the indexes and may show different characteristics. Hayat (2006) found that Islamic mutual funds that invested globally in the period 17 August 2001 to 25 August 2006 earned higher average returns than DJI and DJW, but funds that restricted themselves to Malaysia underperformed not only these indexes, but also their Kuala Lumpur Islamic and conventional benchmarks. The global Islamic funds had a positive alpha vis-à-vis both the DJI and DJW benchmarks and in both cases a beta < 1.[13] They have thus been relatively low-risk investments over the period studied.

6.4.3 Some Special Funds

Some special funds call for attention. First, we have pension funds and, second, hedge funds figure prominently on the financial scene.

Pension funds pose no special problems from an Islamic point of view. They simply have to invest in halal assets. Still, Islamic pension funds are few and far between. One was started by HSBC Amanah in 2004 and another by the South African insurer Old Mutual in 2006. Others are slowly following. HSBC's fund invests 95 per cent in equities and the rest in such things as sukuk. Old Mutual sticks to 75 per cent in equities, as it is held by law to invest at least 25 per cent in cash or interest-bearing instruments. Both funds apply the DJI criteria for selecting stocks (Gelderblom 2006).

Hedge funds take long and short positions in securities and borrow for leverage. The knee jerk reaction of fiqh scholars, not unnaturally, is to oppose hedge funds, but financial institutions every now and then try to introduce Islamic versions. Hedge funds could take long positions with the help of murabaha contracts for asset-backed securities such as sukuk or common stock. Banks could provide finance with the securities as collateral. If the price goes down below the level at which the bank would no longer be protected, the murabaha deal would be unwound, with losses for the fund. Leverage for short positions is possible with the help of arbun contracts. The hedge fund could sell stock for future delivery against a down payment (Gassner 2005). Alternatively, it could sell stocks on a salam basis for future delivery but against immediate payment (Dar 2006). In both cases the stock has to be bought from the market on or just before the agreed delivery date. Such short positions will remain dubious from a sharia point of view, given the ban on selling what one does not own. Some scholars argue that salam should be allowed for all fungible goods, including claims on goods, that is, stocks (see Section 4.3.5). Sharia Standard 21 of the AAOIFI, however, states that salam contracts should not be used for transactions in company shares (see Section 4.2.6). The same standard declares the conventional method of selling short by borrowing stocks and selling these spot not acceptable.

6.5 CONCLUSIONS

The products offered by the specialized institutions, and the similar products offered by banks, all face serious limitations and restrictions when compared with their conventional equivalents. In insurance the prevalent form of takaful often leaves the funds without much reserves and the insured, or rather the participants, cannot be sure that claims will be fully honoured, though managing firms that would be loath to see their clients defect to conventional competitors may come to the rescue in such cases. Islamic home finance is of course seriously handicapped in countries that allow tax deduction of interest paid on mortgage loans. However, in other countries it is no smooth sailing either. Murabaha finance is typically an instrument for short-term trade finance and in the case of home finance severely restricts the freedom of movement, literally, of the home buyer. Ijara wa iqtina and diminishing musharaka may be less problematic in this respect, but will usually be more expensive than conventional home finance, and ijara brings huge risks for the client both if his and if the financier's financial solidity weakens. Investment is restricted to non-interest-bearing securities that furthermore meet the ethical standards of Islam. As there are also non-Muslims that reject interest and/or want their investments to comply with ethical norms, these restrictions may make Islamic funds attractive to them as well. Islamic funds have less scope for diversification than others, but the evidence so far does not point to systematically worse performance. Islamic pensions funds have only just started, but do not seem to face special problems, except that regulators may require them to invest part of their assets in interest-bearing instruments. Hedge funds are an interesting phenomenon in the sense that they can be seen as attempts to stretch the meaning of 'sharia-compliant'.

NOTES

1. Mr Bakri Muhammad is a self-professed salafist who was born in Syria and spent part of his life in Britain, where he was active in the Hizb ut-Tahrir movement before breaking away and setting up his own organization. He has often advocated violence in the Holy War against the non-believers and was not allowed back into Britain after leaving in 2005. There is a Wikipedia entry on him with references to many other sources.
2. Mr Al-Zarqa was a prominent jurist. He wrote an authoritative *Comprehensive Introduction to Islamic Law* (*Al Madkhal al-Fiqhi al-A'am*) and was involved in the formulation of family law and civil law in Syria after it had gained independence from the French. He also served as Minister of Justice and as Minister of Religious Endowments in Syria and helped draft Jordanian civil law. He was associated with the Islamic Fiqh Council in Mecca and the Islamic University of Medina and supervised the preparation of the encyclopaedia of Islamic Fiqh in Kuwait. His approach to the sharia was characterized by flexibility and practicality, as he thought it should be applicable in all societies and at all times and certainly should not aim at going back to the times of the Prophet. Mr Al-Zarqa is credited with formulating the rule that interest received on bank deposits should be donated for the benefit of the poor (Salahi 2003).
3. From a report by Mohammad Ajmal Bhatty, chief executive of Takaful International, excerpted on the Dutch website www.islamic-commerce.net, 11 June 2002.
4. There are no objections in the sharia to the granting of a mortgage or a deed of trust to secure a creditor in his rights (Thomas 2001). Quran 2:283 says: 'If you are on a journey and cannot find a scribe (to write down the transaction), then transact your business by taking possession of a pledge. If one of you entrust another with a pledge, let the trustee deliver the pledged property to its owner, and let him fear Allah, his Lord. Do not conceal testimony, and whoever conceals it, his heart is surely sinful. Allah is aware of all your actions.'
5. It seems possible to circumvent such double payments by having the home buyer first act as the buying agent of the financier and next as his selling agent. If the home buyer as the financier's agent buys and sells in his own name, double payments can be avoided. This construct was used in Britain before the 2003 Stamp Duty Land Tax made it unnecessary (Sinke 2007, p. 52). One wonders whether all this was really sharia-compliant, as the financier should hold title to the property for a time.
6. Derived from information given to Ms Rachida Talal by a British provider of Islamic home finance. I am indebted to Ms Talal for this information.
7. Below a threshold of £125 000, on 2 September 2008 raised to £175 000 for a year, no stamp duty is due.
8. www.hsbcamanah.co.uk/amanahuk/home-finance, 2007.
9. El Diwany (2003a); www.isnacanada.com/ichc.htm.
10. http://muslim-investor.com/, 9 June 2008.
11. www.djindexes.com, 9 June 2008. See for the different norms applied by the Shariah Advisory Council of the Securities and Exchange Commission (SEC) of Malaysia: Ali 2005, pp. 19–20.
12. Dow Jones publishes a great number of Islamic indexes. FTSE's GIIS has been replaced by the FTSE Shariah Global Equity Series, complemented by a number of indexes constructed and published jointly with local stock exchanges, see www.ftse.com/.
13. Alpha and beta are entities that find their place in Michael Jensen's modification of the Capital Asset Pricing Model (CAPM: see Jensen 1968). In his model we may relate the return on an asset or a portfolio to both the return on a risk-free asset and the return on the market portfolio, however defined, as follows:

$$R_{pt} - R_{ft} = \alpha_p + \beta_p (R_{mt} - R_{ft}) + \mu_t,$$

where

R_{pt} = the return on portfolio p at time t
R_{ft} = the return on the risk-free asset at time t
α_p = the intercept of the model, to be estimated using regression analysis
β_p = the systematic risk of portfolio p, to be estimated using regression analysis
R_{mt} = the return of the market portfolio at time t
μ_t = the error term at time t

Alpha is the return on a portfolio over and above that predicted by the CAPM. It reflects pure luck or above average ability of fund managers in picking assets.

7. Public finance and the monetary authorities

7.1 INTRODUCTION

The ban on riba, if interpreted as a ban on conventional interest, poses a problem for the fiscal and monetary authorities. Alternatives for conventional bonds as a means of borrowing money have to be found. In the early days of the ideas on an Islamic economy its advocates advanced ideas that in their naiveté were only equalled by Chilean President Dr Allende's belief that under his Unidad Popular rule (1970–73) people would not work simply because they receive money in return, but from an innate urge to contribute to the wellbeing of society as a whole (Allende 1973). In the same vein, Maulana Maududi (1999, p. 206) thought that in order to meet emergencies, non-productive national expense and war expenditure, an Islamic government could be assured of voluntary donations. The proscription of interest and the establishment of the system of zakat would result in such prosperity that people would not feel such donations as a burden. In addition, people would be glad to provide charitable (quard hasan) loans. But Maududi must have had an inkling that this was a bit starry-eyed after all, as he adds that if more money is needed than is collected in these ways, the government cannot only use capital levies such as the zakat, but also force people to lend part of their bank deposits to the government or even, if the worst came to the worst, resort to inflationary finance.

The ban on riba not only makes financing the government's budget more complicated, it also calls for creative thinking in monetary policy. In conventional monetary systems the central bank manipulates interest rates in its attempts to stimulate commercial banks to increase or reduce lending. For a government that is under pressure to avoid paying and receiving interest, the question is how to find a sharia-compliant equivalent. A similar problem presents itself when the central bank has to act as lender of last resort.

Monetary authorities not only are responsible for monetary policy, but also for supervision of the financial sector, including the sub-section that is Islamic. The rules and standards that apply to conventional financial institutions may require modifications before they can be used for supervision of Islamic ones.

In many of these areas both thinking and practice are still in an experimental phase; developments have not yet crystallized.

7.2 PUBLIC FINANCE

In so far as taxes, fees and property income can be used for financing a government's expenditure, there is no need for specific Islamic solutions. Budget deficits may, however, cause headaches, as interest-bearing bonds and private placements are out of the question if financing is to observe the ban on riba (assuming that riba is considered to be synonymous with interest). The easy way out is to force the central bank to provide free credit, but that makes the money supply grow and, if done on a large scale, fuels inflation.

Financial institutions can offer PLS finance to private companies and they can do the same with the government as their client. This works fine for government-owned companies or other activities that promise an income. It has been resorted to in Iran and Sudan (M.F. Khan 2007, pp. 292–3). For financing other government expenditure PLS is less suitable. One would be hard put to calculate the rate of return on such expenditure, though ingenious solutions have been proposed. In Iran the National Participation Certificates or National Participation Paper (NPP) recommended by Ul Haque and Mirakhor (1998) were designed to solve the calculation problem by linking the rate of return to returns in the private sector. The proposal has been under consideration for a decade or so. So far, it does not seem to have gone off the runway (Sundararajan et al. 1998; M.F. Khan 2007, p. 292). In other Muslim countries the chances for such a project would certainly be slim, as fiqh scholars outside Iran generally reject the idea.

For financing buildings or means of transport, ijara offers a solution. If ijara wa iqtina is chosen, the government agrees to buy the good at the end of the lease period for a given price and the lease payments then provide the financier with a steady income stream, possibly linked to LIBOR or EURIBOR (M.F. Khan 2007). Under a simple ijara contract, by contrast, the rate of return is not known beforehand, as the residual value of the object of the lease would be uncertain. Murabaha loans are of course another possibility. These are, however, at a disadvantage compared with PLS and ijara finance in that the banks cannot easily resell them on the secondary market. They are for all practical purposes illiquid because they are debt. Musharaka, mudaraba and ijara financing by contrast represent ownership of physical goods and can thus be traded on the secondary market.

For financing a government budget deficit that is not attributable to specific projects, one solution is to borrow in the form of quard hasan loans at zero per cent and offer gifts, at the discretion of the issuer, in recompense. In Malaysia the 2003 Government Investment Issues (GII) scheme was based on this principle, as was an earlier version, the Government Investment Certificates scheme introduced by a law passed in 1983. Investors buying government debt under these schemes formally provided a benevolent, or quard hasan, loan to the government, and the government gave a return in the form of a dividend, formally a gift. The committee setting the dividend made it dependent on such variables as inflation, real growth and yields on other financial instruments. These schemes, however, were developed not so much with the government budget deficit in mind as with a view to making liquid instruments available to the Islamic banking sector (at times consisting of one bank only). The sector could hold them as required liquidity or for investing excess reserves (Sundararajan et al. 1998; M.F. Khan 2007, p. 297).

Sukuk, developed by the government of Malaysia in conjunction with HSBC, provide an elegant way of borrowing to finance general expenditure. The ijara securities issued by the Bahrain Monetary Authority (BMA, now Central Bank of Bahrain) in 2000 are close cousins (*Euromoney* 2001). Like sukuk, which may also be based on ijara, these are quite similar to fixed-interest debt, but are at least formally interest free and, moreover, backed by real assets. Also from Bahrain is a scheme that looks like bai'salam combined with elements of tawarruq. It works like this: BMA sells short-term government bonds, or bills, in the form of *sukuk al-salam*, certificates of pre-paid forward sales. Officially, investors pay for the future purchase of some commodity. They are not, however, required to take delivery of the commodity on the bill maturity date, as BMA arranges to sell the commodity on the investors' behalf at a predetermined price. This price equals the purchase price of the bills plus interest, based on LIBOR plus a spread (El-Gamal 2005a). All this implies that BMA first buys and then sells commodities before it can repay the investors, a time-consuming and costly way just to formally comply with the religious requirements. Before BMA pays for the commodities, the funds can be used to finance a governent deficit. The paper is not tradeable, as goods cannot be sold before they are delivered, according to sharia law. With a 91-day maturity, these securities are still sufficiently attractive for the banks with an eye to liquidity management.

If some governments go out of their way to obey the ban on riba, at least formally, the Islamic Republic of Iran hardly bothers to keep up the façade.The Iranian government requires the private sector to eschew riba, but it saw no opportunity to completely do without interest-based financial transactions itself. As the owner of the state banks, it thinks itself justified in neglecting the ban on riba in its dealing with those banks. Its reasoning is built up of two elements. First, it argues that when borrowing from state-owned banks, it really borrows from itself. Second, it has defined riba in such a way that it does not include cases where the debtor and the creditor are not separate legal bodies. Big business is catered for in the same way: for intra-group business loans an identical reasoning applies (Lewis and Algaoud 2001, pp. 103–4).

7.3 MONETARY POLICY

7.3.1 Monetary Policy Instruments

The ban on riba severely restricts a central bank's grip on the economy and may lead to harmful consequences. A central bank that cannot use interest-based measures to control the commercial banking sector's lending activities and money creation may easily be tempted to resort to measures that undermine the efficiency of financial markets, in particular direct credit controls. However, it is not entirely without indirect instruments, as variable cash and liquidity ratios can still be applied (Chandavarkar 1996, ch. 9).

How did the countries that fully Islamized their financial system deal with the problem? The Central Bank of Iran (CBI) is authorized to impose ceilings on the banks' loan and credit volumes, not only in a global sense but for individual economic sectors as well. It may also use required reserve ratios, with different rates for different liabilities and for different fields of activity. Open-market operations are possible through the issuance of CBI Participation Papers, which pay a profit rate, and banks may deposit their excess liquidity in an open deposit account, which again pays no interest but promises a profit rate (CBI 2008). The Iranian authorities apparently are loath to leave things to the market. The banks, in so far as they are government-owned, are not fully free to set the payments on their deposits. The CBI imposes a minimum 'profit' rate which the banks must pay deposit holders (Kia 2006, p. 887).

In Sudan the central bank, the Bank of Sudan, has maintained direct instruments for regulating the money supply. It mainly relied on quantitative controls by fixing a random credit ceiling along with an across-the-board cash ratio on all types of deposits. This has not proven to be an effective way of controlling money supply and neither has it been conducive to economic development. The central bank has, however, developed instruments to conduct open-market operations. Central Bank

Musharaka Certificates (CMCs) have been introduced, following their approval by the High Sharia Supervisory Council of the Bank of Sudan. A special company, Sudan Financial Services Co., was established to hold the shares of the government and the Bank of Sudan in commercial banks and CMCs were issued against their value. These CMCs allow the central bank to conduct open-market operations (Sundararajan et al. 1998, pp. 12–13). CMCs can be issued with or without maturity date. The return on the certificates presumably follows the yield on the shares held by the Sudan Financial Services Co. Under an earlier plan, which was under consideration by the Bank of Sudan's High Sharia Supervisory Council in 1998, CMCs would promise investors a negotiable rate of return linked to developments in government revenue, that is, investors got a claim on a share of government revenue. This method had a long history, as it was, according to Sundararajan et al. (1998, pp. 15–16), a modern version of *qabala*, or tax farming, though the government would not now leave tax collection to its creditors.[1] Arguably, the CMCs that eventually have been adopted deal in a more straightforward way with the ban on riba.

Like the central bank of Sudan, other central banks have also found ways to mimic conventional money market instruments with unconventional methods. The Indonesian Central Bank, Bank Indonesia, for instance, allows banks to deposit funds according to wadia (safekeeping) principles. Formally, the funds are kept in custody by the central bank for 7, 14 or 28 days and the depositor has no right to any remuneration. Bank Indonesia, however, may pay out a bonus, or gift, at its discretion (Bank Indonesia 2004). In Kuwait the central bank has introduced tawarruq as an instrument for open-market policy (Solé 2007). If the central bank wants to tighten the money market, it approaches Islamic banks and asks them to purchase some commodity on its behalf. The banks will contact commodity brokers and purchase the commodity. The central bank agrees to pay the purchase price plus a mark-up to the banks at a future date. The banks make no payment to the brokers. Next the central bank asks the banks to sell the commodities back to the brokers at the same price. The banks pay the central bank. The brokers receive no funds and make no payments (presumably they receive a fee). The end result of this circuitous way is a temporary fall in the banks' liquidity. The central bank can, conversely, pump liquidity into the system by making immediate payments to the banks for the purchase of the commodities and agreeing to receive payment for the sale of the commodities later.[2] The most innovative central bank, however, has been Bank Negara Malaysia, the Malaysian central bank. It allowed in its guidelines on the Islamic Interbank Money Market of 1993, effective as per January 1994, a number of instruments (Hakim 2007):

- The Government Investment Issues (GII), mentioned in Section 7.2. The Malaysian central bank also opened a window to purchase and sell GII on the secondary market, at prices set by them.
- Rahn agreements. These resemble GII and repurchase agreements. The lender provides a quard hasan loan against collateral and the borrower may, at his discretion, provide the lender with a gift. The central bank resorts to Rahn agreements to regulate liquidity on the money market.
- Wadia interbank acceptance. This instrument is used to absorb excess liquidity from the banks. The banks place the money in the custody of the central bank. Custody, or wadia, means that the central bank is not seen as the owner of the funds and is not required to pay something in return. The central bank may, however, pay depositors a return at its own discretion. This is seen as a bonus, or a gift. An Islamic central bank may resort to this method as an alternative to conventional interest-bearing required reserves or open-market policies.
- Bank Negara negotiable notes, created through bai inah (commercial banks grant credit to Bank Negara through a bai inah operation and receive the notes in return). The notes are traded on the secondary market and can be used for open-market operations. They resemble Treasury bills. Prices are set by the central bank on a discount basis.
- Sale and buy-back agreement. Under this agreement one party sells an asset and agrees to buy it back later at a predetermined higher price.

7.3.2 Lender of Last Resort

The ban on riba severely constrains a commercial bank's room of manoeuvre and requires it to safeguard its liquidity, as the conventional interbank money market is out of bounds for a sharia-compliant bank. No interest can be paid by Islamic commercial banks, and other banks will hardly be willing to part with liquidity and receive nothing in return. Consequently, Islamic banks have an incentive to concentrate on investing in short-term assets (El Qorchi 2005). Still, situations may occur where the central bank has to act as lender of last resort. Most countries with Islamic banks are still without provisions for providing liquidity riba free to banks facing liquidity shortages (Grais and Pellegrini 2006b, p. 13). Only a few have central banks that can tide over the banks following the principles of Islamic finance.

In Indonesia Islamic banks may borrow funds from the central bank for periods ranging from 1 to 90 days against collateral. Bank Indonesia demands a return based on the rate of profit of the borrowing bank, for which the realized rate of return on mudaraba time deposits held in that bank acts as a proxy (Bank Indonesia 2003). In Iran commercial banks could at first borrow at a fixed interest rate from the central bank, which clearly conflicts with Islamic principles (Iqbal and Mirakhor 1987, p. 14). With nationalized banks, the hiyal of not considering interest payments between entities belonging to the same owner to be riba could be applied, but the Iranian central bank in the end decided to provide uncollateralized overdraft facilities and it has been extending interest-free short-term loans under a lender-of-last-resort facility (Errico and Farahbaksh 1998, p. 22). Uncollateralized loans imply that the central bank assumes the risk of default. If those loans are not freely available, or if banks doubt whether they can count on it, this further implies that the banks have to hold a high level of unremunerated reserves with the central bank, which according to figures from the 1990s they indeed did (Sundararajan et al. 1998, p. 9). Such reserves eat into the profits of the banks and force them to demand a relatively high remuneration for the funds they supply, which may lead to disintermediation.

7.3.3 Interbank Money Market

Clearly, banks have a need for an interbank money market. Creating sharia-compliant money market instruments is a tall order, but several attempts have been made. In addition to the measures discussed in Section 7.3.1, Bank Negara Malaysia introduced in 1994 the following instruments:

- Mudaraba interbank investment. This facility is called Skim Perbankan Tanpa Faedah (SPTF), literally 'Bank Scheme Without Advantage' (Sundararajan and Errico 2002, p. 7). Periods of investment run from overnight to 12 months. These investments earn a share of the profits for investment of one year of the investee bank, at a negotiable profit-sharing ratio. Mudaraba interbank investments replace Certificates of Deposit and are issued and traded by the banks.
- The GII mentioned above. The Malaysian central bank also opened a window to purchase and sell GII on the secondary market, at prices set by them.
- Islamic Accepted Bills. These resemble banker's acceptances and are based on murabaha (mark-up). A bank selling a good under a murabaha contract draws a bill of exchange on its client and may sell the bill to a third party in a *bai'al-dayn* sale at an agreed

price. *Bai'al-dayn* is debt financing by way of sale/purchase of trade documents and papers. In the case of exports, the exporter sends documentation as required under a letter of credit to the importer's bank and draws a bill of exchange which is bought by the bank. Outside Malaysia, *bai'al-dayn* is not universally accepted as sharia-compliant.

The instruments mentioned in Section 7.3.1 that are traded on the secondary market, CMCs and Bank Negara negotiable notes, can of course also be used by the banks for purposes of liquidity management.

Ways to provide credit that are nominally linked to goods transactions have been developed for the benefit of the non-bank private sector and these could be applied in the interbank sector as well, provided one deems these methods not too much at variance with the precepts of sharia. Banks could thus make use of bai inah and tawarruq for attracting and placing funds among themselves. Bank A, needing funds, might approach bank B and ask it to buy some commodity and sell it (with a mark-up) to itself (that is, bank A). A sells the commodity immediately back to the original seller or the commodities broker. Bank B pays the broker or seller spot and the broker or the seller channels the funds immediately to bank A. A pays B in instalments. This of course is a very cumbersome and circuitous way to generate funds, which would force banks into the role of commodities traders and may conflict with the demands of financial sector regulators. For short-term investment, sukuk are probably much more attractive, and for relieving a liquidity shortage, securitizing ijara loans might be a solution.

7.4 SUPERVISION OF THE FINANCIAL SECTOR

Central banks are not only responsible for monetary policy, but often also for regulating and supervising the banking sector. Alternatively, a separate Financial Sector Authority may have been set up to this end. As for supervision on Islamic financial institutions, it is early stages yet and there clearly still is a long way to go. A few points call for special attention when setting up supervision on an Islamic financial sector.

- Deposit guarantees. Conventional bank deposits benefit from deposit guaranty schemes. These partly conflict with sharia, as investment deposits are formally mudaraba investments, which share in profits and losses, by their very nature excluding any guarantee of the principal. PLS (investment) accounts can therefore in principle not be included in deposit guarantee schemes. However, the sharia board of the Islamic Bank of Britain (IBB), the first wholly Islamic bank in Britain, established in 2004, decided not to sacrifice the whole project for an unattainable ideal and accepts that in the real world compromises have to be made. It had to accept that the definition of 'deposit' as applied by the Financial Services Authority (FSA) was incompatible with the PLS (mudaraba) character of the 'savings deposits' they offered customers. The solution agreed between IBB and the FSA was that IBB would inform customers that they were legally entitled to full repayment, but had the right to refuse deposit protection and choose sharia-compliant sharing not only of profits but also of losses (Chiu and Newberger 2006; Ainley et al. 2007). There don't seem to be such strictures against insurance of demand deposits, though a guarantee system where member banks pay premiums that are invested in interest-bearing instruments would not be acceptable. The Dutch system, where no premiums are paid but banks provide guarantees among themselves, is not tainted with interest payments. It would probably meet with less resistance from the fuqaha. In Jordan demand deposits of Islamic banks are covered by deposit insurance but if banks fail, investment account holders are treated like shareholders, which means that their deposits are not protected. Turkey, in 2003, allowed Islamic banks to create an Islamic deposit takaful that covers holders of demand deposits, whereas investment account holders receive protection only when it is fraudulent mismanagement that brings a bank down (Grais and Pellegrini 2006b; Solé 2007). Most countries with Islamic banks, however, have no explicit deposit insurance scheme. Some provide an implicit guarantee from the conventional insurance system, but that is not satisfying from an Islamic point of view, given that the funds of such a system may be invested in interest-bearing assets. Malaysia is preparing a scheme where premiums collected from Islamic banks will be invested separately from the premiums from conventional banks. However, they are designed to cover PLS accounts as well, which not only exacerbates the moral-hazard problems associated with such forms of finance, but also runs counter to the fundamental idea of risk sharing. The authorities appear to sacrifice religious purity for a lower risk of bank runs (Solé 2007).

- Speculation. As speculation, in the sense of attempting just to make a quick profit without caring for the underlying real asset, is seen as maysir and considered haram, stock market supervisors have to ask themselves whether they should interfere in case of high volatility. Regulators are known to impose limits on price volatility in practice. Limits on the daily movement of stock prices are used in Korea, Malaysia and Japan, in order to prevent speculators pushing prices up or down too fast. Institutions such as the Australian Stock Exchange and the New York Stock Exchange may interrupt trading in individual stocks, for instance, when price-sensitive news is about to be released. The New York Stock Exchange also has 'circuit-breakers' that interrupt trading in the event of large price declines (Naughton and Naughton 2000). Supervisors of Islamic stock markets may draw inspiration from these examples.

- Zakat payments. Zakat payments are due on Islamic deposits. Opinions differ, however, whether it is the financial institution or the depositor who should pay zakat tax (KPMG 2006). It is up to Islamic standard-setting bodies themselves to solve this question, but if zakat is paid by the bank, supervisors understandably want to know where the money goes. After all, as we saw in Section 3.2, there are widely differing views on who should be the beneficiaries of zakat disbursements, ranging from the needy in the immediate environment of the taxpayer to bodies that defend the faith against any foe. The wide interpretation might include organizations that some governments find suspect.
- Sharia boards. Not all firms offering Islamic financial products disclose the powers of their boards and they are not in the habit of publishing the fatawa of these boards on the sharia-compliance of their products. Authors associated with the Dutch supervisory bodies (the central bank and the Autoriteit Financiële Markten, or Netherlands Authority for the Financial Markets) foresee reputational and even legal risks if clients of Islamic financial institutions start to doubt the Islamic character of their products. They also note that qualified potential members of sharia boards are not in abundant supply and they are concerned that conflicts of interest might arise with the same people manning a relatively large number of sharia boards (Verhoef et al. 2008).
- PLS lending. It has been noted that an Islamic bank, when providing funds according to PLS principles, may be considered a fund manager as much as a commercial bank. Some supervisors seem to prefer to treat them as such, though usually PLS takes up a minor share of a bank's activities (El Qorchi 2005).
- The classification of Islamic financial instruments. What conventional instrument do they resemble most, and analogous to what conventional instrument should they be regulated? In the case of mudaraba sukuk, for instance, the British supervisor FSA notes that in each individual case it has to be decided whether they should

be seen as a Collective Investment Scheme, which is unregulated, or as debt instruments, which are regulated (Ainley et al. 2007, pp. 25–6).

Then there are the normal risks that also confront conventional finance, but these may demand a slightly different application of the rules in the case of Islamic finance, in particular as regards capital-asset ratios (see Verhoef et al. 2008; Čihák and Hesse 2008):

- Credit risk, or the risk of default of a counterparty. PLS financing is, as we have seen in Chapter 4, beset with moral-hazard problems. In addition, Islamic financial institutions cannot profit from penalties imposed on debtors that have fallen into arrears and credit risk cannot be mitigated by the use of credit derivatives. Credit risk may therefore be higher than in comparable conventional banks and this may call for higher capital–asset ratios.
- Market risk, that is, the risk of price volatility of marketable assets. This risk is arguably somewhat higher with a portfolio made up of Islamic products, as there is less scope for diversification or for hedging risks with the help of derivatives.
- Financing risk, or the risk of insufficient funding. The ban on riba makes it difficult for Islamic financial institutions that face a lack of liquid funds to take recourse to the interbank money market. This might be a reason for supervisors to insist on a higher volume of own funds or on higher cash and liquidity ratios.
- The character of investment deposits. In so far as these deposits are on a PLS basis and share in the total risk of the financial institution, they are on a par with own funds, or tier-1 capital in the terminology of the Basel Capital Accords. If those deposits are matched by specific investments and depositors only share the risks of those investments, they should not be included in the institution's risk capital. As Islamic financial institutions tend not to shift losses to their clients in practice, for fear that they would defect to competitors, either Islamic or conventional, the conclusion will often be that investment deposits are not comparable to own funds.
- Operational risk. This is the risk of losses resulting from inadequate or failed internal processes, people or systems or from external events. The legal and reputational risks mentioned above might be included under this heading, but another factor, as noted by Čihák and Hesse (2008), is that monitoring PLS arrangements cannot easily be standardized, which may make large Islamic banks in particular vulnerable (provided a large part of their financing is in PLS modes).

> This squares with their finding that large Islamic banks are financially less solid than large conventional banks and than small Islamic banks, whereas for small Islamic banks it is the other way round. Financial solidity is measured by return volatility relative to equity capital and reserves plus average return.[3] The authors also note that financial solidity tends to decline when small banks grow, but to increase when large banks grow. Apparently, there is something like a U-shaped relationship. Their hunch is that, when large banks grow, increased diversification and a larger share of income from non-lending activities compensate for the negative effects of the high monitoring costs.

One fundamental question that the monetary authorities have to solve when Islamic financial institutions are set up in their jurisdiction is what supervisory approach to take. Two main approaches can be discerned. One, followed by regulators in Malaysia and Yemen, for example, is that the supervision and regulation of Islamic financial institutions should be entirely different from that of conventional banks. The second approach is to treat the sector as a variant of the conventional one and putting them under the same central bank supervision and regulatory regime, with only slight modifications and special guidelines for which occasional central bank circulars suffice. This is the approach followed in, among others, Bahrain and Qatar (El Qorchi 2005). Institutions such as the IFSB and the IIFM (see Section 5.4.4) can help in developing and harmonizing standards and norms.

7.5 CONCLUSIONS

Banks and governments have proven to be very innovative in designing ways for financing the government. Still, governments that fully rely on sharia-compliant financial instruments face some restrictions that their colleagues using conventional instruments do not have to cope with. First, borrowing must, at least formally, be backed by real goods, which leads to cumbersome procedures. Second, rescheduling government debt will be difficult, as Islamic contracts cannot easily be renegotiated.

As for monetary policy, the options open to the central bank are far more restricted than under conventional finance, but there have been enough innovations to make monetary policy at least possible, be it probably at higher cost and in more complicated ways than under conventional finance. Setting up an Islamic interbank money market in particular is bound to be a laborious process.

Finally, financial sector regulators have to face the fact that their standards and norms cannot always be applied to Islamic financial products without taking the special character of these products into consideration.

NOTES

1. See Fritschy (2008) on the history of tax farming in the Ottoman empire.
2. Presumably this counts as tawarruq and not as bai inah because the brokers may sell the commodities to other parties than the original sellers.
3. More precisely, the authors calculate z scores using $z \equiv (k + \mu)/\sigma$, where k is equity capital and reserves as per cent of assets, μ is average return as per cent of assets and σ is standard deviation of return on assets as a proxy for return volatility. The z score measures the number of standard deviations the return over a period has to fall in order to deplete equity, under the assumption of normality of banks' returns. A higher z score means a lower probability of insolvency (Čihák and Hesse 2008, p. 7).

8. Islamic finance: a tentative verdict

8.1 INTRODUCTION

What does Islamic finance bring us? We can ask this question with different things in mind. First, one may wonder how Islamic finance scores in a technical sense when compared with conventional finance. This is not the only yardstick along which Islamic finance should be measured. Islamic finance was not primarily introduced because of an alleged technical superiority, even if the wildest claims have been made by its advocates. It was first and foremost propagated as an alternative for, and as a radical departure from, conventional finance, enabling its practitioners and its clients to follow the commandments of God. A legitimate question then is whether it really delivers the goods, from an Islamic point of view. We first discuss the first question, but before we turn to the second one, we have a look at the potential demand for Islamic financial products. All the time, it must be kept in mind that judgements can only be of a tentative character, as one cannot be sure how Islamic banking and finance will develop in the future. Much is still in an experimental phase.

8.2 PROS AND CONS IN COMPARISON WITH CONVENTIONAL FINANCE

8.2.1 Claimed Benefits

Seen through the eyes of the non-Muslim observer, applying Islamic principles in finance comes down to submitting economic activity to a number of restrictions. This cannot but have at least some negative effects. There are potential positive effects as well. Let us start with the latter. We concentrate on four issues:

- danger of insolvency
- financial crises
- participation in the official financial system
- speculation.

1. Lower danger of insolvency. Under PLS banking, if strictly applied, fluctuations in a bank's income are passed on to depositors in the form of fluctuating payments. This should reduce the danger of insolvency. PLS financing, however, is generally only a minor part of an Islamic bank's asset portfolio. Moreover, losses are not in fact always passed on to holders of PLS accounts. Quite often there is an implicit promise of some minimal return on deposits, or a de facto guarantee of non-negative returns. The bank may in that case suffer losses after all. Such a guarantee of non-negative returns is of course explicit as far as transaction accounts, that is, zero-yield current accounts, are concerned. Ideally, money on these accounts is given in amanah, custody, or wadia, safekeeping, and should be backed for the full 100 per cent by liquid funds or even base money (accounts held with the central bank). If, however, the money is lent on, there is a risk for the bank which cannot easily be passed on to depositors. Alternatively, if losses are suffered on the bank's assets and these are fully passed on to PLS depositors, these will see a more than proportionate fall in the value of their deposits. Consider a bank with a credit and investment portfolio amounting to 100, transaction accounts amounting to 20 and PLS deposits amounting to 80. If losses on the asset portfolio are 10 and these are fully passed on to PLS depositors, the latter will see the value of their deposits fall by 12.5 per cent instead of 10 per cent. Banks will, however, try to prevent their customers switching to other banks and depositors will therefore generally be given a positive return.

   PLS banking may protect a bank against interest risk and credit risk to some extent, but not against operational risk. Malfunctioning computer systems or fraudulent behaviour of a bank's officers still may bring on serious losses. And even if insolvency would be less of a problem, PLS banking will do little to prevent liquidity problems. If a bank's liabilities have on average a shorter time to maturity than its assets, and depositors shift funds to other banks because of poor yields, rumours about investments turning sour or doubts about the integrity of the bank's management, it may be faced with a shortage of liquid funds and must fall back on the central bank's lender-of-last-resort facilities.
2. Protection against financial crises. It has been argued by Chapra (2002) that PLS might go a long way to prevent financial crises, as it would substantially reduce the moral-hazard problems associated with prudential supervision of banking, in particular the incentive given by deposit guarantees for high-risk lending and investment. Under PLS, there would be more discipline in the system. Depositors would be more interested in the soundness of the banks and in the quality of the banks' assets, in order to prevent having to accept negative returns, and banks

would have a better incentive to be careful in selecting borrowers and projects. Depositors will invest their funds with banks having the best risk/return profile, and possible negative outcomes have a higher weight in their decisions, as they will not be compensated by the monetary authorities. One may doubt, however, whether depositors have sufficient information to see and understand how a bank is performing before it is too late. Even sharia boards and large depositors can be misled, let alone small depositors. Several large Islamic financial institutions had deposited considerable amounts of money with the Bank of Credit and Commerce International (BCCI) but were unable to see its collapse in 1991 coming (Grais and Pellegrini 2006a, p. 8).

3. Increase of participation in the official financial system. The benefits of PLS banking in preventing solvency problems and crises claimed by its proponents are fine in theory but often turn out to be no more than pious hopes. Still, Islamic finance can point to at least one other positive result. There are many people who could never bring themselves to enter a conventional bank's office and make use of the bank's services. If an Islamic bank sets up shop in their neighbourhood, the fact that it is Islamic might be just the incentive they need to enter the world of formal finance (Scheepens 1996; Demir et al. 2004). That was one of the reasons for Turkey's government under Turgut Özal to set up Islamic finance houses in 1983 (Jang 2005, p. 141). In this way Islamic banks have contributed to a higher degree of financial intermediation, which both economic theory and econometric research say generally fosters economic development (Christopoulos and Tsionas 2004; Levine 2004; Ang 2008). Islamic investment funds may fulfil a similar role. These also offer an alternative for some non-Muslims seeking ethical investment opportunities, even though the wholesale rejection of the amusement industry might strike some as overly strict. Unfortunately, a number of less than trustworthy characters have misused the 'Islamic' moniker to lure unsuspecting people into depositing their money with them and then used those funds for risky or un-Islamic investments. Turkey's Ihlans Finans, for instance, was liquidated in 2001 after it had channelled funds, against the rules, to in-group companies that squandered the money. The BCCI had promised to invest the funds deposited by other Islamic financial institutions in sharia-compliant commodity contracts. After the collapse of the BCCI it turned out that they had failed to do so, and apparently this had escaped the attention of their sharia board (Grais and Pellegrini 2006a, p. 8).
4. Less speculation. Another claim made for Islamic finance is that it would substantially reduce speculative activities, as credit expansion decoupled from the production of and trade in real goods and services

is not possible in principle (Chapra 2002). Basically, Islamic finance should always involve real goods and services and the use of derivates is, to say the least, discouraged. Two counterarguments can be made. First, finance is sometimes provided on the basis of fictitious real transactions or on real transactions that do not really contribute to GDP but are undertaken only for the sake of making a financial transaction formally sharia-compliant, think of tawarruq and bai inah. The money thus transferred can easily be used for speculative activities. Second, if speculative activities are hindered, hedging, which reduces uncertainty, may he hindered at the same token. One person's speculation may be another person's hedging. Furthermore, speculation may help to stabilize markets or even be necessary for stabilization. For instance, if prices on any market are plummeting, speculators may expect a recovery at a later date, step in as buyers and thus help to reverse the price movement.

In the same vein, it has been argued that interest-based debt leads to over-indebtedness, resulting in loan defaults and bankruptcies and possibly in a cyclical downturn made worse by deflation; the ban on such debt by Islamic finance might result in a lessened danger of this phenomenon (Keen 1997; Ebrahim and Rahman 2005).[1] Even if it were true that Islamic finance is less prone to cycles of over-indebtedness and debt liquidation than conventional finance, it does not follow that it is consequently superior. As will be argued below, the concentration on debt matched by real activities has serious negative effects. If we do without other debt, we will also miss the benefits of such debt. It is a bit like banning motor cars. If we have no cars, we have no car accidents, but is it worth the sacrifice? Still, it must be admitted that Islamic banks will not so easily fall prey to the temptations of such things as the derivatives market, even if they would perhaps love to do so.

It thus appears that the benefits of Islamic finance, when measured by conventional yardsticks, do not amount to much, apart perhaps in the sense that they are shielded from some of the excesses and hypes of markets in complicated products. Also, in countries with an effective system of bank supervision, which is able to keep swindlers out, Islamic financial institutions might help lower people's psychological barriers against financial institutions.

8.2.2 Negative Effects

The basic idea underlying economics is that there is no such thing as a free lunch. This maxim can also be applied to Islamic finance; the pros, in so far as real rather than imaginary, have to be weighed off against the cons. We look at a number of negative points. With all these negative points, one may wonder whether large-scale adoption of Islamic finance might not be detrimental to economic growth. The negative points include:

- risks for depositors
- higher costs
- principal–agent problems and their effects on growth
- inadequate financing of SMEs
- limited supply of consumer credit
- insurance with pitfalls
- less scope for diversification and hedging, and its effects on growth.

1. Risk for depositors. If PLS principles, strictly applied, reduce the danger of insolvency for banks, the flip side of the coin is that depositors run a higher risk. A strict application of PLS principles would shift the risk of losses from shareholders to depositors. They often are less able to monitor the banking firm and even if they do, they are not in a position to replace managers. The only thing they can do is vote with their feet. And even if the banks are well managed, PLS principles make the recompense for deposit holders more volatile than some depositors might like. They simply have no choice but to accept fluctuating payments, even if many Islamic banks stabilize profit distributions to deposit holders to a great degree.
2. Higher costs. Islamic finance will often be more expensive than conventional finance. The most widespread form of bank finance is murabaha. This involves two sales transactions instead of one and in addition may saddle the financier with the burden of physically handling goods, that is, see to it that they are properly stored and insured. More generally, Islamic contract law stipulates that each transaction requires a separate contract, which makes for higher costs. Furthermore, the circuitous ways that sometimes have to be followed to mimic conventional finance, think of bai inah and tawarruq, cannot but have financial consequences. Islamic finance also requires the setting up of separate legal entities or at least organizing a firm in such a way that clients can be sure that a financial firm's Islamic assets are financed by halal funds. Next, the room of manoeuvre of clients of Islamic financial institutions is sometimes seriously restricted. Here the virtual impossibility to sell a home before the end of the agreed loan period under a murabaha mortgage comes to mind. Sellers may incur prohibitive losses.

A totally different factor adds to the cost disadvantage of Islamic banks. This is the fact that Islamic banks have only limited opportunity, if at all, to borrow on the interbank money market and therefore are obliged to hold a larger percentage of their assets in liquid funds.

Probably the cost disadvantage can be reduced if Islamic financial institutions grow or merge and exploit economies of scale. Supervisory authorities and the industry itself can contribute to a lowering of costs by stepping up the pace of harmonization of standards.

3. Principal–agent problems. Islamic banks are less well equipped than conventional banks to deal with principal–agent problems. Under PLS finance, there is a higher moral-hazard risk than under conventional interest-based finance and Islamic finance in general struggles with the limited scope for penalty clauses under sharia law. Long-term financing seems to suffer, as a result (Aggarwal and Yousef 2000). If bank credit is not available, capital markets may provide funds, in particular in the form of sukuk, but this is only suitable for large projects. Long-term growth may suffer, as a result.
4. SMEs are not served well by Islamic banks. Islamic finance may be fine for financing the purchase of specific goods, but the lack of overdraft facilities makes it less suitable for providing working capital. Moreover, bookkeeping of SMEs in countries where Islamic banks operate is often very elementary, which works against the use of musharaka and mudaraba finance. Small-scale entrepreneurs often are not too keen on the close monitoring implied by PLS partnerships anyway, and PLS finance again does not fill the need for fluctuating funds. A more general problem for SMEs, not peculiar to Islamic finance, is the lack of suitable security. Understandably, even Islamic banks that specialize in small-scale credit tend to restrict themselves to murabaha and bai'salam finance.[2]
5. Consumer credit. Just like SMEs, consumers are not well catered for. For financing goods purchases, in particular durable goods, murabaha and ijara present themselves as the natural solution. Overdraft facilities are another matter. In Britain overdraft facilities for students are available, as we have seen, but for the rest banks have to take recourse to instruments that some Muslims will be inclined to see as involving hiyal (tricks): bai inah and tawarruq. These instruments are also likely to be more expensive than conventional consumer credit.
6. Insurance. Islamic insurance, takaful, may in case of high claims during any book year leave claimants with less than full compensation of damages. It is not impossible to build up reserves, and if reserves are absent or insufficient the managing firm may provide credit facilities,

but policy holders or participants cannot take this for granted and may be in for unpleasant surprises.

7. Diversification, hedging and growth. A ban on forward contracts and other derivatives may reduce speculation and add to the stability of the financial system, but it also reduces the opportunities to hedge risks or optimize the risk–return profile of a wealth portfolio. With less scope for hedging and more uncertain returns on savings and investment accounts, it is not completely clear how the supply of funds for high-risk, high-return projects, and with it possibly economic growth, reacts, but there are bound to be negative effects. Investors and business firms also suffer from the ban on trading in risk and the difficulties that brings for hedging all kinds of risks. This too cannot but have a negative effect on economic growth. Investors suffer more generally from a restriced freedom of choice under Islamic finance. A restricted choice means a reduction in welfare. It must be conceded, though, that the industry has been inventive enough to develop instruments that offer stable returns and in that respect resemble conventional interest-bearing financial instruments. Sukuk and ijara investments come to mind, though these are primarily available to wealthy investors.

Given all these restrictions, one may wonder whether Islamic finance is able to provide a spectrum of financial instruments sufficiently wide to serve the needs of a developed, or even developing, economy, at least without circumventing the principles it pretends to obey. If not, a country considering across-the-board introduction of Islamic finance and the organization of the economy exclusively along Islamic principles might be condemned to permanent low growth rates. We have mentioned a couple of mechanisms that are likely to hinder growth and the outcome might well be negative, but it is not a priori clear to what extent growth would be lowered. Similar questions have been raised about the relationship between Islam and the relative decline of the Muslim world over the past millennium or so. Surely there are links, but again it is not clear to what extent these are inherent to Islam per se rather than caused by specific manifestations in specific historical periods. One factor deemed important by Kuran (1997) is the closure of 'the gate of ijtihad' between the ninth and eleventh centuries. It was declared that independent judgement was no longer permissible because all the answers were available; hardly an incentive for free discussion and the development of new ideas, the breeding grounds for the Schumpeterian 'new combinations' on which long-term growth depends. He also points to the absence in classical Islamic law of room for corporations as separate legal entities and further to weak property rights and an inheritance system that limited concentration of wealth. Investing one's money in business enterprises was relatively unattractive compared with setting up a waqf, a charitable trust. Such a waqf, resembling a modern foundation, provided services to society and was not so easily plundered by the taxman. The founder could give both himself as the trustee and manager and family members in various positions handsome salaries and appoint an heir as his successor, in that way keeping the family fortune intact (Kuran 2004). In the Ottoman empire by the way, the ban on riba does not seem to have played a significant role. Money lenders could openly charge interest, but for the financing of businesses mudaraba was the preferred mode (Pamuk 2004). Large-scale business did not develop, possibly because of the reasons mentioned by Kuran.

There is no strong evidence that economic development is incompatible with Islam, but a large part of the historical forms of Islam since roughly the twelfth century does not appear to have been conducive to economic development. As for the late twentieth century, Noland (2005) could not find a systematic negative correlation between Islam and economic growth. His samples exclude such countries as Egypt, Iraq, Libya, Saudi Arabia and Yemen and thus a sizeable part of the Middle East. Attitudes and institutions may vary widely across regions. Anyhow, Islamic finance is a phenomenon that has only just taken off, and in most countries it still does not dominate the financial system, so hard facts on the relationship between Islamic finance and economic growth are hard to obtain. Theoretical considerations and casual empiricism would suggest that there is little reason to fear that Islamic finance would lead to serious economic stagnation, but negative effects might nevertheless result from higher costs, reduced possiblities for hedging risks, less long-term finance provided by financial institutions and insufficient funding of SMEs.

8.3 THE DEMAND FOR ISLAMIC FINANCIAL PRODUCTS

Obviously, there is a demand for Islamic financial products, otherwise there would be no Islamic financial institutions, at least not in countries where people have a choice between Islamic and conventional banks. We try to get an idea of the demand for Islamic products by looking at market shares, though data are not readily available. A picture of potential demand can be formed by looking at the results of surveys. These will be discussed next.

Islamic finance is spreading to regions where Muslims are a minority, including North America, Europe and South Africa. Even in the UK, with its Muslim population of roughly 1.8 million people and a fiscal system that does not punish Islamic home finance, they have only captured a very small slice of the market. In 2007 the FSA mentioned an estimate of the size of the Islamic home finance market of £500 million out of a total stock of mortgage lending of over £1.1 trillion (Ainley et al. 2007, p. 22). In all fairness, it must be granted that the share is likely to grow, as some fiscal impediments to Islamic home finance were only removed in Gordon Brown's 2003 budget. The USA offer an even less positive picture. LARIBA has been offering home finance and car and business finance since 1987, but in 2003 it could underwrite no more than roughly $100 million in mortgage, car and business loans, even though it had a licence for all states barring New York. This in spite of the fact that any financial constraints that it may have felt were much loosened when in December 2002 Fannie Mae, an institution devoted to buying mortgages on the secondary market, made LARIBA eligible for its facilities. A younger firm, Guidance Financial Group in Reston, Virginia, says it funded transactions totalling $400 million in 2004 (Smith 2005).

More telling, perhaps, is the relatively small part of the market held by Islamic financial institutions in Malaysia, despite the support of the government and the innovative activities of the industry. In 2005 only 10 per cent of all banking assets were held in sharia-compliant accounts (KPMG 2006, p. 11). Given that 60 per cent of Malaysians are Muslim, that would mean that Muslims only put some 17 per cent of their money in Islamic accounts, if bank deposits were evenly spread across the population groups. As average income of *bumiputra*, the mainly Muslim ethnically Malay inhabitants, is lower than that of Chinese and Indian Malaysians, the true percentage is bound to be somewhat higher, but it will probably remain in the low 20s. In the Gulf States the share of the Islamic finance industry is estimated to be between 15 per cent and 25 per cent (Khalaf 2008). It is, however, set to grow substantially, thanks to large-scale government support and government initiatives. Developments in Saudi Arabia certainly offer hope to the industry: Islamic banks and Islamic windows of conventional, or mixed, banks took 56 per cent of total credit to the private sector at the end of 2006, up from 30 per cent at the end of 2000 (England 2007).

Surveys on the demand for Islamic financial instruments do not always give the impression that the Muslim population can't wait a day longer for Islamic finance to become available. One thorough study is a survey conducted by Dr Humayon Dar, then of Loughborough University, among over 500 Muslims. He found that only 5 per cent of UK Muslims were seriously interested in Islamic finance and that an additional 23 per cent would be interested in Islamic financial services such as mortgages if these were comparable in price with conventional interest-based mortgages (Dar

2004). Other initiatives were developed in Belgium. A Dutch company, Intermediate Marketing Services (IMS), opened a website in Belgium where those interested in Islamic financial products could sign up after paying €25. The site was said to be commissioned by Islamic banks from the Middle East that considered setting up shop in Belgium if at least 100 000 people would sign up (de Jong 2004). The attempt foundered, but others had also been busy in the meantime. In the final months of 2002 the Cercle d'Études et de Recherche en Économie Islamique CEREI of Brussels conducted a survey among Muslims in mosques and via the Internet, focusing on home finance. No more than some 700 out of the more than 4000 copies of the questionnaire distributed were returned and it was found that 65 per cent of Belgian Muslims rent their homes, against 30 per cent of the whole Belgian population. Asked why they rent and did not buy, 61 per cent gave riba as the reason. This would mean that at least 61 per cent out of 65 per cent, or close to 40 per cent, of the Muslim population would be seriously interested in Islamic forms of home finance. Of home owners, 35 per cent of the Muslim population, 66 per cent had taken out a conventional mortgage, but 77 per cent of those 66 per cent said they only had done so out of necessity. This means that an additional 77 per cent of 66 per cent of 35 per cent, that is, nearly 18 per cent of the Muslim population, would be interested. Some of those that did not take out a conventional mortgage would no doubt be interested as well, which would lead to the conclusion that the potential market might be as large as 60 to 70 per cent of Belgian Muslims. However, with only 17.5 per cent of the questionnaires returned this would be a rash conclusion. Most of the non-returners can probably be assumed to be indifferent, and the situation might after all not be that much different than found in Dr Dar's survey.

In the Belgian survey 53 per cent of the respondents did not invest their savings because of a fear of becoming tainted by riba or getting involved in haram activities. This abhorrence of riba has been found in the Netherlands as well, as mentioned in Section 6.3.1. For the USA, Abdelkader Thomas states that 'AJIF, First Takaful, UBK, CAIR and Falaika surveys coalesce around 25% core consumer base seeking Islamic products with a similar number open to conversion to Islamic products based upon competitiveness and clarity of presentation' (Thomas 2001, p. 1 n. 1).[3] Of these surveys on the demand for Islamic investments, only the Failaka one is easily available (Failaka 2000). It was conducted at the annual Islamic Circle of North America (ICNA) conference in Pittsburgh, Pennsylvania. Though this is a gathering of 10 000 to 20 000 Muslims from the USA and Canada, no more than 100 bothered to fill in their questionnaires (ibid.). That does not point to a heartfelt need for Islamic financial products.

Against this, a survey by the Dutch Rabobank indicated that some 200 000 Dutch Muslim households might be interested in Islamic home finance products (Verhoef et al. 2008, p. 25). Given that the total Muslim population in the Netherlands is around 900 000, this would mean a majority, and at least a doubling when compared to Dr Dar's results. It is not clear, however, to what extent this survey was representative.

It appears that any financial firm considering whether to enter this market outside the Muslim world, and in large parts of the Muslim world as well, does not only need a good marketing strategy, but time and patience as well. Knowledge of financial matters was generally found to be low in surveys, especially among migrants groups, and with rising educational levels among second- and third-generation immigrants this may improve over time, which may help foster interest in the Islamic financial sector. Even then, firms offering Islamic financial products cannot be sure of a sunny future. In Muslim countries no less than elsewhere, cost and quality of services often is as much a decisive factor in choosing between Islamic and conventional banks as religious considerations (Gait and Worthington 2007). As far as these religious aspects are concerned, a fundamental question is to what extent Islamic finance really fills the bill.

8.4 ISLAMIC FINANCE: HOPES FULFILLED?

Islamic finance has sprung up out of a desire by salafi reformists to create an economy functioning along Islamic principles (see Chapter 2). Finance and insurance are the only areas where results can be shown. In other respects, nothing has been achieved, see the fruitless attempts to propagate zakat as a viable alternative to Western-style social security (see Chapter 3).

The relative success of Islamic finance has its downside, at least in the eyes of some of its well-wishers. Some true believers in Islamic finance claim that PLS finance would bring a totally different world. Interest brings injustice, and Islamic forms of finance that resemble interest, and even make use of interest as a benchmark, are hardly better, in their eyes. If PLS finance were embraced across the board, that would not only mean that divine commandments were obeyed, but also that depositors received higher returns, allocation of resources for economic growth would be optimized and individual and social welfare would get a boost (Siddiqui 2002). In view of the agency problems discussed in Chapter 4 and the limited range of transactions for which PLS finance is suitable, these are vacuous claims. The minor share of PLS finance in Islamic banks' total assets is not because of its attractiveness.

Bankers have been extremely inventive in developing non-PLS products that mimic conventional ones while avoiding interest, at least formally. But it is exactly this phenomenon that makes the existing Islamic financial industry suspect to some, disappointing to others. As for the suspicion, more than one half of the respondents in Dr Dar's survey had doubts about the sharia compatibility of Islamic financial services (Dar 2004). Some scholars who initially had been staunch supporters later became disappointed. Dr M. Umer Chapra, for instance, argues that Islamic finance ideally implies PLS but that financial institutions mainly provide credit and eschew the risk of fluctuating returns from PLS finance (Chapra 2007, p. 327).[4] The same goes for Dr S.H. Siddiqui (2002).[5] Professor M.A. Choudhury, on a more fundamental level, deplores the fact that Muslim scholars have been unable to develop a distinct Islamic worldview, starting from an Islamic epistemology that is based on the Quran and the sunna (Choudhury 2007).[6] They simply follow Western paradigms. Another leading author, Mahmoud A. El-Gamal, sees 'an Islamic finance movement that is at best an economically inefficient replication of the conventional finance for which it purports to be a substitute' (El-Gamal 2003b, p. 17).[7] He could not escape the conclusion that Islamic finance brings higher transaction costs and lower efficiency with nothing worth mentioning in return, as Islamic financial instruments are sharia-compliant in form but not in substance. Moreover, the Islamic norms observed by the Islamic finance industry are, in his eyes, those of a hopelessly outdated, medieval jurisprudence that also contributes to an unfortunate separatist Islamic identity fanning feelings of superiority (El-Gamal 2007a). He would now favour cooperative forms of finance that meet ethical norms and contribute to development and no longer cares for a separate Islamic financial sector (El-Gamal 2005b, 2006, 2007a, 2007b). Others are not so much disappointed as simply deeply hostile to Islamic finance in its present form, as it does not radically distance itself from debt-based money. They yearn for a return to a metal-based currency system without fractional-reserve banking (El Diwany 2003b; see also Section 3.6) and consider the existing Islamic banks as no more than conventional banks in disguise (El Diwany 1997). Their ideas are an echo of the 100 per cent reserve banking system as advocated in the 1930s by US economists such as Irving Fisher (1936), Henry Simons (see Friedman 1969) and Laughlin Currie (2004).

Ideas of radical breaks with the existing monetary system must be seen as pipe dreams. Any attempt to develop a separate religion-based epistemology will also almost certainly turn out to be a wild goose chase.[8] Muslims are, it would seem, stuck with a choice between (1) conventional financial firms, either invoking darura or following liberal interpretations of the ban on riba, (2) an Islamic financial sector making concessions to the needs of the twenty-first century by mimicking conventional financial products and (3) denying oneself many of the services of a financial system.

NOTES

1. The debt deflation phenomenon as first described by Irving Fisher is a cycle of over-indebtedness, debt liquidation, distress selling, falling money supply, falling prices and declining net worth, bankruptcies and unemployment, loss of confidence and continued downward spiralling movements, later adopted by Hyman Minsky as the pivotal element in his theory of inherent instability of the market economy (I. Fisher 1933; Minsky 1986). Ebrahim and Rahman (2005) mention the negative view on interest-based debt, but do not themselves subscribe to it.
2. Personal information from the manager of PT BPR Syariah Asad Alif at Sukorejo, Central Java. BPR is Bank Perkreditan Rakyat, or People's Credit Bank; PT is Perseroan Terbatas, or Ltd.
3. AJIF is *American Journal of Islamic Finance*, UBK is United Bank of Kuwait, CAIR is Council on American–Islamic Relations.
4. Dr M. Umer Chapra is a research adviser at the Islamic Research and Training Institute (IRTI) of the IDB, Jeddah. Earlier he worked for several decades at the Saudi Arabian Monetary Agency (SAMA).
5. Dr Shahid Hassan Siddiqui is a prominent Pakistani banker and economist.
6. Dr Masudul Alam Choudhury is a Canadian citizen and professor at the School of Business at Cape Breton University, Sydney, Nova Scotia, Canada and at Trisakti University Jakarta, Indonesia.
7. Dr Mahmoud Amin El-Gamal is an Egyptian-born US citizen and a professor at Rice University, Houston, Texas.
8. Serious attempts have been made at the VU University, Amsterdam (see Chapter 3, n. 1).

Appendices

A. THE QURAN ON RIBA

***Sura* 2, Al-Baqara (The Cow)**

275. Those that live on usury shall rise up before Allah like men whom Satan has demented by his touch; for they claim that usury is like trading. But Allah has permitted trading and forbidden usury. He that receives an admonition from his Lord and mends his way may keep what he has already earned; his fate is in the hands of Allah. But he that pays no heed shall be consigned to Hell-fire and shall remain in it for ever.
276. Allah has laid His curse on usury and blessed almsgiving with increase. He bears no love for the impious and the sinful.
278. Believers, have fear of Allah and waive what is still due to you from usury, if your faith be true.

***Sura* 3, *Al-Imran* (The Imrams; from Amram, the father of Moses and Aaron)**

130. Believers, do not live on usury, doubling your wealth many times over. Have fear of Allah and you shall prosper.

***Sura* 4, *Al-Nisa* (Women)**

160. Because of their iniquity, We forbade the Jews good things which were formerly allowed them; because time after time they have debarred others from the path of Allah;
161. Because they practise usury – although they were forbidden it – and cheat others of their possessions, We have prepared for those of them that disbelieve a stern chastisement.

***Sura* 30, *Al-Rum* (The Greeks, that is, the Byzantines)**

39. That which you seek to increase by usury shall not be blessed by Allah; but the alms you give for His sake shall be repaid to you many times over.

From: *The Koran* (1959), translated by N.J. Dawood, Harmondsworth, Middlesex: Penguin.
Note that riba here has been translated as usury.

B. THE QURAN ON MAYSIR

Sura 2, *Al-Baqara*

219. They ask you about drinking and gambling. Say: 'There is great harm in both, although they have some benefit for men; but their harm is far greater than their benefit.'

Sura 5, *Al-Ma'ida* (The Table)

90. Believers, wine and games of chance, idols and divining arrows, are abominations devised by Satan. Avoid them, so that you may prosper.
91. Satan seeks to stir up enmity and hatred among you by means of wine and gambling, and to keep you from the remembrance of Allah and from your prayers. Will you not abstain from them?

From: *The Koran* (1959), translated by N.J. Dawood, Harmondsworth, Middlesex: Penguin.

C. THE BIBLE ON INTEREST

The Old Testament (Tenach):

Exodus 22

24. If you lend money to one of your poor neighbors among my people, you shall not act like an extortioner toward him by demanding interest from him.

Leviticus 25

35. When one of your fellow countrymen is reduced to poverty and is unable to hold out beside you, extend to him the privileges of an alien or a tenant, so that he may continue to live with you.
36. Do not exact interest from your countryman either in money or in kind, but out of fear of God let him live with you.

Deuteronomy 23

20. You shall not demand interest from your countrymen on a loan of money or of food or of anything else on which interest is usually demanded.
21. You may demand interest from a foreigner, but not from your countryman, so that the LORD, your God, may bless you in all your undertakings on the land you are to enter and occupy.

Nehemiah 5:7

7. After some deliberation, I called the nobles and magistrates to account, saying to them, 'You are exacting interest from your own kinsmen!' I then rebuked them severely . . .

Psalms 15

. . . lends no money at interest, accepts no bribe against the innocent. Whoever acts like this shall never be shaken.

Proverbs 28

8. He who increases his wealth by interest and overcharge gathers it for him who is kind to the poor.

Ezekiel 18

5. If a man is virtuous – if he does what is right and just,
8. if he does not lend at interest nor exact usury; if he holds off from evildoing, judges fairly between a man and his opponent;
9. if he lives by my statutes and is careful to observe my ordinances, that man is virtuous – he shall surely live, says the Lord GOD.

Ezekiel 22

12. There are those in you who take bribes to shed blood. You exact interest and usury; you despoil your neighbors violently; and me you have forgotten, says the Lord GOD.

The New Testament:

Matthew 25

27. Should you not then have put my money in the bank so that I could have got it back with interest on my return?

Luke 6

34. If you lend money to those from whom you expect repayment, what credit (is) that to you? Even sinners lend to sinners, and get back the same amount.
35. But rather, love your enemies and do good to them, and lend expecting nothing back; then your reward will be great and you will be children of the Most High, for he himself is kind to the ungrateful and the wicked.

Luke 19 (Same Parable as in Matthew 25:27)

23. why did you not put my money in a bank? Then on my return I would have collected it with interest.

Source: *The New American Bible*, US Conference of Catholic Bishops, www.nccbuscc.org/nab/bible/.

D. USEFUL WEB ADRESSES

islamic-finance.startpagina.nl/	Dutch portal
www.al-islaam.com	Conservative Dutch-language website
www.cpifinancial.net/	Islamic Business & Finance online
www.djindexes.com	Dow Jones Islamic Market Index series
www.failaka.com	Site of an Islamic consultancy; many articles on the theory and practice of Islamic banking and finance
www.ftse.com/indices	Various Shariah Index series
www.gcu.edu.pk/Library/islam.htm	Islamic Resources of the library of Government College University, Lahore; includes complete Hadith collections

www.irti.org	Islamic Research and Training Institute (IRTI), Jeddah; thorough studies in the Institute's online Occasional Paper Series
www.iifm.net	International Islamic Financial Market (IIFM)
www.iirating.com	Islamic International Rating Agency (IIRA)
www.isdb.org	Islamic Development Bank; parent organization of IRTI
www.islamicity.com/finance	US site devoted to Islamic economics
www.islamic-finance.com	Information on Islamic finance, edited by Tarek El Diwany
www.islamicmint.com	Site propagating Islamic gold dinars
www.islamic-world.net/economics/	News and articles
www.islamonline.com	US site with information on Islam and Muslim life, including Islamic business
www.jamaat.org	Site of Pakistan's Jamaat-e-Islami organization
www.lmcbahrain.com/global-table.asp	Lists sukuk issues
www.minaret.org	Minaret of Freedom Institute, Bethesda, Maryland, which is close to the Austrian School
www.muslim-investor.com	Information on investment, banking and so on
www.muslimphilosophy.com	Islamic Philosophy Online
www.siddiqi.com/mns	Dr Mohammad Nejatullah Siddiqi's site
www.suedasien.net/themen/islam	Studies on Islam and society in South Asia
www.tariqramadan.com	Tariq Ramadan's site, with a number of articles
www.uga.edu/islam/	The University of Georgia's Islamic sources, including complete Hadith collections
www.usc.edu/dept/MSA	The University of Southern California's Islamic sources, including Hadith collections and a glossary

References

A Field Guide to Islamic Activists (2001 or 2002), www.muhajabah.com/fieldguide.htm.

Adams, Charles J. (1966), 'The ideology of Mawlana Mawdudi', in D.E. Smith (ed.), *South Asian Politics and Religion*, Princeton, NJ: Princeton University Press, ch. 17.

Aggarwal, Rajesh. K. and Tarik Yousef (2000), 'Islamic banks and investment financing', *Journal of Money, Credit, and Banking*, **32** (1), 93–120.

Ahmad, Aziz (1967), *Islamic Modernism in India and Pakistan, 1857–1964*, London: Oxford University Press.

Ahmad, Imad-ad-Dean (n.d.), 'Islam and markets', www.minaret.org/acton.htm.

Ahmad, Imad-ad-Dean (1995), 'Islam and the medieval progenitors of Austrian economics', www.minaret.org/austrian.htm.

Ahmad, Imad-ad-Dean (1996), 'Riba and interest: definitions and implications', Minaret of Freedom Institute Preprint Series 96-5, Minaret of Freedom Institute, Bethesda, paper presented at the 22nd conference of American Muslim Social Scientists, Herndon, VA, 15–17 October 1993, www.minaret.org/riba.htm.

Ahmad, Imad-ad-Dean (1998), 'The dinar: indispensibility of hard money to the Islamic monetary regime', paper presented to the American Muslim Social Scientists, Chicago, 30 October, www.minaret.org/OLD/MONETARY.HTM and www.islamicmint.com/newsarticles/minaret.html (abstracts, not identical).

Ahmad, Imad-ad-Dean (2004), 'Conflict within the Islamic civilization: the challenge of disentangling culture from religion', *Global Dialogue*, **6** (1–2), www.minaret.org/gd.pdf.

Ahmad, Khursid (n.d., probably 1997), 'Deliverance from the curse of interest (riba): the real hindrance', www.jamaat.org/issues/riba.html.

Ahmad, Mahmud (1999), *Towards Interest-Free Banking*, Delhi: Adam.

Ahmed, Shoayb (2005), 'The development of Islamic jurisprudence (fiqh) and reasons for juristic disagreement among Schools of Law', Master's Thesis, University of South Africa, http://etd.unisa.ac.za/ETD-db/theses/available/etd-06062006-134114/unrestricted/dissertation.pdf.

Ainley, Michael, Ali Mashayekhi, Robert Hicks, Arshadur Rahman and Ali Ravalia (2007), *Islamic Finance in the UK: Regulation and Challenges*, London: Financial Services Authority.

Akhtar Aziz, Tan Sri Dato' Sri Dr. Zeti (2007), conference speech held on 18 October, www.bnm.gov.my/index.php. Ms Akhtar Aziz is the governor of the Malaysian central bank, Bank Negara Malaysia.

Al-Ameen Al-Dhareer, Siddiq Mohammad (1997), 'Al-Gharar in contracts and its effects on contemporary transactions', Eminent Scholars' Lecture Series no. 16, Islamic Research and Training Institute, Islamic Development Bank, Jeddah, www.irti.org.

Ali, Salman Syed (2005), 'Islamic capital market products: developments and challenges', Occasional Paper no. 9, Islamic Research and Training Institute, Islamic Development Bank, Jeddah, www.irti.org.

Allende, S. (1973), 'The purpose of our victory', *Chile's Road to Socialism*, Harmondsworth: Penguin, ch. 2, translation of inaugural address as President of Chile, 5 November 1970.

Al-Mukhtar Al-Salami, Muhammad (1999), 'Al-Qiyas (analogy) and its modern applications', Islamic Research and Training Institute, Islamic Development Bank, Jeddah, www.irti.org. Mr Al-Mukhtar Al-Salami is a former Grand *Mufti* of Tunisia.

Al-Rifai, Tariq and Aamir Khan (2000), 'The role of venture capital in contemporary Islamic finance', www.failaka.com.

Al-Suwailem, Sami (2006), 'Hedging in Islamic finance', Occasional Paper no. 10, Islamic Research and Training Institute, Islamic Development Bank, Jeddah, www.irti.org.

Ang, James B. (2008), 'A survey of recent developments in the literature of finance and growth', *Journal of Economic Surveys*, **22** (3), 536–76.

Anielski, M. (2003), *The JAK Members Bank Sweden: An Assessment of Sweden's No-Interest Bank*, Edmonton: Anielski Management, www.anielski.com/Documents/The%20JAK%20Bank%20Report.pdf.

Aquinas, St Thomas (1965), 'Summa Theologica', in A.E. Monroe, *Early Economic Thought*, 8th impr., Cambridge, MA: Harvard UP, ch. 3.

Ariff, Mohamed (2001), 'Islamic banking', www.islamicity.com/finance/IslamicBanking. Mr Ariff was associated with the University of Malaya.

Aristotle (1992), *The Politics*, translated by T.A. Sinclair, revised by T.J. Saunders, Harmondsworth: Penguin.

Baker, J.W. (1974), 'Heinrich Bullinger and the idea of usury', *Sixteenth Century Journal*, **5** (1), 49–70.

Bakri Muhammad, Omar (n.d.), 'Why Islam declares war against insurance?', www.as-sahwa.com/leaflets/21/index.htm (no longer available on this URL).

Bälz, Kilian (2004), 'A Murabaha transaction in an English court – the London High Court of 13th February 2002 in Islamic Investment Company of the Gulf (Bahamas) Ltd. V. Symphony Gems N.V. & Ors', *Islamic Law and Society*, **11** (1), 117–34.

Bank Indonesia (2003), Regulation number: 5/3/PBI/2003 concerning the short-term financing facility for Sharia Banks, www.bi.go.id/biweb/utama/peraturan/pbi-5-3-2003-eng.pdf.

Bank Indonesia (2004), 'Regulation number: 6/7/PBI/2004 concerning Bank Indonesia Wadiah Certificates', www.bi.go.id/biweb/utama/peraturan/pbi-6-7-04_engl.pdf.

Barenberg, Andrew (2004–05), 'Islamic financing impacts on development and equality', *Oeconomicus*, **VII**, 17–23.

Benthall, Jonathan (1999), 'Financial worship: the Quranic injunction to almsgiving', *Journal of the Royal Anthropological Institute*, **5** (1), 27–42.

Best, A., J.M. Hanhimäki, J.A. Maiolo and K.E. Schulze (2004), 'The rise of political Islam 1928–2000', *International History of the Twentieth Century*, London: Routledge, ch. 19.

Beutels, R. (1990), 'Over de usura-doctrine of het kerkelijk renteverbod', *Maandschrift Economie*, **54** (4), 316–26.

Billah, Mohd Ma'sum (2002), 'Takaful (Islamic insurance): an economic paradigm', http://islamic-insurance.com/t-paradigm.

Billah, Mohd Ma'sum (2007), 'Islamic banking and the growth of *takaful*', in M. Kabir Hassan and Mervyn K. Lewis (eds), *Handbook of Islamic Banking*, Cheltenham, UK and Northampton, MA, USA: Edward Elgar, pp. 401–18.

Bjelanovic, Jelena and Kevin Willis (2007), 'Takaful may stimulate Middle East insurance growth but business model is unproven, says S&P', Standard and Poor's, press release, 10 April, www2.standardandpoors.com/spf/pdf/media/.

Bokhari, Jawaid (1984), 'One-window lending operation by Pakistani banks – II', *The Muslim*, 23 September.

Bokhari, F. (2002), 'Moves to tighten rules on borrowing', *Financial Times*, 27 October.

Botje, Harm (1987), 'Aanval geopend op islamitisch establishment in Egypte', *NRC Handelsblad*, 18 April.

Botje, Harm (1988), 'Egyptische rechter: rente niet in strijd met islam', *NRC Handelsblad*, 18 August.

Boxberger, Linda (1998), 'Avoiding riba: credit and custodianship in nineteenth- and early-twentieth century Hadramawt', *Islamic Law and Society*, **5** (2), 196–213.

Brooke-Rose, C. (1971), *A ZBC of Ezra Pound*, London: Faber & Faber, ch. 11.

Brown, Kym, M. Kabir Hassan and Michael Skully (2007), 'Operational efficiency and performance of Islamic banks', in M. Kabir Hassan and Mervyn K. Lewis (eds), *Handbook of Islamic Banking*, Cheltenham, UK and Northampton, MA, USA: Edward Elgar, pp. 96–115.

Bukhari (Muhammad ibn Ismail al-Bukhari), *Sahih Bukhari*, translated by M. Muhsin Khan, www.usc.edu/dept/MSA/fundamentals/hadithsunnah/bukhari/.

CBI (2008), 'Monetary policy instruments in Iran', www.cbi.ir/section/1370.aspx, retrieved 23 June 2008.

Chandavarkar, A. (1996), *Central Banking in Developing Countries*, London and Basingstoke: Macmillan.

Chapra, M. Umer (1998), 'The major modes of Islamic finance', paper presented at the 6th Intensive Orientation Course on 'Islamic Economics, Banking and Finance', held at the Islamic Foundation, Leicester, UK, 17–21 September, www.kantakji.org/fiqh/Finance.htm.

Chapra, M. Umer (2000), 'Is it necessary to have Islamic economics?', *Journal of Socio-Economics*, **29** (1), 21–37.

Chapra, M. Umer (2002), 'Alternative visions of international monetary reform', in Munawar Iqbal and David T. Llewellyn (eds), *IslamicBanking and Finance: NewPerspectives on Profit-Sharing and Risk*, Cheltenham, UK and Northampton, MA, USA: Edward Elgar, pp. 219–38.

Chapra, M. Umer (2006), 'The nature of riba in Islam', lecture course on 'Principles and Practices of Islamic Economics and Banking', Azerbaijan State Economic University, Baku, 27–30 November, http://rufat edu.castel.az/islam/IRTI%20Course%202006/Chapra3.pdf. A slightly revised version of chapter 2 of M. Umer Chapra (1985), *Towards a Just Monetary System*, Leicester, UK: The Islamic Foundation.

Chapra, M. Umer (2007), 'Challenges facing the Islamic financial industry', in M. Kabir Hassan and Mervyn K. Lewis (eds), *Handbook of Islamic Banking*, Cheltenham, UK and Northampton, MA, USA: Edward Elgar, pp. 325–57.

Chiu, Shirley and Robin Newberger (2006), 'Islamic finance: meeting financial needs with faith based products', *Profitwise News and Views*, Federal Reserve Bank of Chicago, February, www.chicagofed.org/community_development/files/02_2006_islamic_finance.pdf.

Choudhury, Masudul Alam (1986), *Contributions to Islamic Economic Theory*, Basingstoke and London: Macmillan.

Choudhury, Masudul Alam (1996), 'The nature of globalization and the Muslim world', *Managerial Finance*, **22** (5–6), 7–30.

Choudhury, Masudul Alam (1997), *Money in Islam: A Study in Islamic Political Economy*, London and New York: Routledge.

Choudhury, Masudul Alam (2007), 'Development of Islamic economic and social thought', in M. Kabir Hassan and Mervyn K. Lewis (eds), *Handbook of Islamic Banking*, Cheltenham, UK and Northampton, MA, USA: Edward Elgar, pp. 21–37.

Christopoulos, D.K. and E.G. Tsionas (2004), 'Financial development and economic growth: evidence from panel unit root and cointegration tests', *Journal of Development Economics*, **73** (1), 55–74.

Čihák, Martin and Heiko Hesse (2008), 'Islamic banks and financial stability', IMF Working Paper No. 08/16.

Comptroller of the Currency (1997), 'Letter on the permissibility of Ijara transactions for US banks; Interpretive Letter #806', December, www.failaka.com.

Comptroller of the Currency (1999), Letter on the permissibility of Murabaha transactions for US banks; Interpretive Letter #867, November, www.failaka.com.

Coutsoukis, P. (2004), 'Sudan; Islamic banking', www.photius.com/countries/sudan/economy/sudan_economy_islamic_banking.html. Based on *The Library of Congress Country Studies* and the *CIA World Factbook*.

Cragg, Kenneth (1964), *The Call of the Minaret*, New York: Oxford University Press.

Currie, Laughlin (2004), 'The 100 percent reserve plan', *Journal of Economic Studies*, **31** (3/4), 355–65, First published 1938.

Dante Alighieri (1955), *The Divine Comedy, I: Hell*, translated by D.L. Sayers, Harmondsworth: Penguin. First published 1949.

Dar, Humayon A. (2004), 'Demand for Islamic financial services in the UK: chasing a mirage?', Economics Research Paper no. 04-11, Loughborough University, http://hdl.handle.net/2134/335.

Dar, Humayon A. (2006), 'Shari'ah issues with hedge funds', www.cpifinancial.net/v2/print.aspx?pg=magazine&aid=7.

Dar, Humayon A. (2007), 'Incentive compatibility of Islamic financing', in M. Kabir Hassan and Mervyn K. Lewis (eds), *Handbook of Islamic Banking*, Cheltenham, UK and Northampton, MA, USA: Edward Elgar, pp. 85–95.

de Bruijn, J.T.P. (2008), 'De sji'itische islam in het moderne Iran', in Jacques Waardenburg (ed.), *Islam: Norm, Ideaal en Werkelijkheid*, 6th edn, Houten and Antwerp: Fibula/Unieboek, pp. 424–31.

de Jong, R. (2004), 'Commotie over islamitisch bankieren', *Het Financiëele Dagblad*, 11 September.

Demir, Ömer, Mustafa Acar and Metin Toprak (2004), 'Anatolian Tigers or Islamic capital: prospects and challenges', *Middle Eastern Studies*, **40** (6), 166–88.

Deutsche Bank (2007), 'Pioneering innovative shari'a compliant solutions', Deutsche Bank Academic Paper, www.db.com/presse/en/download/White_Paper.pdf.

Devi, Sharmila (2008), 'Scholars and harmony in short supply', *Financial Times*, 18 June.

Douwes, Dick (2004), 'Richtingen en stromingen', in Henk van Dries (ed.), *In het huis van de islam*, Nijmegen/Amsterdam: SUN, pp. 162–81.

Driessen, Henk (ed.) (2008), *In het huis van de islam*, 4th edn, Nijmegen/Amsterdam: SUN.

Drummond, J. (2000), 'Survey – Islamic banking', *Financial Times*, 26 October.

Ebrahim, M. Shahid and Shafiqur Rahman (2005), 'On the pareto-optimality of futures contracts over Islamic forward contracts: implications for the emerging Muslim economies', *Journal of Economic Behavior & Organization*, **56** (2), 273–95.

El Diwany, Tarek (1997), 'Fractional reserve banking', *The New Straits Times*, August, www.islamic-finance.com.

El Diwany, Tarek (2003a), 'The great Islamic mortgage caper?', www.islamic-finance.com/item122_f.htm.

El Diwany, Tarek (2003b), 'Travelling the wrong road patiently', *Banker Middle East*, September, www.islamic-finance.com.

El-Gamal, Mahmoud A. (2000), 'A basic guide to contemporary Islamic banking and finance', www.ruf.rice.edu/~elgamal.

El-Gamal, Mahmoud A. (2001a), 'An economic explication of the prohibition of *Ribā* in classical Islamic jurisprudence', in *Proceedings of the Third Harvard University Forum on Islamic Finance*, Harvard University Center for Middle Eastern Studies, www.ruf.rice.edu/~elgamal. Also published in *Islamic Finance: Local Challenges, Global Opportunites: Proceedings of the Third Harvard University Forum on Islamic Finance*, Cambridge, MA: Center for Middle Eastern Studies, Harvard University, 2001, pp. 29–40.

El-Gamal, Mahmoud A. (2001b), 'An economic explication of the prohibition of gharar in classical Islamic jurisprudence', paper presented at the 4th International Conference on Islamic Economics, Leicester, 13–15 August, www.ruf.rice.edu/~elgamal.

El-Gamal, Mahmoud A. (2002), 'Islamic jurisprudence and finance: trends of the past, and promises of the future', slides address, Geneva, 22 July, www.ruf.rice.edu/~elgamal.

El-Gamal, Mahmoud A. (2003a), 'The recent Azhar fatwa: its logic, and historical background', presentation in Dubai and California, www.ruf.rice.edu/~elgamal/files/azharfatwa.pdf.

El-Gamal, Mahmoud A. (2003b), '"Interest" and the paradox of contemporary Islamic law and finance', *Fordham International Law Review*, http://www.ruf.rice.edu/~elgamal/files/interest.pdf.

El-Gamal, Mahmoud A. (2005a), 'Islamic finance in the Middle East', prepared statement for the US Senate Committee on Banking, Housing and Urban Affairs, 13 July, www.ruf.rice.edu/~elgamal/files/Testimony.pdf.

El-Gamal, Mahmoud A. (2005b), 'Mutuality as an antidote to rent-seeking Shari'a-arbitrage in Islamic finance', www.ruf.rice.edu/~elgamal/files/Mutuality.pdf.

El-Gamal, Mahmoud A. (2006), *Islamic Finance: Law, Economics, and Practice*, New York: Cambridge University Press.

El-Gamal, Mahmoud A. (2007a), 'Incoherent pietism and Sharia arbitrage', *Financial Times*, 23 May.

El-Gamal, Mahmoud A. (2007b), 'Mutualization of Islamic banks', in M. Kabir Hassan and Mervyn K. Lewis (eds), *Handbook of Islamic Banking*, Cheltenham, UK and Northampton, MA, USA: Edward Elgar, pp. 310–24.

El-Hawary, Dahlia, Wafik Grais and Zamir Iqbal (2007), 'Diversity in the regulation of Islamic financial institutions', *Quarterly Review of Economics and Finance*, **46** (5), 778–800.

El Qorchi, Mohammed (2005), 'Islamic finance gears up', *Finance and Development*, **42** (4), 46–50.

Elhiraika, Adam B. (2003), 'On the experience of Islamic agricultural finance in Sudan: challenges and sustainability', Research Paper no. 63, Islamic Research and Training Institute, Islamic Development Bank, Jeddah, www.irti.org.

Emmanuel, A. (1969), *L'échange inégal*, Paris: Maspero.

Engen, D. (2004)., 'The economy of Ancient Greece', in Robert Whaples (ed.), *EH.Net Encyclopedia*, http://eh.net/encyclopedia/article/engen.greece.

Engineer, Asghar Ali (2000), 'Islam and secularism', *Secular Perspective*, 1–15 October, Centre for Study of Society and Secularism, Mumbai, http://ecumene.org/IIS/csss42.htm.

England, Andrew (2007), 'Demand leads to dominance', *Financial Times*, 23 May.

Ergene, Bogac (n.d.), 'Sources and schools of Islamic law', http://college.hmco.com/currentconflict/instructors/history/islamic_activities/islamic_law/islamic_law.pdf. 'A guide to the current conflict' (http://college.hmco.com/currentconflict) was a site with teaching material of Houghton Mifflin publishers, which opened after September 11, 2001. Mr Ergene is with the University of Vermont.

Errico, L. and M. Farahbaksh (1998), 'Islamic banking: issues in prudential regulations and supervision', Working Paper WP/98/30, IMF.

Esposito, John L. (ed.) (2003), *The Oxford Dictionary of Islam*, New York: Oxford University Press.

Euromoney (2001), 'Islamic banks tap a rich new business', December.

Euromoney (2007a), 'Outstanding contribution to Islamic finance: Sheikh Nizam Yaquby', February.

Euromoney (2007b), 'Best new product: Abu Dhabi commercial bank's meethaq mudarabah overdraft facility', February.

Failaka (2000), 'Survey results: demand for Islamic investments in America', www.failaka.com.

Fatwa Bank (2000), 'Fatwa on life insurance', 10 July, www.islamonline.net/fatwa/english/FatwaDisplay.asp?hFatwaID=11158.

Fatwa Bank (2001), 'Fatwa on insurance', 27 December, www.islamonline.net/fatwa/english/FatwaDisplay.asp?hFatwaID=58824.

Fisher, Irving (1933), 'The debt-deflation theory of great depressions', *Econometrica*, **I** (4), 337–57.

Fisher, Irving (1936), *100% Money*, revised edn, New York: Adelphi Company. The first edition appeared in 1935.

Fisher, Oman Clark (2001), 'Seven misconceptions about insurance and takaful', Bank Al Jazira Takaful Taawuni, 14 August, www.failaka.com.

Friedman, Milton (1969), 'The monetary theory and policy of Henry Simons', in *The Optimum Quantity of Money and Other Essays*, London: Macmillan, ch. 4. First published in the *Journal of Law and Economics*, **10**, 1967.

Fritschy, Wantje (2008), 'Indirect taxes and public debt in the world of Islam before 1800', in S. Cavaciocchi (ed.), *La fiscalità nell'economia europea secc. XIII–XVIII*, Florence: Firenze University Press, pp. 51–74.

Fyzee, Asaf A.A. (2005), *Outlines of Muhammadan Law*, 4th edn, New Delhi: Oxford University Press.

Gafoor, A.L.M. Abdul (1996), *Interest-Free Commercial Banking*, Kuala Lumpur: A.S. Noordeen.

Gafoor, A.L.M. Abdul (2000), 'Islamic banking & finance; another approach', http://islamic-finance.net/riba-free-banking/gafoor.html.

Gainor, T. (2000), 'A practical approach to product development', paper presented at the Fourth Harvard University Forum on Islamic Finance, 30 September to 1 October, www.failaka.com.

Gait, A. and A.C. Worthington (2007), 'An empirical survey of individual consumer, business firm and financial institution attitudes towards Islamic methods of finance', Faculty of Commerce, University of Wollongong, Australia, http://works.bepress.com/acworthington/30.

Gardet, Louis (1967), *De Islam*, Utrecht/Antwerpen: Het Spectrum. First published as *Connaître l'Islam*, Paris: Librairie Arthème Fayard, 1958.

Gassner, Michael Saleh (2005), 'Islamic hedge funds: recipes, merits and critics', *Banker Middle East*, **63**, September, www.bankerme.com/bme/2005/sep/islamic_hedge_funds.asp.

Gassner, Michael Saleh (2007a), 'Developing common standards for Islamic finance', *Business Islamica Magazine*, May, www.islamica-me.com.

Gassner, Michael Saleh (2007b), 'Islam & hedge funds', www.islamica-me.com.

Gelderblom, A. (2006), 'Islamic finance and the feasibility of a Dutch Islamic pension fund', Master's Thesis, RSM Erasmus University, Rotterdam.

Gelpi, R.M. and F. Julien-Labruyère (2000), *The History of Consumer Credit: Doctrines and Practices*, London: Macmillan.

George, Sir Edward (2003), speech given for the Islamic Home Finance Seminar, London, 27 March, www.bankofengland.co.uk. Also published in *New Horizon*, **130**, May.

Gesell, Silvio (1931), *Die natürliche Wirtschaftsordnung durch Freiland und Freigeld*, Hochheim: Stim-Verlag Hans Timm.

Ghazanfar, S.M. and A. Azim Islabi (1990), 'Economic thought of an Arab scholastic: Abu Hamid al-Ghazali (A.H. 450–505/A.D. 1058–1111)', *History of Political Economy*, **22** (2) 381–403.

Gibbon, Bill and Trevor Norman (2008), 'Hedge funds and Shari'ah compliance in the GCC', www.cpifinancial.net/, 12 August.

Gillespie, Piers (2007), 'Current issues in Indonesian Islam: analysing the 2005 Council of Indonesian Ulama Fatwa No. 7 opposing pluralism, liberalism and secularism', *Journal of Islamic Studies*, **18** (2), 202–40.

Girard, Eric and M. Kabir Hassan (2006), 'Faith-based ethical investing: the case of Dow Jones Islamic Indexes', paper presented at the 2006 Financial Management Association International (FMA) Annual Meeting, Salt Lake City, 11–14 October, www.fma.org/SLC/Papers/Faith-BasedEthicalInvesting.pdf.

Goodhart, C.A.E. (1995), 'Why do banks need a central bank?', in C.A.E. Goodhart, *The Central Bank and the Financial System*, Basingstoke: Macmillan. Originally in *Oxford Economic Papers*, **39**, 1987, 3–18.

Gordon, Barry (1993), 'Aristotelian economic analysis and the medieval schoolmen', *History of Economics Review*, **20**, summer, 1–12.

Grais, Wafik and Matteo Pellegrini (2006a), 'Corporate governance in institutions offering Islamic financial services: issues and options', World Bank Policy Research Working Paper 4052.

Grais, Wafik and Matteo Pellegrini (2006b), 'Corporate governance and stakeholders' financial interests in institutions offering Islamic financial services', World Bank Policy Research Working Paper 4053.

Haase, Michael (2001), 'Fatwa', Südasien-Informationsnetz e.V., www.suedasien.net.

Hakim, S. and M. Rashidian (2002), 'Risk and return of Islamic stock market indexes', paper presented at the 9th Economic Research Forum Annual Conference, Sharjah, U.A.E., 26–28 October, www.erf.org.eg/cms.php?id=conferences_details&conference_id=6.

Hakim, S. and M. Rashidian (2004), 'How costly is investor's compliance to Sharia?', paper presented at the 11th Economic Research Forum Annual Conference, Sharjah, U.A.E., 14–16 December, www.erf.org.eg/CMS/getFile.php?id=543.

Hakim, S.R. (2007) , 'Islamic money market instruments', in M. Kabir Hassan and Mervyn K. Lewis (eds), *Handbook of Islamic Banking*, Cheltenham, UK and Northampton, MA, USA: Edward Elgar, pp. 161–71.

Haladjian, Mardig (2006), 'How Moody's rates', *Islamic Business & Finance*, **6**, 24–5.

Haque, Ziaul (1995), *Riba, The Moral Economy of Usury, Interest and Profit*, Kuala Lumpur: S. Abdul Majeed for Ikraq.

Hassan, Hussein (2002), 'Contracts in Islamic law: the principles of commutative justice and liberality', *Journal of Islamic Studies*, **13** (3), 257–97.

Hassan, M. Kabir and Mervyn K. Lewis (eds) (2007), *Handbook of Islamic Banking*, Cheltenham, UK and Northampton, MA, USA: Edward Elgar.

Hayat, Raphie (2006), 'An empirical assessment of Islamic equity fund returns', Master's Thesis, VU University Amsterdam, www.failaka.com.

Henning, J.J. (2000), 'Aspects of the law of partnership and the usury doctrine in historical perspective', *Theological Forum*, **28** (1 and 2), http://rec.gospelcom.net/TF-May2000Henning.html.

Henry, C.M. and R. Wilson (eds) (2004), *The Politics of Islamic Finance*, Edinburgh: Edinburgh University Press.

Hoebink, Michel (2008), 'Het denken over vernieuwing en secularisatie', in Henk Driessen (ed.), *In het huis van de islam*, 4th edn, Nijmegen/Amsterdam: SUN, pp. 199–217.

Horne, J. (2002), 'Malaysia's Islamic global first', *FinanceAsia*, www.financeasia.com/articles/3CC0F47D-84A8-11D6-81E00090277E174B.cfm).

Hosseini, H. (1995), 'Understanding the market mechanism before Adam Smith. Economic thought in medieval Islam', *History of Political Economy*, **27** (3), 539–61.

Iley, K. and M. Megalli (2002), 'Analysis – Western banks eye billion dollar Islamic market', 8 August, www.reuters.com/printerfriendly.jthml?type=search&StoryID=1306099.

Iqbal, Munawar and David T. Llewellyn (eds) (2002), *Islamic Banking and Finance: New Perspectives on Profit-Sharing and Risk*, Cheltenham, UK and Northampton, MA, USA: Edward Elgar.

Iqbal, Zamir (1997), 'Islamic financial systems', *Finance and Development*, **34** (2), 42–5.

Iqbal, Z. and A. Mirakhor (1987), 'Islamic banking', Occasional Paper 49, IMF.

'Islamic finance (a UAE legal perspective)' (n.d.), www.tamimi.com/publications/islam-fin.htm.

IFSB (Islamic Financial Services Board) (2006), 'Guiding principles on corporate governance for institutions offering only Islamic financial services (excluding Islamic insurance (takaful) institutions and Islamic mutual funds)', www.ifsb.org.

Islamic Mint (n.d.), 'Introducing the Islamic dinar and dirham', www.islamicmint.com, retrieved 2006.

Ismail, Sufyam Gulam (n.d.), 'Insurance revisited – the Shariah view', www.1stethical.co.uk/pages/rp-insurance-revisited, retrieved 21 August 2008.

Israël, F.A. (2006), 'Wettelijke belemmeringen bij het sluiten van een fiscaal vriendelijke "halal hypotheek"', *Weekblad fiscaal recht*, **135** (6688), 5 November, 1142–4.

Jang, Ji-Hyang (2005), 'Taming political Islamists by Islamic capital: the passions and the interests in Turkish Islamic society', PhD dissertation, The University of Texas at Austin, www.lib.utexas.edu/etd/d/2005/jangj05548/jangj05548.pdf.

Jensen, Michael C. (1968), 'The performance of mutual funds in the period 1945–1964', *Journal of Finance*, **23** (2), 389–416.

Jobst, Andreas A. (2007), 'The economics of Islamic finance and securitization', Working Paper 07/117, IMF.

Jobst, Andreas, Peter Kunzel, Paul Mills and Amadou Sy (2008), 'Islamic bond issuance – what sovereign bond managers need to know', IMF Policy Discussion Paper PDP/08/3.

Jones, Norman (2004), 'Usury', in Robert Whaples (ed.), *EH.Net Encyclopedia*, http://eh.net/encyclopedia/?article=jones.usury.

Jum'a, Ali (2005), 'Response to Tariq Ramadan's Appeal', in Tariq Ramadan, 'A response to Shaykh Dr. Ali Jum'a, Mufti of Egypt', www.tariqramadan.com.

Kahf, Monzer (2004), 'Islamic banks: the rise of a new power alliance of wealth and *Shari'a* scholarship', in C.M. Henry and R. Wilson (eds), *The Politics of Islamic Finance*, Edinburgh: Edinburgh University Press, pp. 17–36.

Karim, Adiwarman A. (2002), 'Incentive-compatible constraints for Islamic banking: some lessons from Bank Muamalat', in Munawar Iqbal and

David T. Llewellyn (eds), *Islamic Finance and Banking: New Perspectives on Profit-Sharing and Risk*, Cheltenham, UK and Northampton, MA, USA: Edward Elgar, pp. 95–108.

Keen, S. (1997), 'From prohibition to depression: the Western attitude to usury', *Accounting, Commerce and Finance: The Islamic Perspective*, **1** (1), 26–55, www.acfip.com/vol1j.htm#vol1jb:Steve (no longer available on this URL).

Kerridge, Eric (2002), *Usury, Interest and the Reformation*, Aldershot: Ashgate.

Keynes, John Maynard (1936 [1961]), *The General Theory of Employment, Interest and Money*, London: Macmillan.

Khalaf, Rouala (2007), 'Experts see need for a common approach', *Financial Times*, 23 May.

Khalaf, Rouala (2008), 'Grappling with problems of success', *Financial Times*, 19 June.

Khalil, Abdel-Fattah A.A., Colin Rockwood and Victor Murinde (2002), 'Evidence on agency-contractual problems in *mudarabah* financing operations by Islamic banks', in Munawar Iqbal and David T. Llewellyn (eds), *Islamic Banking and Finance: New Perspectives on Profit-Sharing and Risk*, Cheltenham, UK and Northampton, MA, USA: Edward Elgar, pp. 57–92.

Khan, A. (2002), 'Developing Shariah-compliant product & services to fit today's market', slides for a presentation at the Islamic Finance Summit 2002, EuroMoney Seminars, 23–24 January, www.failaka.com/Library/Articles/Euro%20IFS%2002.pdf.

Khan, M. Fahim (1997), 'Islamic futures and their markets; with special reference to their role in developing rural financial market', Research Paper no. 32, Islamic Research and Training Institute, Islamic Development Bank, Jeddah, ww.irti.org.

Khan, M. Fahim (2007), 'Islamic methods for government borrowing and monetary management', in M. Kabir Hassan and Mervyn K. Lewis (eds), *Handbook of Islamic Banking*, Cheltenham, MA, USA: Edward Elgar, pp. 285–301.

Kia, Amir (2006), 'Deficits, debt financing, monetary policy and inflation in developing countries: internal or external factors? Evidence from Iran', *Journal of Asian Economics*, **17** (5), 879–903.

Kiezen voor de stad: Kwalitatief onderzoek naar de vestigingsmotieven van de allochtone middenklasse (2007), Ministerie van VROM, www.vrom.nl/.

Kinninmont, Jane (2007), 'Rise of the female factor', *Gulf News*, 27 August, http://archive.gulfnews.com/supplements/financial_review_3_2007/sub_story/10149526.html.

KPMG (2006), 'Making the transition from niche to mainstream; Islamic banking and finance: a snapshot of the industry and its challenges today', www.us.kpmg.com/microsite/FSLibraryDotCom/docs/Islamic%20Banking%20and%20Finance.

Kranenborg, R.P. and R. Talal (2007), 'Islamitisch financieren – en de zgn. Eigenwoningregeling van art. 3. 111 Wet IB 2001. Dualiteit of perspectief?', *Weekbiad Fiscaal Recht*, **36** (6472), 1259–69.

Kuran, Timur (1995), 'Islamic economics and the Islamic subeconomy', *Journal of Economic Perspectives*, **9** (4), 155–73, reprinted as ch. 2 in Timur Kuran (2006), *Islam and Mammon: The Economic Predicaments of Islamism*, 3rd edn, Princeton, NJ: Princeton University Press, pp. 38–54.

Kuran, Timur (1996), 'The discontents of Islamic economic morality', *American Economic Review*, **86** (2), 438–42.

Kuran, Timur (1997), 'Islam and underdevelopment', *Journal of Institutional and Theoretical Economics*, **15** (3), 41–71, reprinted as ch. 6 in Timur Kuran (2006), *Islam and Mammon: The Economic Predicaments of Islamism*, 3rd edn, Princeton, NJ: Princeton University Press, pp. 121–47.

Kuran, Timur (2004), 'Why the Middle East is economically underdeveloped: historical mechanisms of institutional stagnation', *Journal of Economic Perspectives*, **18** (3), 71–90.

Kuran, Timur (2006), *Islam and Mammon: The Economic Predicaments of Islamism*, 3rd edn, Princeton, NJ: Princeton University Press.

Layish, Aharon (2004), 'The transformation of the *Shari'a* from jurists' law to statutory law in the contemporary Muslim world', *Die Welt des Islams*, **44** (1), 85–113.

Le Goff, Jacques (1979), 'The usurer and purgatory', in *The Dawn of Modern Banking* (Proceedings of conference held at the University of California at Los Angeles, 23–25 September 1977), New Haven, CT: Yale University Press, pp. 25–52.

Levine, Ross E. (2004), 'Finance and growth: theory and evidence', NBER Working Paper W10766.

Lewis, M.K. (2007), 'Comparing Islamic and Christian attitudes to usury', in M. Kabir Hassan and Mervyn K. Lewis (eds), *Handbook of Islamic Banking*, Cheltenham, UK and Northampton, MA, USA: Edward Elgar, pp. 64–81.

Lewis, M.K. and L.M. Algaoud (2001), *Islamic Banking*, Cheltenham, UK and Northampton, MA, USA: Edward Elgar.

Libson, Gideon (1997), 'On the development of custom as a source of law in Islamic law', *Islamic Law and Society*, **4** (2), 131–55.

Lubis, Nur Ahmad Fadhil (2004), 'Financial activism among Indonesian Muslims', in Virginia Hooker and Amin Saikal (eds), *Islamic Perspectives on the New Millennium*, Singapore: ISEAS, pp. 91–112.

Malley, Mohammed (2004), 'Jordan: a case study of the relationship between Islamic finance and Islamist politics', in C.M. Henry and R. Wilson (eds), *The Politics of Islamic Finance*, Edinburgh: Edinburgh University Press, pp. 191–215.

Masud, Muhammad Khalid, Brinkley Messick and David S. Powers (1996), 'Muftis, fatwas, and Islamic legal interpretation', in Muhammad Khalid Masud, Brinkley Messick and David S. Powers (eds), *Islamic Legal Interpretation: Muftis and their Fatwas*, Cambridge, MA: Harvard University Press, ch. 1.

Maududi, S. Abul A'la (1941), 'The economic problem of man and its Islamic solution', address delivered at the Muslim University, Aligarh, 20 October, in S. Abul A'la Maududi (1999), *Economic System of Islam*, 4th edn, Lahore: Islamic Publications, pp. 8–36.

Maududi, S. Abul A'la (1963), 'Economic and political teachings of the Qur'an', in M.M. Sharf (ed.), *A History of Muslim Philosophy*, vol. 1, Wiesbaden: Otto Harrassowitz.

Maududi, S. Abul A'la (1999), *Economic System of Islam*, 4th edn, edited by Khurshid Ahmad, English translation by Riaz Husain, Lahore: Islamic Publications.

Maurer, Bill (2003), 'Articulating Islamic knowledge to an American dream: Islamic home financing alternatives after September 11, 2001', Russell Sage Foundation Grant Proposal, *PoLAR*, **26** (2), 196–222.

Mazari, Shireen M. (1998), 'The JI & Pakistan! A historical perspective', *Globe*, **12** (10), December, www.defencejournal.com/globe/dec98/ji-pak.htm.

McBride, Sarah (2000), 'Islamic funds proliferate, and results prove divine', *The Wall Street Journal Interactive Edition*, 18 May.

Meherally, Akbarally (2007), 'Understanding "Riba" (usury) – Revised', www.mostmerciful.com/riba-revised.htm.

Mehmood, Aurangzeb (2002), 'Islamisation of economy in Pakistan: past, present and future', *Islamic Studies*, **41** (4), 675–704.

Mills, Paul S. and John R. Presley (1999), *Islamic Finance: Theory and Practice*, Basingstoke and London: Macmillan.

Minsky, H.P. (1986), *Stable and Unstable Economy*, New Haven, CT: Yale University Press.

Motzki, Harald (2008), 'Het ontstaan van het Islamitisch recht', in Henk Driessen (ed.), *In het huis van de islam*, 4th edn, Nijmegen/Amsterdam: SUN, pp. 240–58.

Muslim (Abul Husain Muslim bin al-Hajjaj al-Nisapuri), *Sahih Muslim*, translated by Abdul Hamid Siddiqui, www.usc.edu/dept/MSA/fundamentals/hadithsunnah/muslim/.

Najjar, Fauzi (2005), 'The Arabs, Islam and Globalization', *Middle East Policy*, **12** (3), 9–106.

National Information Center, Federal Reserve System (2008), 'Top 50 bank holding companies', www.ffiec.gov/nicpubweb/nicweb/Top50Form.aspx.

Naughton, S. and T. Naughton (2000), 'Religion, ethics and stock trading: the case of an Islamic equities market', *Journal of Business Ethics*, **23** (2), 145–59.

Netzer, Miriam Sophia (2004), 'Riba in Islamic jurisprudence: the role of interest, in discourse on law and state', MA Thesis, Fletcher School, Tufts University, http://fletcher.tufts.edu/research/2004/Netzer-Miriam.pdf.

New Horizon (2003), 'IFSB and its new challenges', **125/126**.

Nienhaus, Volker (2007), 'Governance of Islamic banks', in M. Kabir Hassan and Mervyn K. Lewis (eds), *Handbook of Islamic Banking*, Cheltenham, UK and Northampton, MA, USA: Edward Elgar, pp. 128–43.

Noland, Marcus (2005), 'Religion and economic performance', *World Development*, **33** (8), 1215–32.

O'Brien, George (2001), *An Essay on Mediaeval Economic Teaching*, Kitchener, Ontario: Batoche Books, socserv.mcmaster.ca/econ/ugcm/3ll3/obrien/mediaeval.pdf. First published London 1920.

Oahalou, R. and M. Bouissaghouane (2003), 'Islamitische financiering en haar mogelijkheden in Nederland', Master's Thesis, VU University, Amsterdam.

Obaidullah, Mohammed (2005), 'Islamic financial services', Islamic Economics Research Center at King Abdul Aziz University, Jeddah, http://islamiccenter.kau.edu.sa/english/publications/Obaidullah/ifs/ifs.html.

Opwis, Felicitas (2008), 'The construction of *Madhhab* authority: Ibn Taymiyya's interpretation of juristic preference (*Istihsān*)', *Islamic Law and Society*, **15** (2), 219–49.

Otto, Torsten (2001), 'Maulana Maududi und die Ideologie der Jamaat-i-Islami', www.suedasien.net/themen/islam/maududi.htm.

Pal, Izzud-Din (1999), *Pakistan, Islam, and Economics: Failure of Modernity*, Karachi: Oxford University Press.

Pamuk, Şevket (2004), 'The evolution of financial institutions in the Ottoman Empire, 1600–1914', *Financial History Review*, **11** (1), 7–32.

Pound, Ezra Loomis (1968), *The Cantos*, 2nd impr., London: Faber & Faber.

Presley, J.R. and J.G. Sessions (1994), 'Islamic Economics; the emergence of a new paradigm', *Economic Journal*, **104** (424), 584–96.

Qureshi, Anwar Iqbal (1991), *Islam and the Theory of Interest*, revised edn, Lahore: Sh. Muhammad Ashraf.

Ramadan, Tariq (2004), *Western Muslims and the Future of Islam*, New York: Oxford University Press.

Raphaeli, Nimrod (2006), 'Islamic banking – a fast-growing industry', Middle East Media Research Institute (MEMRI), Inquiry and Analysis Series no. 297, www.//memri.org.

Sadeq, Abu Al-Hasan (2002), 'A survey of the institution of Zakah: issues, theories and administration', Discussion Paper No. 11, 2nd edn, Islamic Research and Training Institute, Islamic Development Bank, Jeddah, www.irti.org.

Sadr, Kazem and Zamir Iqbal (2002), 'Choice between debt and equity contracts and asymmetrical information: some empirical evidence', in Munawar Iqbal and David T. Llewellyn (eds), *Islamic Banking and Finance: New Perspectives on Profit-Sharing and Risk*, Cheltenham, UK and Northampton, MA, USA: Edward Elgar, pp. 139–51.

Salahi, Adil (2003), 'Scholar of renown: Professor Mustafa Al-Zarqa', *Arab News*, 19 May, www.arabnews.com.

Saleh, Nabil A. (1986), *Unlawful Gain and Legitimate Profit in Islamic Law*, Cambridge: Cambridge University Press.

Sarker, A.A. (1999), 'Islamic business contracts, agency problem and the theory of the Islamic firm', *International Journal of Islamic Financial Services*, **1** (2), 12–28.

Schacht, Joseph (1949), 'A revaluation of Islamic traditions', *Journal of the Royal Asiatic Society*, pp. 143–54, http://answering-islam.org.uk/Books/Schacht/revaluation.htm.

Schacht, Joseph (1975), *Origins of Muhammadan Jurisprudence*, 5th edn, Oxford: Oxford University Press.

Schacht, Joseph (1982), *An Introduction to Islamic Law*, Oxford: Oxford University Press. First published 1964.

Scheepens, M.F.H. (1996), 'Prospects for an international Islamic financial market and Islamic-approved derivatives', Master's Thesis, VU University, Amsterdam.

Schoon, Dr Natalie (2007), 'Money in the bank: the impact of Basel II on Islamic institutions', *Business Islamica*, 30 April, www.zawya.com/story.cfm/sidZAWYA20070509111523.

Schumpeter, J.A. (1967), *History of Economic Analysis*, 6th edn, London: George Allen & Unwin. First published 1954.

Sentürk, Recep (2007), 'Review of *Hadith: Origins and Developments*, ed. Harald Motzki', *Journal of Islamic Studies*, **18** (1), 97–9.

Shayesteh, Abdi (2007), 'American justice', *Banker Middle East*, 31 July, www.zawya.com.

Siddiqi, Mohammad Nejatullah (1994), 'Nature and methodology of Islamic political economy in a globalized world environment', paper presented at the International Workshop on Islamic Political Economy in Capitalist Globalization: An Agenda for Change, Pulau Pinang, 12–14 December, www.siddiqi.com/mns.

Siddiqi, Muhammad Nejatullah (2001), 'Towards a grass-roots based islamic finance for all', Keynote Address 8th Annual International Conference Lariba Islamic Banking, Los Angeles, 16 June, www.siddiqi.com/mns.

Siddiqi, Mohammad Nejatullah (2002), 'Comparative advantages of Islamic banking and finance', paper presented at the Harvard University Forum on Islamic Finance, 6 April pp. 11–24, www.siddiqi.com/mns.

Siddiqui, Shahid Hasan (2002), 'Islamic banking: true modes of financing', *Journal of Islamic Banking & Finance*, **19** (1), www.islamic-banking.com.

Sinanovic, Ermin (2004), 'The majority principle in Islamic legal and political thought', *Islam and Christian–Muslim Relations*, **15** (2), 237–56.

Sinke, Marjorie J. (2007), *Halal Mortgage: Islamic Banking and Finance (Also Containing Islamic Contract Law)*, Tilburg: Celsus Legal Publishers.

Slomp, Jan (2002), 'Conservatieve geleerden winnen nog aan invloed', *Trouw*, 4 October.

Slomp, Jan (2003), 'The "political equation" in *Al-jihad fi al-Islam* of Abul A'la Mawdudi (1903–1979)', in David Thomas and Clare Amos (eds), *A Faithful Presence: Essays for Kenneth Cragg*, London: Melisende, pp. 237–55.

Slomp, Jan (2005), *Islam*, 3rd edn, Kampen: Kok.

Smith, Elliot Blair (2005), 'Dream fulfilled helps Muslims realize theirs', *USA Today*, 24 February www.usatoday.com/money/perfi/general/2005-02-24-islamic-finance-usat_x.htm.

Sneller, Z.W. (1968), 'Economische inzichten van Maarten Luther', in Z.W. Sneller, *Bijdragen tot de economische geschiedenis*, Utrecht/Antwerpen: Het Spectrum, pp. 53–79.

Solé, Juan (2007), 'Introducing Islamic banks into conventional banking systems', Working Paper 07/175, IMF.

Soy, Sudip (2006), 'A product without a market', *Euromoney*, **37** (450), October.

State Bank of Pakistan (2005), 'Essentials and model agreements for Islamic modes of financing', press release, 15 April, www.sbp.org.pk.

Stein, Yoram (2005), 'Klassieke denkers achter de polderterrorist', *Trouw*, 22 February.

Suleiman, Nasser M. (2005), 'Corporate governance in Islamic banks', www.al-bab.com/arab/econ/nsbanks.htm.

Sundararajan, V. and L. Errico (2002), 'Islamic financial institutions and products in the global financial system: key issues in risk management and challenges ahead', Working Paper WP/02/192, IMF.

Sundararajan, V. and D. Marston (2002), 'IMF facilitates establishment of Islamic Financial Services Board', *IMF Survey*, 13 May.

Sundararajan, V., D. Marston and G. Shabsigh (1998), 'Monetary operations and government debt management under Islamic banking', Working Paper WP/98/144, IMF.

Supreme Court of Pakistan (2003), *Annual Report 2002*, www.scp.com.pk.

Tag El-Din, Seif El-Din and M. Kabir Hassan (2007), 'Islam and speculation in the stock exchange', in M. Kabir Hassan and Mervyn K. Lewis (eds), *Handbook of Islamic Banking*, Cheltenham, UK and Northampton, MA, USA: Edward Elgar, pp. 240–55.

Talal, Rachida (2007), 'Het ribāverbod in de moderne periode: "ribā versus rente?"', Bachelor's Thesis, Radboud University, Nijmegen, supervised by Professor Harald Motzki.

Tawney, R.H. (1960), *Religion and the Rise of Capitalism*, London: John Murray. First published 1926.

Tett, Gillian (2006), 'Make money, not war', *FT Magazine*, 23 September.

The New American Bible, US Conference of Catholic Bishops, www.nccbuscc.org/nab/bible/, retrieved 2008.

Thomas, A. (2001), 'Methods of Islamic home finance in the United States; beneficial breakthroughs', research paper, www.failaka.com.

Timewell, Stephen and Joe Divanna (2007), 'How fast is the Islamic finance industry growing?', *The Banker*, **96**, November.

Tourani Rad, Alizera (1989), 'The interest-free banking and the impact of abolition of interest on the economic system', PhD Thesis, Vrije Universiteit, Brussels.

Udovitch, A.L. (1979), 'Bankers without banks: commerce, banking, and society in the Islamic world of the Middle Ages', in *The Dawn of Modern Banking* (Proceedings of conference held at the University of California at Los Angeles, 23–25 September 1977), New Haven, CT: Yale University Press, pp. 255–73.

Ul Haque, N. and A. Mirakhor (1998), 'The design of instruments for government finance in an Islamic economy', Working Paper WP/98/54, IMF.

Usmani, Muhammad Taqi (n.d.), 'Islamic finance: murabahah', http://www.darululoomkhi.edu.pk/fiqh/islamicfinance/murabaha.html#bai, retrieved 29 July 2008.

Usmani, Muhammad Taqi (2000), 'The text of the historic judgment on interest given by the Supreme Court of Pakistan' (the part written by Justice Usmani), www.failaka.com.

Uzair, Mohammad (1978), *Interest-Free Banking*, Karachi: Royal Book Company.

Valeri, M. (1997), 'Religion, discipline, and the economy in Calvin's Geneva', *Sixteenth Century Journal*, **28** (1), 123–42.

Valibeigi, M. (1993), 'Islamic economics and economic policy formation in post-revolutionary Iran: a critique', *Journal of Economic Issues*, **27** (3), 793–812.

van Asselt, W.J. (2007), *Voetius*, Kampen: Kok.

van der Aa, Gerbert (2007), 'Interview with Jonathan Benthall', *Internationale Samenwerking*, **9**.

van der Kooy, T.P. (1952), 'Het vraagstuk van de rechtvaardige prijs', *De Economist*, **100**, 321–40, 428–52.

van der Kooy, T.P. (1957), 'Economie', in F.W. Grosheide and G.P. van Itterzon (eds), *Christelijke Encyclopedie*, Kampen: J.H. Kok N.V., pp. 534–7.

van Deursen, A.Th. (2005), *Een hoeksteen in het verzuild bestel*, Amsterdam: Bert Bakker.

van Dooren, P.J. and G.J. Kerkhoven (1987), 'The role of cooperatives in Sudan's agricultural and horticultural development', mimeo, Royal Tropical Institute, Amsterdam.

van Straaten, A.J. (2002), *Woeker en het verbod op rente*, Amsterdam: Boom.

Verhoef, B., S. Azahaf and W. Bijkerk (2008), 'Islamitisch financieren en toezicht: een verkennende analyse', Occasional Studies 6:3, De Nederlandsche Bank, Amsterdam.

Versteegh, Kees (2008), 'Wetenschap in de islamitische samenleving', in Henk Driessen (ed.), *In het huis de islam*, 4th edn, Nijmegen/Amsterdam: SUN, 278–95.

Visser, Hans (1998), 'Islamitisch bankieren', *Maandschrift Economie*, **62** (6), 402–13.

Visser, Hans (2004), *Islamic finance*, Financial and Monetary Studies, vol. 22, no. (3), Amsterdam: NIBE-SVV.

Visser, Hans (2007), 'Is Islamic finance feasible in Europe?', *Buletin Ştiinţific* of the George Bacovia University, vol. 10, no. 2; Proceedings of the 9th ISINI Conference, Bačau, Romania, 22–26 August.

Waardenburg, Jacques (2008), 'De historische ontwikkeling tot 661', in Jacques Waardenburg (ed.), *Islam: Norm, ideaal en werkelijkheid*, 6th edn, Houten and Antwerp: Fibula/Unieboek, pp. 27–38.

Wahyuni, Sri (2003), 'Muhammadiyah cool on Islamic bank edict', *The Jakarta Post*, 18 December.

Wigglesworth, Robin (2006), 'From strength to strength', interview with Mishari Al-Mishari, CEO of Aljazira Bank, *Islamic Business & Finance*, **6**, 9–11.

Wijaksana, D. and A. Junaidi (2003), 'MUI commission bans bank interest', *The Jakarta Post*, 17 December.

Williams, J.A. (ed.) (1961), *Islam*, London and New York: Prentice-Hall International and George Braziller.

Wilson, Rodney (2002), 'The interface between Islamic and conventional banking', in Munawar Iqbal and David T. Llewellyn (eds), *Islamic Banking and Finance: New Perspectives on Profit-Sharing and Risk*, Cheltenham, UK and Northampton, MA, USA: Edward Elgar, pp. 196–212.

Wilson, Rodney (2007), 'Islamic finance in Europe', RSCAS Policy Papers 2007/02 European University Institute, San Domenico di Fiesole, www.iue.it/RSCAS/WP-Texts/07_02p.pdf.

Wolters, Willem G. (2005), 'Is een Islamitische economie mogelijk?', valedictory lecture, Radboud University, Nijmegen, dare.ubn.kun.nl:8080/dspace/handle/2066/26924.

Wood, Diana (2002), *Medieval Economic Thought*, Cambridge: Cambridge University Press.

Yaqubi, Sheikh Nizam (2000), 'Requirements to be fulfilled when conventional banks set up Islamic banks, "windows" or "Islamic funds"', www.failaka.com.

Yasseri, Ali (2002), 'Islamic banking contracts as enforced in Iran', in Munawar Iqbal and David T. Llewellyn (eds), *Islamic Banking and Finance: New Perspectives on Profit-Sharing and Risk*, Cheltenham, UK and Northampton, MA, USA: Edward Elgar, pp. 155–67.

Yudistira, Donsyah (2004), 'Efficiency in Islamic banking: an empirical analysis of eighteen banks', *Islamic Economic Studies*, **12** (1), 1–19.

Zubair, Sohail (2008), 'How Islamic banks are different from conventional ones', http://islamicfinanceandbanking.blogspot.com/, 30 March.

Glossary

amana (also: *amanah, amanat*): custody, deposit on trust
arbun or *urbun*: a premium paid by the buyer in order to obtain the right to decide at a later moment whether to buy or not
ayatollah: honorific title for an outstanding legal scholar in the Twelver sect of Shiism; literally, Sign of God

bai al-dayn: debt financing by way of sale/purchase of trade documents and papers
bai bithamin ajil: credit sale
bai inah, bai-al-einah: repurchase by the seller
bai'muajjal: credit sale (shortened form of *bai bithamin ajil*)
bai'salam: pre-paid purchase

caliph: successor of Muhammad as ruler of the Islamic world

dar al-ahd: the abode of treaty, countries that have a treaty with Muslim countries
dar al-harb: the territory of war
dar al-Islam: the territory or abode of Islam, where Islamic law prevails
dar al-kufr: the house or territory of the infidels
darura: necessity

faqih, pl. *fuqaha*: *fiqh* scholar
fard: obligatory duties
fatwa, pl. *fatawa*: legal opinion, that is, an authoritative, but not binding, ruling on a point of Islamic law issued by a qualified scholar (*mufti*) or group of scholars
fiqh: the science of Islamic law, consisting of interpretation of the *sharia*

gharar: uncertainty, risk

hadith, pl. *ahadith*: tradition, that is, record of actions and sayings of the Prophet and his Companions; collectively known as *Hadith*
hajj: pilgrimage to Mecca, which Muslims should do at least once in their life if they possibly can

halal: lawful, or permitted according to the *sharia*
haram: forbidden by the *sharia*
hiba: gift
hijra: emigration, that is, the migration of Muhammad and his Companions from Mecca to Medina in 622, which marks the start of the Muslim era
hiyal: legal stratagem
hudud Allah: boundaries established by Allah

ibadat: devotional matters
ijara: leasing
ijara wa iqtina: lease purchase, lease to own
ijma: the consensus of the scholars
ijtihad: independent reasoning by a qualified jurist deriving new legal rules
illah: reason for something
imam: leader of the Friday mosque services, in Sunni Islam a title also used for the founders of the law schools; in Shia Islam the successor of Muhammad as leader of the Muslim community
Islam: literally, submission (to the will of Allah)
istihsan: juristic preference
istislah: taking account of the public interest (*maslaha*)
istisna: a contract of manufacture with progressive financing

jahiliyyah: Time of Ignorance, prior to the coming of Islam, pre-Islamic Arabian society; the modern world in the eyes of fundamentalist Muslims[1]
ja'iz: ethically or morally deemed indifferent by the *sharia*

kafir, pl. *kuffar*: unbeliever

madhhab, pl. *madhahib*: law school
madrassa: school or college of Islamic studies
makruh: undesirable, advisable not to do
mandub: desirable, advisable to do
maslaha: public interest
maulana: a scholar of Persian and Arabic (in India, Pakistan)
maysir: gambling
muamalat: dealings in the political, economic and social spheres
mudaraba: trust financing
mudarib: agent-manager, managing trustee
mufti: a lawyer who is authorized to issue a *fatwa*, jurisconsult
muqarada: *mudaraba*, applied to bonds

murabaha: cost-plus or mark-up financing
musaqat: *musharaka*-like contract in orchard keeping
musawama: a sale that differs from *murabaha* in the sense that no reference is made to the price paid or the cost incurred by the seller
musharaka: partnership financing
musharaka mutanaqisah: diminishing partnership
muzara: *mudaraba*-like contract in farming

qabala: tax farming.
qirad: *mudaraba*, q.v.
qiyas: deduction from analogy
qimar: gambling, including stock market speculation
Quran: literally, recitation; the Holy Book of Islam, revealed to Muhammad by the archangel Jibril, or Gabriel, between 610 and Muhammad's death in 632
quard hasan: beneficence loans

rabb al-mal: the financier or sleeping partner in a *mudaraba* partnership
rahn: repurchase agreement with collateral
ray: personal interpretation
retakaful: *takaful* reinsurance
riba: increase, excess
riba al-fadl: *riba* by way of excess in simultaneous exchange
riba al-nasia: *riba* by way of deferment
riba al-jahiliyya: pre-Islamic *riba*

sadaqa, pl. *sadaqaat*: voluntary alms giving
salat: prayer, required five times daily
sawm: observation of the fast of the month of Ramadan
shahada: profession of faith
Shaik al-Islam: highest-ranking official *mufti* in a country
sharia: Islamic law, based on the *Quran* and the *sunna*
Shia: Party, that is, Party of Ali, the fourth Caliph and cousin and son-in-law of Muhammad
sukuk: certificates, Islamic bonds
sukuk al-salam: certificates of pre-paid forward sales
sunna: the whole of the *ahadith*; in full: *sunnat al-nabî*, or habit of the Prophet; sayings and practices of the Prophet
sura: chapter from the *Quran*

ta'awon: mutual assistance
tabarru: voluntary contribution

takaful: cooperative or mutual insurance; literally, mutual support among the members of a society or group of people
takfir: the act of declaring a Muslim an unbeliever, that is, an apostate
tawarruq: literally, monetization (that is, of the traded commodity); purchase of a good on credit followed by a sale to a third party (can be done by a bank on behalf of the clients)
tawheed: the oneness of God

'*uhda*: an exchange of a cash payment for temporary custodianship and use of property
ulama, sing. *alim*: religious scholars
umma: the community of the believers
urbun, *arbun*: a premium paid by the buyer in order to obtain the right to decide at a later moment whether to buy or not
urf: custom
usul al-fiqh: the 'roots' of Islamic law: *Quran*, *sunna*, *ijma* and *qiyas*

wa'd: unilateral promise
wadia: safekeeping
wakala: attorney-client contract, agency
wakil: agent (pure agent, not a *mudarib* who shares in the profits)
waqf: charitable trust

zahir: literal meaning (of the *Quran* and the *sunna*)
zakat: charity tax, required alms giving

NOTE

1. Actually, it seems that *jahiliyyah* means 'time of wildness' or 'intrepidity' rather than 'time of ignorance' (see Fyzee 2005, p. 6).

Index